Niti Mehta

Rural Transformation in the Post Liberalization Period in Gujarat

Economic and Social Consequences

Niti Mehta
Sardar Patel Institute of Economic and Social Research
Ahmedabad, Gujarat, India

ISBN 978-981-10-8961-9   ISBN 978-981-10-8962-6   (eBook)
https://doi.org/10.1007/978-981-10-8962-6

Library of Congress Control Number: 2018944582

Cover illustration: Sagar Lahiri, Kolkata West Bengal/Getty Images

Printed on acid-free paper

This Palgrave Macmillan imprint is published by the registered company Springer Nature
Singapore Pte Ltd. part of Springer Nature.
The registered company address is: 152 Beach Road, #21-01/04 Gateway East, Singapore
189721, Singapore

PRAISE FOR *RURAL TRANSFORMATION IN THE POST LIBERALIZATION PERIOD IN GUJARAT*

"The book in the classical tradition deals with agriculture and rural development in a fast growing economy, deftly managing diversification, infrastructure besides the rural-urban space. It is for a real life example, Gujarat, making it a must read. I did this for India; but India is too big and the models and simulations remain abstract. The book is important for the businessman, policy maker, scholar and student."
—Professor YK Alagh, *Eminent Economist and Former Union Minister*

"The rural transformation process in going on for quite some time, but it appears that the speed has accelerated with the advent of improved connectivity. Many rural areas by definition have amenities in common with small towns. I am happy that this book brings forth several of these dimensions."
—Professor SP Kashyap, *Eminent Economist having extensive work on issues related to economic development*

"The book vividly demonstrates how urbanization can turn a powerful vehicle of rural transformation if we address the problems faced by small towns and promote rural and urban linkages through them. As agriculture has limited capacity to generate gainful employment, rural diversification of the sources of income and employment opportunities is the need of the hour. This book would be very useful in guiding the policy makers in ameliorating agrarian distress and promoting rural development."
—Professor RB Bhagat, *Head, Department of Migration and Urban Studies, International Institute for Population Sciences, Mumbai*

"...The running theme of the book is 'inclusive and sustainable urbanisation'. Based on the case studies of 15 diverse towns in Gujarat, the author tries to understand the intricacies of urban growth and its socio-economic ramifications. The policy makers could take a leaf of two from the work, especially when the exercise of crafting a National Policy for Urban Development is currently underway in the country".

—Professor Dinesh Awasthi, *Former Director, Entrepreneurship Development Institute of India, Ahmedabad*

PREFACE

Rapid structural changes are evident in the rural sector with economic reforms as manifested in the expanding share of rural non-farm employment to almost one-third of rural employment. Concomitantly rural incomes have shown a dramatic shift towards non-primary activities. Such changes in rural economic sector have also had an impact on the urbanization process in India, notably the rising numbers of census towns that are also emerging as a major source of overall urbanization. The focus of the study is on these newly emerging urban settlements that have not been re-designated as statutory towns and economic factors underlying the growth of villages leading to their reclassification. Rural transformation is driven by the diversification of rural economies away from the reliance on agriculture, growth of non-agricultural activities, adoption of multiple livelihood strategies by individuals and households, urban ward migration as well as urbanization of rural regions that reduces the relative isolation of rural areas and people.

In Gujarat as in some other pockets of the nation, urbanization is getting equitably spread out besides the concurrent process of peripheral expansion. The momentum of urban growth is fuelled by the lower levels of settlement hierarchy or the smaller towns. It is also evident that structural changes and employment diversification has enabled a large number of villages to be elevated to town status. The present study makes an attempt at understanding the on-going changes in the rural economic structure of Gujarat as manifested in emergence of large numbers of census towns and the underlying economic, social and environmental dimensions. A large chunk of the urban population remains unrecognised that leads to problems of service provision, resource generation and governance. Clearly, policy focus is desired on all of these fronts for a smooth process of rural transformation. This is also imperative in the interest of emergence of a sustainable settlement system that eases the constraints being faced by the explosive metropolitan expansion. Timely policy interventions are desirable to make agriculture a more profitable venture for the communities dependent on the sector. In addition expansion and provision of urban amenities and regulation of land use changes in these settlements are of utmost importance for equitable growth.

The study is the result of financial support received from the Indian Council of Social Science Research, New Delhi (ICSSR) under the major research programme scheme. We acknowledge with gratitude the financial support from ICSSR and administrative support received from Mrs. Revathy, Director at the ICSSR. This report has been prepared with the help of several individuals whose help is acknowledged. First and foremost, I would like to express my gratitude to Prof. S.P. Kashyap for his advice in designing the methodology of the study. He also offered insightful comments on all the chapters. The support of Research Associates, Ms. Monu Yadav and Ms. Indu Pareek, along with the Research Assistants, Mr. Ashwin Rawal and Mr. Pradeep Chauhan, in conducting the field surveys, focus group discussions and in tabulating the primary and secondary information has been invaluable. The involvement of Ms. Reena Narendran and Mr. Satheesan in providing timely computational and secretarial assistance is also gratefully acknowledged.

The study has benefitted immensely from the comments and suggestions made by Professor Dinesh Awasthi and Professor AK Singh as members of the Research Advisory Committee appointed for the Project. Their valuable insights have given direction to the research work. The components of the study have been presented in seminars organized by NIRD&PR, Hyderabad, SPIESR, Ahmedabad, and ISLE, New Delhi. For that, we are thankful to the organizers and to the discussants for their sharp comments. The study also benefitted from the suggestions of two anonymous referees.

Last but not the least, discussions with numerous officials, Panchayat functionaries and the residents and enterprise owners of the towns selected as case studies have enriched the final outcome. The respondents of the field investigation spared their valuable time in parting with information and also deserve our heartfelt gratitude. The support offered by the publishing team at Springer (Palgrave Macmillan) India, especially Ms. Sagarika Ghosh and Ms. Sandeep Kaur has enabled the study to be published and be available for wider dissemination. Any shortcomings, and there are bound to be numerous, are entirely the author's.

Ahmedabad, Gujarat, India   Niti Mehta

CONTENTS

ABOUT THE AUTHOR

Niti Mehta is Professor of Economics and officiating Director at the Sardar Patel Institute of Economic and Social Research (SPIESR), Ahmedabad, Gujarat, India. She is an alumni of Delhi School of Economics, CEPT University and Gujarat University. Prior to her current job, she was associated with the Agro-Climatic Regional Planning Project of the Planning Commission wherein she was involved in formulating resource based decentralized agro-climatic plans for the country. Her research interests are agriculture development, employment issues, agrarian growth and rural transformation, urbanisation and related areas. Dr. Mehta has authored and co-authored several research papers in journals and books on these subjects. Her books relate to hired labour use in agriculture, sources of agricultural growth and total factor productivity, and human development.

LIST OF TABLES AND FIGURE

CHAPTER 1

Introduction

Conceptual Framework

Rural transformation is defined "as a process of comprehensive societal change whereby rural societies diversify their economies and reduce their reliance on agriculture; become dependent on distant places to trade and to acquire goods, services, and ideas; move from dispersed villages to towns and small and medium cities; and become culturally more similar to large urban agglomerations" (Berdegué et al. 2014). Rural transformation involves reorganization of a society in a given space, rather than emptying of space and the moving away of people and economic activities (Timmer and Akkus 2008). It is also believed that the transformation process is imbued within the larger changes in economic structure in a country that is recording a decline in the relative importance of agriculture in the overall economy, migration towards urban areas, and is accompanied with a transitory phase of demographic growth. Furthermore, rural transformation incorporates a slow blurring of the sharp economic, social, and cultural differences between rural and urban areas and their merger along a continuous continuum or gradient. Timmer and Akkus (2008) also underscore that despite the presence of such common elements across nations, rural transformation results in varying levels of economic growth, of social inclusion and environmental sustainability.

Up to the 1970s decade, rural transformation was co-terminus with the structural changes as countries shifting from agriculture towards greater reliance on industry and services. In the initial phase, agricultural sector is

© The Author(s) 2018

N. Mehta, *Rural Transformation in the Post Liberalization Period in Gujarat*, https://doi.org/10.1007/978-981-10-8962-6_1

1

considered a provider of labour, wage goods/food grains and raw materials for the expanding industrial and tertiary sectors. An economy facing structural transformation it is contended, experiences a reduction in the income and subsequently employment share of primary sector and expansion of the share of secondary and tertiary sectors (Johnston and Mellor 1961). Urbanization resulted as people moved from rural areas to places where industry and services were located. During this stage, rural development initiatives were aimed at attaining modernization in agriculture, whose growth would drive the well-being of rural populations. Green Revolution can be seen as one such transformative policy innovation (Lipton 1968; Schultz 1968; Hayami and Ruttan 1971). Since the 1970s the concept of "rural" lost its strict identification with agriculture, and was increasingly associated with diversified economies, inter-sectoral linkages, and rural–urban linkages, and the unit of analysis was no longer the farm sector alone, but encompassed broader, interacting systems (Berdegué et al. 2014). Today rural transformation and rural development are no longer synonymous with agriculture, agricultural modernization or agricultural development. In fact, the 2008 World Development Report (Agriculture for Development), classified developing countries as "agriculture-based," "transforming," and "urbanized." According to this classification, only 14 percent of the world's rural population lived in agriculture-based countries, 77 percent are in transforming countries such as India, and nine per cent are in urbanized developing countries such as Brazil (World Bank 2007).

As per the International Fund for Agricultural Development (IFAD 2016), rural transformation is a sub set of the larger trend of structural transformation contoured by the inter-linkages between agriculture, the rural non-farm economic sector including both manufacturing and service activities. It also believes that rural transformation is an essential component, as is accompanied by increasing agricultural productivity, commercialization and diversification of production and livelihood opportunities within primary sector and the rural non-farm sector. Rising output in agriculture and the rural non-farm economy provide the surplus food to meet the demands of urban growth (Ibid.). Haggblade et al. (2007) note that the rising labour productivity in agricultural sector releases workers to undertake non-farm activities such as manufacturing and services. Simultaneously, increasing farm incomes are invested outside agriculture, and also raise demand stimulating diversification of economic activities. The enhanced share of people involved in non-farm sector supports the

growth of towns and cities. Furthermore, the authors opine that respond-
ing to the growing demand for labor in the towns and cities, agricultural
workers shift location thereby linking towns with their hinterlands, often
encouraging daily or seasonal commuting. Such a process is often termed
'a virtuous cycle' of growth. Amongst the drivers of rural transformation
of utmost the importance reportedly are employment diversification,
changes in the rural economic base, adoption of multiple livelihood strategies along with their enabling conditions and finally, urbanization of rural
regions that reduces the relative isolation of rural areas and people. In the
case of stagnant rural regions, conditions are far less positive, as there is
outmigration of poor rural people who are forced out of the subsistence
agriculture (Ibid.).

Rural non-farm activities are highly diverse and variegated, depending
on whether they are distress induced or are an outcome of a vibrant primary sector (Basu and Kashyap 1999; Kashyap and Mehta 2007). Non-
farm sector spans allied activities such as forestry, natural resource
extraction, food processing, non-food manufacturing and also tertiary
activities, including retail trade, transport, tourism and business, personal
and community services. These activities involve tradable or non-tradable
non-farm goods and services. Except for capital-intensive activities, such
as processing of agricultural commodities, the non-farm goods and services produced are usually labour intensive and their production takes
place in micro/small enterprises, often involving only a single own-account
worker (IFAD 2016). Hence the size of rural non-farm sector ranges from
household based and village primary production of low-quality products
that use local raw materials (e.g. rice milling and handloom weaving) to
small factories that use mechanical power and technology, and units
involved in production of higher-quality products (such as metalworking,
machinery and farm equipment repair shops) (Ranis and Stewart 1999).
In terms of organisation, activities in the rural non-farm sector may include
sub-contracting work to farm families by urban based firms (embroidery,
garment stitching and other artisanal work done by women), non-farm
activity in village and rural town enterprises (diamond polishing, factory
workers), and activities that require commuting between rural residences
and urban jobs (Lanjouw and Lanjouw 2001; Chandrasekhar and Sharma
2014). The characteristics of agriculture and the rural non-farm sector
play decisive roles in the pace and quality (mainly, inclusiveness) of rural
transformation, as does the capacity of manufacturing to productively and
quickly absorb the labour released by agriculture (IFAD 2016).

However, for an inclusive rural transformation process it is imperative that there is adoption of distinct agricultural policies and modernizing approaches. These should be designed to facilitate the transition to greater specialization and diversification in production and trade for increasing numbers of smallholder farmers and small rural enterprises (Ibid.). It has been noted that India is experiencing the type of rural transformation where the movement of labour between agriculture and the rural non-farm sector is associated with higher labour productivity and wages thereby favouring poverty reduction (Binswanger-Mkhize 2013).

The rural transformative forces often create conditions for favourable social impacts—betterment of health, nutrition and life expectancy, improvements in education, and empowerment of women. Additional aspects are increased access to public services and development of roads and telecommunications services. Since structural transformation is the cause and effect of economic growth, it may lead to profound economic, cultural, social and environmental imbalances and inequities as well, that present major challenges in addition to offering opportunities for investments to promote growth and sustainable development (IFAD 2016).

Urbanisation is intrinsically linked to the economic growth and development process as postulated by von Thünen (1826) and Christaller (1966). The developing regions of Asia, Africa, and Latin America are experiencing a decline in the rural population, with the emergence of numerous small and medium urban centres that are growing faster than the rate of population growth of large urban agglomerations and megacities (Currie-Alder et al. 2014). The emergence of these provincial small and medium urban centers, and their linkages with 'deep' rural areas, is a critical feature of the rural transformation process (Tacoli 2006). These towns and their rural hinterlands are functionally related in a rural-urban continuum in terms of products, labour, markets and services. Rural workers commute to work or study in the urban center, shop in it and urban merchants rely on these consumers. Small and medium farmers engage in trading activities in this nearby town, and the latter may also attract skilled workers, technicians, teachers, doctors and other service sector workers.

Research indicates a two-way causation from economic growth to urbanisation. Economic agglomeration increases efficiency, which entices more enterprises and generates well-paid jobs. Urbanisation thus creates additional avenues to move up the income ladder for workers earlier working in farms (Solarin and Yen 2016). As per the World Bank (2013) urbanisation can be considered an instrument rather than an indicator of economic development. However, for effective and sustainable contribution of urbanisation to economic development there is a need to invest in social and physical infrastructure of the urban centres, including roads, water, energy, waste management, health care, street lighting etc. Empirical studies report a strong relationship between infrastructure development, economic growth, rural development and poverty reduction (Ellis et al. 2003; Jayaraman and Lanjouw 1998; Zimmerman and Carter 2003).

In Indian context, with the proportion employed in agriculture falling, a substantial part of the increase in non-farm employment is located in rural settlements. According to the National Sample Survey Office (NSSO) data, 54 per cent of the unincorporated non-farm enterprises were located in rural areas. The growth of census towns, rural locations reclassified as urban, are also a phenomenon pointing to increased non-farm activity in rural areas. Between 2001 and 2011, the number of census towns increased by more than 200 per cent from 1271 to 3894, accounting for up to 29 per cent of total urban population growth of 90 million. Nonetheless, the underlying character of urbanisation in India continues to be "metropolitan," as many of the census/new towns have emerged in close proximity to the already existing large towns (Pradhan 2013; World Bank 2013).

RURAL NON-FARM SECTOR AND PROCESS OF URBANISATION

Successful agrarian and rural transformation is linked with industrialization and transition from an agriculturally dominant economy towards the modern secondary and tertiary sectors (Lewis 1956; Kuznets 1966; Mellor 1986). However, the trajectory of growth in India is accompanied by a distinctive process of change that incorporates persistently large rural population and workforce. Yet the agrarian economy in India is witnessing transformation, and the rural sector, particularly after the onset of reforms, is undergoing rapid structural changes. According to Binswanger-Mkhize (2012) unlike the experience of most of the countries where the growth of the economies and the growth of non-farm employment with it leads to shift of labor from rural to urban locations, in India the growth of non-farm employment in recent decades is more in the form of Rural Non-Farm Employment (RNFE), which is referred to as a unique feature of India's rural transformation.

With the land constraint becoming binding and the ever widening gap in incomes emanating from agricultural and non-agricultural sectors, it is essential that jobs in the non-farm sector are created in fairly large numbers for economic growth to be sustainable and for inclusive development outcomes. The rural economy is undergoing structural changes which are manifested in terms of changes in the employment pattern (Himanshu 2011; Majumdar 2012). The occupational diversification of the rural sector noticed by the 1981 Census and various NSS rounds, has continued at a varying pace and assumes greater significance in the recent past. The employment share of non-farm sector in the total rural employment has risen from 18.7 per cent (1983) to 35.4 per cent (2011–2012) as shown by the NSSO data (Table 1.1). The share has accelerated to 42 per cent (UPS) in 2015. The rate of change has been particularly rapid since the onset of reforms, as the rural non-farm employment share jumped from 21.6 per cent (1993–1994) to more than one-third of rural employment by 2011–2012. As per the Labour Bureau data in 2015, while 58.1 per cent of workers (usual principal status) were in agriculture, within the non-agricultural sector dominant sectors were construction (11.6%), manufacturing (7.9%) and, trade and repair (7.1%) (Basole 2017).

Data reveals an absolute decline in labour force accompanied with a decline in agricultural employment for both male and females. Further the decline in female workforce in agriculture is significantly higher than male workforce. The key drivers of changes are the higher growth in infrastructure and construction, improved transportation and communication, differential wage rates. Improved literacy levels have also aided such a change. The result of the significant movement of rural workers to non-farm activities and migration from rural areas to cities, especially by male workers to relatively higher wage work, is tightening of the labour market. Thus the scarcity of farm labour is currently emerging as a major constraint to increasing agricultural production in India. This has several implications on agriculture in terms of rise in farm wages along with the rising input costs, making an impact on the cost of production (Reddy et al. 2014).

Table 1.1 Distribution of rural workers (in per cent)

NSS Round	Primary	Non-primary
32 (77–78)	83.3	18.7
38 (83)	81.4	18.6
50 (93–94)	78.4	21.6
55 (99–00)	76.3	23.7
61 (04–05)	73.2	26.8
68 (11–12)	64.6	35.4

Source: Derived from NSSO, various rounds

Employment trends are mirrored sharply in the emerging changes in the rural income generation structure (Table 1.2). While rural income data is not available as easily unlike employment data, it can be observed that in the rural incomes, the share of rural non-farm or non-primary activities has increased from 28 per cent (1970–1971) to 62 percent of the rural net domestic product (NDP) as early as 2004–2005. Thus rural incomes too have shown a noticeable shift towards non-primary activities.

Consistent with the significant shift in the rural occupational distribution from agriculture sector, the sector is also marked by poor performance in terms of growth in gross value added (Table 1.3). Sectoral growth rates show that growth of gross value added in this sector has been below those of other sectors in the economy. Thus agriculture while being the largest sector in terms of employment, has performed worse than the

Table 1.2 Sectoral distribution of rural incomes (per cent)

Year	Primary	Non-primary
1970–1971	72.4	27.6
1980–1981	64.4	35.6
1993–1994	57.0	43.0
1999–2000	51.4	48.6
2004–2005	38.3	61.7

Source: Papola and Sahu (2012)

Table 1.3 Sectoral growth rates (at constant prices)

Year	Primary sector	Manufacturing construction & utilities	Trade, transport & communication	Financial, real estate & business services	Personal & community services	GVA at factor cost
1999–2000 to 2004–2005	1.9	6.8	8.8	5.9	4.9	5.7
2004–2005 to 2011–2012	4.1	9.1	9.8	11.6	7.1	8.5
2011–2012 to 2015–2016	2.4	5.8	8.9	10.7	5.8	6.6

Source: Calculated from CSO data at 2004–05 prices. Row 4 at 2011–12 series

economy as a whole. As rightly pointed out by Basole (2017) in addition to the declining importance of agriculture in supporting decent livelihoods even within households that are considered "agricultural" as per the NSSO definition, Labour Bureau data shows that 22 per cent reported wage employment and 4.7 per cent reported non-agricultural enterprises as their principal source of income. On an average of the total income from all sources, 32 per cent was contributed by wages or salaries. It is quite clear that currently the non-farm sector is no longer a residual sector, but an emerging driver of rural development and transformation.

It is also evident that with liberalization and economic reforms rapid structural changes are taking place in the rural sector of the country that are accompanied by dramatic rise in the share of employment in non-primary activities as well as the income coming from them. Such changes in the rural economy have had an impact on the urbanization process in India as well, as revealed by the Census 2011. In 2011, the urban population in the country grew to 377 million, showing a growth rate of 2.8 per cent per annum over 2001. It may be stressed that acceleration in urbanization hinges on rural and urban population growth differentials (Kashyap 2011). Bhagat (2011) reported that for the first time in Census 2011 the absolute growth in urban population (91 million) was estimated more than its rural counterpart and slightly higher than expected. He attributed this decline in rural population mainly to rural-urban classification rather than rural to urban migration. Noteworthy was the increase in number of census towns termed "missing or unacknowledged urban settlements" by Pradhan (2013), and "denied" urbanisation by Denis, Mukhopadhyay and Zérah. In the South Asian region such a phenomenon is popularly known as "rural urbanisation" (Wang and Hu 2007; Zhu et al. 2009; Zhu 2014). It can be described as an "in situ" process of settlement transformation whereby people retain their geographical location, uproot themselves from agriculture and replant themselves in non-agricultural pursuits (Chakraborty et al. 2017). Thus reclassification in 2011 census as opposed to its negligible contribution in 1981 (Pant and Mohan 1982), has been a major driver of urbanisation, with migration rates remaining roughly the same. This process of identification of villages as census towns is a "retrospective approach" followed by the census authority. There is lag of a decade between the actual attainment of urban characteristics by a village and its recognition as an urban settlement. During 2001 to 2011 period the census identified new towns that increased from 1362 to 3894, even though the number of statutory towns increased marginally from 3799 to

4041. Thus of the additional 2774 towns enumerated for the country in 2011, nearly 2532 were census towns and only 242 were statutory towns. Up to 2001 the share of these towns in the total urban population was low (7.4%) and their numbers were growing gradually (Pradhan 2013). Nearly 29.5 per cent of urban population growth in India was fundamentally owed to this unique process of rural to urban classification. Evidently the changing structure of employment enabled a large number of villages to be elevated to town status, and this phenomenon has played an important role in increasing the overall urbanization levels (Kundu 2011a, b).

The linkage between changing rural employment structure and urban growth is apparent from this process of recognition of large villages as urban settlements. It is important to note here that settlements in the census are designated as urban areas on the basis of certain demographic and economic criteria. A village is transformed into a town by satisfying the three criteria of (a). Size (population of 5000 or more), (b). Density (at least 400 per sq km), and (c). Nature of work (at least 75 per cent of the male workers engaged in non-farm work) (Sivaramakrishnan et al. 2005). If a rural settlement satisfies the demographic and economic criteria alone, the census recognizes it as a 'census town'. Once the settlement receives state government recognition, it is recognised as a 'statutory town'. The current thrust of the government on developing 'rurban' areas—semi-urban areas in the vicinity of cities or the emphasis on 'PURA' (providing urban amenities in rural areas) is significant when viewed in context of the growth of census towns in such large numbers (see Table 1.4 for details of towns).

Table 1.4 Number of towns, 2011 & 2011

Type of urban unit	2011 Census	2001 Census
India		
Towns	7935	5161
Statutory town	4041	3799
Census town	3894	1362
Gujarat		
Towns	348	242
Statutory town	195	168
Census town	153	74

Source: Census of India, 2011

It has been noted that the largest size class cities were showing rapidly declining decadal urban growth rates (Jan van Duijne 2017). The formation of new towns is indicative of dispersed and complex urbanisation processes occurring at the bottom of the urban hierarchy. Such trends are active without disturbing the distribution scales of the total urban population in their favour (Ibid.). According to literature, there are several factors that have contributed to the process of rural urbanisation in the country (Sarkar 2006; Khasnabis 2008; Kundu 2011a; Samanta 2014). A commonly cited factor (as in the case of West Bengal) is that the adoption of neo-liberal policy by the government discouraged state support for small peasants and reduced the subsidies on inputs to an extent that the operational costs increased making agriculture non-profitable. This provided an impetus to the movement of farmers away from farm to non-farm activities. Concomitantly, inadequate support to marketing, exports and falling price of food grains forced many cultivators to leave agriculture. On the other hand, it has also been shown that towns have emerged and are flourishing on account of a mechanism of capital transfer from the agricultural sector to commercial sector. There is an apparent paradox between these two views. However, it is also true that the number and area under marginal holdings over the years have recorded an increase. Inadequacy of agricultural earnings might have allowed farmers, who previously practised agriculture, to engage in petty informal non-farm economic activities such as rural transport, retail trade, vegetable vending etc. without entirely giving up agriculture related activities.

Kundu (1983) contended that the distribution of urban population across size class of towns in the country was "top-heavy," and that large-sized towns and cities were the main drivers of the urbanisation process, with the small- and medium-sized towns barely registered growth. Thus on the methodological consideration, Kundu launched a debate against this extraordinary and unprecedented increase in the number of new census towns in 2011 and referred it as "census activism" by pointing out that the "directorate of census operations has become a bit more enthusiastic in identifying new urban centres" (2011b: 15).

The other important phenomenon concomitant to the urbanization process in India is the fact that villages located outside the boundaries of cities or those with peripheral locations are getting included within the municipal boundaries over time and are becoming part of the urban agglomerations. India is on the path of rapid urbanization and the urban development authorities of all the cities are planning to draw more and more villages into their nets. The causes and consequences of this phenomenon therefore require careful analysis. Even after a village is included in the city's administrative boundary, the problems of rural-urban linkages remain and makes the categorization as "rural" and "urban" quite fuzzy (Shah 2012). The substantial growth of peri-urban areas or urban agglomerations has been fuelled by the growth of peripheral 'new towns' and the population growth in the urban agglomeration has been more than that in the primary metros (Sita and Bhagat 2005; Shaw 2005).

Gandhi and Pethe (2017) contend that certain problems are associated with the peripheral urban growth (outside municipal boundaries), chiefly relating to land conversion from agricultural to non-agricultural uses and development of real estate for residential and commercial purposes. Since such areas are largely governed by rural panchayats or smaller municipal councils, they have limited capacity to develop the infrastructure or the service requirements of the expanding population. Most of the new urban centres face severe shortage in service delivery such as connections for water supply, sewerage networks, and solid waste management. Moreover, absence of proper development regulations in these areas, existence of a strong builder–politician nexus, corruption, and lack of monitoring lead to unauthorised development and urban sprawl (Ibid.). These problems need to be addressed through proper planning and enforcement at the regional level.

Finally, several scholars have also underscored the fact that the population statistics generated by the census are not dynamic or temporal, but occur once per decade. As such the population census are not conducted with the intension to capture the rapidly unfolding and complex urbanisation processes. Samanta (2014) and Jan van Duijne (2017) believe that available evidence points to the fact that the contemporary urban realities have become more differentiated, polymorphic, and variegated, and the boundaries of the urban and rural have become less sharp. Having stated this, it is also true that urbanisation is associated with important societal transformations and is integral to modernisation and progress. It results in greater geographic mobility, elements of demographic transition (including lower fertility, longer life expectancy, and population ageing), higher levels of literacy and education, greater access to health and social services and public amenities, and enhanced opportunities for cultural and political participation (Glaeser 2011). To capture some of these on-going transitions, narratives of areas showing fast demographic as well as morphological changes and empirical regional case studies based on large-scale primary data collection is needed. Only these can provide insights into the complex process of urbanisation.

SELECTION OF CASE STUDY

Gujarat presents an interesting case to study the underlying dimensions of rural transformation process. Gujarat state was selected for the in-depth study as the state's economy performed well in terms of growth of state domestic product in the first decade of economic reforms. It was celebrated as one of the dynamic regional economies of India, with an above average net state domestic product (NSDP) and its growth rate. The growth rate of NSDP remained stable at 4.6 percent in the 1970s and 1980s. Gujarat improved its growth performance remarkably thereafter. The growth acceleration was very noticeable after 1999–2000 as can be seen from the trend growth at 9.3 per cent in the overall NSDP between 1999–2000 to 2008–2009 (Arya and Mehta 2011). Such high growth can be attributed to economic policy reforms. Apparently, Gujarat benefited from liberalization much more than the other states (Dholakia 2007). There has been much debate on the economic performance of Gujarat and the reasons for the same, apart from the significance of the growth on overall development of the state and its residents (Bagchi et al. 2005; Dholakia 2000, 2007; Hirway 1995, 2000; Mehta 2006). Implementation of economic reforms in Gujarat, based on its socio-economic, cultural and political environment, turned the state into one of the fastest-growing states in the country. However, it is increasingly felt that despite this success, inclusive growth was not forthcoming easily; this along with problems related to redistribution, human development indicators and neglect of the environmental dimension of growth—may prove the path being followed to be unsustainable (Shah and Pathak 2014; Hirway et al. 2014). Post liberalization, great regional disparities in the levels of development were seen in the state, with an observable bias in favour of developed regions and better-off sections of the populations, coupled with the distortion of the agriculture-industry linkage and severe resource degradation.

There was an uneven pattern of growth across the sectors. Arya and Mehta (2011) noted that the primary sector in Gujarat from 1960–1961 onwards showed fluctuating growth. Up to 1980–1981 the agriculture sector grew at 0.3 per cent. In 1990s decade up to mid-2000s, long term agriculture growth rate hovered at 1.6 per cent. Thus value added from agriculture sector showed hardly any upward growth trend. The linear growth rate of the primary sector after 1999–2000 accelerated to nine per cent. Agriculture sector alone grew at nearly ten per cent. This phenomenon has been widely documented by others as well (Gandhi and

Namboodiri 2010; Shah et al. 2009; Kumar et al. 2010; Mehta 2012a, 2014). In the 2000s decade—the period of high growth in the agricultural sector—the primacy of agriculture in the overall growth acceleration in the state cannot be denied. Amongst the causes identified for the remarkable growth in agricultural sector in the last decade, water management efficiency, regular power supply (due to Jyotigram programme), adoption of cash crops and impetus to horticulture and animal husbandry, introduction of new crop technology chiefly Bt cotton and favourable prices for agricultural products are chiefly cited. Growth was further enhanced by the Narmada project and ample rainfall in the period under consideration. Analysis (Mehta 2012a) indicates that the high growth in yields was mainly an outcome of favourable weather conditions. However, it has been contended (Mehta 2013) that with the adoption of higher yielding varieties and transgenic crop varieties (cotton), expansion of cultivation is happening even on marginal lands with degraded and fragile soils and with uncertain availability of irrigation facilities, that has made agriculture prone to volatility. Vast in-migration to the state and increasing use of capital-intensive machinery may also have helped Gujarat. Unlike other industrialised states that had lost their comparative advantage with growth in per capita incomes, a reflection of rising labour costs for agriculture, on account of the factors stated above Gujarat was able to maintain and enhance its comparative advantage in agriculture (Morris 2014).

Urbanization, considered an index of development, has shot up in Gujarat in the last ten years, according to data of Census 2011. The data reveals that the state's urban population as a percentage of its total population grew from 37.4 per cent in 2001 to 42.6 per cent in 2011. This remarkable growth of 5.2 per cent in the urban population in the last one decade is the highest in the country and much ahead of Tamil Nadu (4.4%), Maharashtra (2.8%) and even the national average of 3.4 per cent. Ahmedabad, Surat, Rajkot, Valsad, Porbandar, Jamnagar and Gandhinagar districts have the largest shares of urban population. The largest increase in urbanisation level and rate has been recorded in the three adjoining districts of Valsad, Surat and Bharuch in the last decade. These are also the districts with concentration of industrial investments during the economic reforms period. Traditionally, Gujarat's urbanisation is considered to be dichotomous in nature, referred to as 'core-periphery'. Development is concentrated in the transport corridor connecting Ahmedabad, the largest city of the state with Mumbai (Patel 1991). About 55 per cent of the state's urban population lived in the four metros (Ahmedabad, Surat, Vadodara and Rajkot), showing a somewhat skewed urbanisation pattern in 2011. In the reforms period, the coastal region also attracted investments and new pockets of economic development emerged in the districts of Rajkot, Jamnagar, Kachchh and Porbandar, these districts also having the locational advantage of the coast. Unlike urbanisation, industrialisation is spread across the state, as can be seen by comparing urbanisation levels (2011) with the industrial investments by districts (Mahadevia 2014).

A phenomenal increase in urban population growth was registered between 2001 to 2011 even in the agrarian and the tribal hinterlands of Gujarat (notably the districts of Valsad, Sabarkantha, Banaskantha). This points to the fact that urbanization in the state is becoming more equitable and the momentum of urban growth is being fuelled by smaller urban settlements. It may be added that in the state of Gujarat the process of reclassification of large villages into census towns has been triggered by the increasing prosperity of the agricultural population. With increasing prosperity, lifestyles are acquiring elements of urban cultures (Shah 2002, 2012). The challenges in this context are creation of social, economic and physical infrastructure (Alagh 2012) and investment in rural education and skill development that makes the rural workforce employable (Lobo and Shah 2012; Mehta 2012b). Another ramification of the high growth experience in the state is the scale of labour mobility- both long term and short spells of migration. It is important to mention here that Gujarat acts as an important magnet that attracts migrants from other states like Rajasthan and Madhya Pradesh (Kundu and Gupta 1996; Srivastava 1998). There is also substantial flow of intra-state migration from less to more developed regions. The increased labour mobility- both intra-state and inter-state is spurred by vibrancy in both agriculture and industry-infrastructure sectors and by 2007–2008, Gujarat was among the five states with the highest incidence of net migration (Shah and Dhak 2014). Both inter-regional disparity within Gujarat and rapid increase in the rate of urbanisation may be important factors leading to labour mobility in the state.

OBJECTIVES AND METHODOLOGY

This book makes an attempt at understanding the on-going transformational changes in the rural economic structure, as manifested in the emergence of large numbers of census towns- these being a major source of overall urbanization, and the underlying economic, social and environmental dimensions of such a change. Given the complexity of the situation at the country level, the book takes recourse to a case study and a thorough in-depth exploration of the situation in the western state of Gujarat. The economic, social and environmental consequences of the on-going process of structural changes in the rural economy and concomitant urbanisation have been examined through analysis of secondary data and field based primary data. Given the all-pervasive nature of the phenomenon and national character, as well as the diversity of the underlying processes aiding the rural transformation, a study at the macro (country) level would pose severe limitations in unravelling the causal dimensions. For this reason an attempt is made to do so by means of a case study of a developed state, namely Gujarat and its census towns. The empirical findings from the micro level can help in arriving at generalisations that explain the processes of change sweeping through the rest of the country and what should be the policy responses. The study, including the field work seeks to add a granular understanding of the economic and social dynamics of non-farm employment growth across varied locations. The idea was to capture the possible diversities that the growth of the non-farm economy possesses and try to ascertain whether the growth of non-farm economy indeed provides an impetus for urbanisation of a "subaltern" kind (Denis et al. 2012) in addition to peripheral growth in already urbanized and industrialized districts ? Does it also possess the potential of transforming a region into a modern social and economic formation?

It is apparent that besides the demographic causes, the growth in rural non-farm sector (in terms of changing employment and income structure) is fuelling the process of urbanisation. Moreover, the emergence of a large number of census settlements is on account of such changes in the village economy. It is also true that transformation in rural landscape would have far reaching social and environmental implications, in addition to the economic implications. Thus the study begins with the following premises:

- It is believed that the economic consequences of rural transformation pertain to reduced dependence on land, or are driven by higher land productivity, larger settlement size encouraging emergence of non-primary economic activities due to scale economies, and agricultural diversification. Obviously the consequences vary depending on locational factors (such as proximity to cities, location along corridors, remoteness of location etc.).
- The social consequences of rural transformation are related to the census towns being a replica of village society in terms of the existing

social relations. It may also happen that urbanisation is accompanied by weakening of some of the social relations, particularly with respect to caste, religion, social norms etc. Possibly the 'sanskritization' process in the newly emerging urban centres may prevail more vigorously and this dimension merits focus.

- Environmental effects of the current trends are mainly related to reduction in land availability and its competing uses for agriculture, industry and residential purposes, population pressure and the need to raise labour productivity. Together these forces may result in enhanced encroachment of forests, use of marginal lands, and degradation of land and water resources due to increase in industrial and urban activity. The absence of urban amenities in the newly emerging urban centres pose threats for wellbeing and sustainable urban living.

In order to examine the above hypotheses a comprehensive methodology has been adopted in the chapters to follow. Preliminary data has been sourced from secondary and government agencies; mainly Census of India, National Sample Survey Office, Economic Census, State line departments etc. for demography and employment, and the Central Statistical Organisation for information on income, in addition to the use of published reports, books and journal articles, as well as digital and web resources (CMIE, Indiastat). The secondary information is supplemented with primary data and field observations. The book includes the results of a field based research conducted for a representative set of census towns. The sample primarily includes large villages that have transformed as census towns and some of the urban areas that have been designated as statutory towns. For a comprehensive coverage of varied situations, selection of the settlements took cognizance of the different agro-climatic conditions, as well as locational factors viz., proximity to cities, location in an agricultural hinterland or industrial district, along a growth axis or transportation corridor, tribal belt, or having a dispersed location. A primary household survey was conducted to ascertain the changes in consumption habits and societal norms by administering a detailed household questionnaire. Recourse was also taken to participatory methods of data gathering (notably, focus group discussions) from different stakeholders, mainly agriculturalists, labourers, panchayat and block level officials, entrepreneurs, and traders. The focus of such exercises was to unravel the nature of changes taking place in the rural/urban economy. The stress areas in terms of environmental and social impacts, particularly where negative externalities are emerging have been highlighted in the book.

It merits mentioning here that the nature of enquiry for the present work is primarily limited to fact finding rather than rigorous hypothesis testing. Techniques such as exploratory factor analyses are useful tools to identify and categorize underlying dimensions, such as the economic, social and environmental impacts of the rural transformation process. However, the nature of data available from secondary and field based enquiry did not permit adoption of such techniques in the book. Nonetheless, wherever required correlation and regression analysis have been incorporated to explain and test the occurrence of identified phenomena. It is envisaged that the insights derived would lead to policy consequences for steering the Indian as well as the regional economy towards an inclusive development process. It would enable planning and aid investment decisions for creation and location of physical and social infrastructures in the newly emerging urban centres. Opportunities required for skill development, creation of markets, services etc. can be identified in a manner that regional economic structure is strengthened and growth process is benign and distributive in nature.

The analysis and findings are presented in seven chapters. Apart from the introductory chapter, the rest of the book comprises of the following chapters; Chap. 2 based on a review of literature and secondary data sources discusses the rural transformation process and analyses the factors responsible for occupational diversification and growth of non-farm economy across the states. Chapter 3 presents stylised facts on the employment situation in Gujarat using the census and NSSO information and also an in-depth analysis of the emerging economic activities with regard to their nature, location, and size in Gujarat. The next chapter is focussed on assessing the implications of structural changes in the rural economy on the urbanization levels, and identifying the challenges therein. The latter part of the book discusses the results of the primary research that has been integral to identifying the undercurrents and consequences of rural transformation. Chapter 5 hence is concerned with highlighting the changing socioeconomic profile of the urbanised villages (Census Towns) that have been selected for the purpose. Chapter 6 is devoted to summarising the economic, social and environmental effects of rural transformation as seen through the field study of census towns in Gujarat. The last chapter summarises the findings and draws out the areas requiring focus of policy interventions.

REFERENCES

Alagh, Yoginder K. 2012. *Rural-Urban Continuum*. Inaugural Address at ITDC-TTI Workshop on Rural-Urban Linkage, at Institute of Rural Management, Anand, 21 August, Mimeo.

Arya, Anita, and Niti Mehta. 2011. *Performance of Gujarat Economy: An Analysis of the Instability Aspect*. SPIESR Working Paper No 7, November.

Bagchi, Amiya Kumar, Panchanan Das, and Sadhan Chattopadhyay. 2005. Growth and Structural Change in the Economy of Gujarat, 1970–2000. *Economic and Political Weekly* 40 (28): 3039–3047.

Basole, Amit. 2017. What Does the Rural Economy Need. *Economic and Political Weekly* 52 (9).

Basu, D.N., and S.P. Kashyap. 1999. Rural Non-Agricultural Employment in India: Role of Development Process and Rural-Urban Employment Linkages. *Economic and Political Weekly* 27 (51/52): 19–26.

Berdegué, Julio A., Tomás Rosada, and Anthony J. Bebbington. 2014. The Rural Transformation. In *International Development: Ideas, Experience, and Prospects*, ed. Bruce Currie-Alder, Ravi Kanbur, David M. Malone, and Rohinton Medhora. Oxford Scholarship Online.

Bhagat, R.B. 2011. Emerging Pattern of Urbanization in India. *Economic and Political Weekly* 46 (34): 10–12.

Binswanger-Mkhize, Hans P. 2012. India 1960–2010: Structural Change, the Rural Non-Farm Sector, and the Prospects for Agriculture. In *Stanford Symposium Series on Global Food Policy and Food Security in the 21st Century*. Stanford: Center for Food Security and the Environment, Stanford University.

———. 2013. The Stunted Structural Transformation of the Indian Economy Agriculture, Manufacturing and the Rural Non-Farm Sector. *Economic and Political Weekly* 47 (26&27): 5–13.

Chakraborty, Saurav, Subhanil Chowdhury, Utpal Roy, and Kakoli Das. 2017. Declassification of Census Towns in West Bengal Empirical Evidences from Patuli, Bardhaman. *Economic and Political Weekly* 52 (25&26): 25–31.

Chandrasekhar, S., and Ajay Sharma. 2014. *Urbanization and Spatial Patterns of Internal Migration in India*. Mumbai: Indira Gandhi Institute of Development Research.

Christaller, Walter. 1966. *Central Places in Southern Germany*. Englewood Cliffs, NJ: Prentice-Hall.

Currie-Alder, Bruce, Ravi Kanbur, David M. Malone, and Rohinton Medhora. 2014. *International Development: Ideas, Experience, and Prospects*. Oxford Scholarship Online.

Denis, Eric, P. Mukhopadhyay, and Marie-Helene Zerah. 2012. Subaltern Urbanization in India. *Economic and Political Weekly* 47 (30): 52–62.

Dholakia, R.H. 2000. Liberalisation in Gujarat—Review of Recent Experience. *Economic and Political Weekly* 35 (35–36): 3121–3124.

———. 2007. Sources of Economic Growth and Acceleration in Gujarat. *Economic and Political Weekly* 42: 770–778.

Ellis, Frank, Milton Kutengule, and Alfred Nyasulu. 2003. Livelihoods and Rural Poverty Reduction in Malawi. *World Development* 31 (9): 1495–1510.

Gandhi, V.P., and N.V. Namboodiri. 2010. The Economics and Contribution of Cotton Biotechnology in the Agricultural Growth of Gujarat. In *High Growth Trajectory and Structural Changes in Gujarat Agriculture*, ed. R.H. Dholakia and S.K. Datta. Macmillan Publishers India Ltd.

Gandhi, Sahil, and Abhay Pethe. 2017. Emerging Challenges of Metropolitan Governance in India. *Economic and Political Weekly* 52 (27): 55.

Glaeser, E.L. 2011. The Challenge of Urban Policy. *Journal of Political Analysis and Management* 31: 111–122.

Haggblade, Steven, Peter B.R. Hazell, and Thomas Reardon. 2007. *Transforming the Rural Nonfarm Economy Opportunities and Threats in the Developing World*. Baltimore, MD: International Food Policy Research Institute, The Johns Hopkins University Press.

Hayami, Y., and V.W. Ruttan. 1971. *Agricultural Development: An International Perspective*. Baltimore, MD: Johns Hopkins Press.

Himanshu. 2011. Employment Trends in India: A Re-Examination. *Economic and Political Weekly* 46 (37): 3729–3748.

Hirway, Indira. 1995. Selective Development and Widening Disparities in Gujarat. *Economic and Political Weekly* 30 (41–42): 2603–2618.

———. 2000. Dynamics of Development in Gujarat: Some Issues. *Economic and Political Weekly* 35 (35).

Hirway, Indira, Amita Shah, and Ghanshyam Shah, eds. 2014. *Growth or Development – Which Way Is Gujarat Going?* Oxford University Press.

International Fund for Agricultural Development. 2016. *Rural Development Report 2016: Fostering Inclusive Rural Transformation*. Rome: Quintily, September.

Jayaraman, Raji, and Peter Lanjouw. 1998. *The Evolution of Poverty and Inequality in Indian Villages*. Policy Research Working Paper, 1870, The World Bank.

Johnston, B.F., and J.W. Mellor. 1961. The Role of Agriculture in Economic Development. *American Economic Review* 51 (4): 566–593.

Kashyap, S.P. 2011. Emerging Tendencies in Rural Non-Farm Enterprise Sector: Role of Policy. *Sampada* 67 (9).

Kashyap, S.P., and Niti Mehta. 2007. Non-Farm Sector in India: Temporal & Spatial Aspects. *Indian Journal of Labour Economics* 50 (4): 611–632.

Khasnabis, Ratan. 2008. The Economy of West Bengal. *Economic and Political Weekly* 43 (52): 103–115.

Kumar, Dinesh M., A. Narayanamoorthy, O. Singh, M.V.K. Sivamohar, Manoj Sharma, and Nitin Bossi. 2010. *Gujarat's Agricultural Growth Story: Exploding Some Myths*. Occasional Paper No.2-0410, Hyderabad: Institute of Resource Analysis & Policy.

Kundu, Amitabh. 1983. Theories of City Size Distribution and Indian Urban Structure – A Reappraisal. *Economic and Political Weekly* 18 (31): 1361–1368.

———. 2011a. Politics and Economics of Urban Growth. *Economic and Political Weekly* 46 (20): 10–12.

———. 2011b. Method in Madness: Urban Data from 2011 Census. *Economic and Political Weekly* 46 (40): 13–16.

Kundu, Amitabh, and Shalini Gupta. 1996. Migration, Urbanisation and Regional Inequality. *Economic and Political Weekly* 31 (52): 3391–3398.

Kuznets, S. 1966. *Modern Economic Growth: Rate, Structure and Spread*. New Haven: Yale University Press.

Lanjouw, Jean, and Peter Lanjouw. 2001. The Rural Non-Farm Sector: Issues and Evidence from Developing Countries. *Agricultural Economics* 26: 1–23.

Lewis, W.A. 1956. *Theory of Economic Growth*. Great Britain: George Allen & Unwin Ltd.

Lipton, M. 1968. Strategy for Agriculture: Urban Bias and Rural Planning. In *The Crisis of Indian Planning*, ed. P. Streeten and M. Lipton. London: Oxford University Press.

Lobo, Lancy, and Jayesh Shah, eds. 2012. *Globalization, Growth and Employment: Challenges and Opportunities*. New Delhi: Rawat Publications.

Mahadevia, Darshini. 2014. Dynamics of Urbanization in Gujarat. In *Growth or Development: Which Way Is Gujarat Going?* ed. I. Hirway, A. Shah, and G. Shah. New Delhi: Oxford University Press.

Majumdar, Surajit. 2012. *Agriculture-Industry Dynamics and Rural Transformation in India*. Presented at ITDC-TTI Workshop on Rural-Urban Linkage, at Institute of Rural Management, Anand, 21 August.

Mehta, Niti. 2006. Imbalances in Development Between Regions and Social Groups: Evidences from Gujarat. *Anvesak* 36 (1): 1–12.

———. 2012a. Performance of Crop Sector in Gujarat During High Growth Period: Some Explorations. *Agricultural Economics Research Review* 25 (2): 195–204.

———. 2012b. Food Security Aspects and Diversification of Demand in the Context of Gujarat. *Anvesak* 42 (1&2).

———. 2013. Employability of Rural Labour in the Neo-Liberal Era: A Study of Gujarat. *Indian Journal of Labour Economics* 56 (2): 243–267.

———. 2014. *Gujarat Over Time: Progress Towards Growth, Development and Inclusiveness*. Paper Presented at the Seminar on "Status of Social Science Research in Western India: Critical Engagement and Future Direction", November 14–16, 2014, ICSSR Western Regional Centre, Vidyanagari, SantaCruz (E), Mumbai.

Mellor, J.W. 1986. *Agriculture on the Road to Industrialisation*. Washington, DC: IFPRI.

Morris, Sebastian. 2014. A Comparative Analysis of Gujarat's Economic Growth. In *Growth or Development: Which Way Is Gujarat Going?* ed. I. Hirway, A. Shah, and G. Shah. New Delhi: Oxford University Press.

Pant, Chandrashekhar, and Rakesh Mohan. 1982. Morphology of Urbanisation in India – Some Results from 1981 Census. *Economic and Political Weekly* 17 (39).

Papola, T.S., and P.P. Sahu. 2012. *Employment Growth and Structure: Policies, Performance and Prospects*. (Mimeo). New Delhi: Institute for Studies in Industrial Development.

Patel, Surendra. 1991. Growing Regional Inequalities in Gujarat. *Economic and Political Weekly* 26 (26): 1618–1623.

Pradhan, K.C. 2013. Unacknowledged Urbanisation – New Census Towns of India. *Economic and Political Weekly* 48 (36): 43–51.

Ranis, Gustav, and Frances Stewart. 1999. V-Goods and the Role of the Urban Informal Sector in Development. *Economic Development and Cultural Change* 47 (2): 259–288.

Reddy, D.N., Amarender A. Reddy, N. Nagaraj, and C. Bantilan. 2014. *Rural Non-Farm Employment and Rural Transformation in India*. Working Paper Series No 57. Patancheru: International Crops Research Institute for the Semi-Arid Tropics.

Samanta, Gopa. 2014. The Politics of Classification and the Complexity of Governance in Census Towns. *Economic and Political Weekly* 49 (22): 55–62.

Sarkar, Abhirup. 2006. Political Economy of West Bengal. *Economic and Political Weekly* 41 (4).

Schultz, T.W. 1968. Institutions and the Rising Economic Value of Man. *American Journal of Agricultural Economics* 50 (5): 1113–1122.

Shah, A.M. 2002. *Exploring India's Rural Past: A Gujarat Village in the Early Nineteenth Century*. Delhi: Oxford University Press.

———. 2012. The Village in the City, the City in the Village. *Economic and Political Weekly* 47 (52): 17–19.

Shah, Amita, and Biplab Dhak. 2014. Labour Migration and Welfare in Gujarat: Recent Evidence and Issues. In *Growth or Development: Which Way Is Gujarat Going?* ed. I. Hirway, A. Shah, and G. Shah. New Delhi: Oxford University Press.

Shah, Amita, and Jharna Pathak, eds. 2014. *Tribal Development in Western India*, 344. New Delhi: Routledge.

Shaw, Annapurna, ed. 2005. *Indian Cities in Transition*. Hyderabad: Orient Longman.

Shah, Tushaar, Ashok Gulati, P. Hemant, Ganga Shreedhar, and R.C. Jain. 2009. Secret of Gujarat's Agrarian Miracle After 2000. *Economic and Political Weekly* 44 (52): 45–55.

Sita, K., and R.B. Bhagat. 2005. Population Change and Economic Restructuring in Indian Metropolitan Cities: A Study of Mumbai. In *Indian Cities in Transition*, ed. Annapurna Shaw. Hyderabad: Orient Longman.

Sivaramakrishnan, K.C., Amitabh Kundu, and B.N. Singh. 2005. *Handbook of Urbanisation in India*. Delhi: Oxford University Press.

Solarin, Sakiru Adebola, and Yuen Yee Yen. 2016. A Global Analysis of the Impact of Research Output on Economic Growth. *Scientometrics* 108 (2): 855–874.

Srivastava, Ravi. 1998. Migration and the Labour Market in India. *Indian Journal of Labour Economics* 41 (4): 583–616.

Tacoli, C., ed. 2006. *The Earthscan Reader in Rural–Urban Linkages*. London & Sterling, VA: Earthscan.

Timmer, C. Peter, and Selvin Akkus. 2008. *The Structural Transformation as a Pathway out of Poverty: Analytics, Empirics and Politics*. Working Paper Number No 150, July. Washington, DC: Centre for Global Development.

van Duijne, Robbin. 2017. What Is India's Urbanisation Riddle? *Economic and Political Weekly* 52 (28): 76–77.

von Thünen, J.H. 1826. *The Isolated State*. English Translation by C.M. Wartenberg (1966). Oxford: Pergammon Press.

Wang, Gabe T., and Xiaobo Hu. 2007. Small Town Development and Rural Urbanization in China. *Journal of Contemporary Asia* 29 (1): 76–94.

World Bank. 2007. *World Development Report 2008: Agriculture for Development*. Washington, DC: The World Bank.

World Bank and the International Monetary Fund. 2013. *Global Monitoring Report 2013: Rural-Urban Dynamics and the Millennium Development Goals*. Washington, DC: The World Bank.

Zhu, Yu. 2014. *In-Situ Urbanisation in China: Processes, Contributing Factors and Policy Implications*. World Migration Report 2015. www.iom.int/sites/default/fi les/our_work/ICP/MPR/WMR-2015.

Zhu, Yu, X. Qi, H. Shao, and K. He. 2009. *The Evolution of China's In Situ Urbanization and Its Planning and Environmental Implications: Case Studies from Quanzhou Municipality*. www.ciesin.columbia.edu/repository/pern/papers/urban_pde_zhu_etal.

Zimmerman, Frederick J., and Michael Carter. 2003. Asset Smoothing, Consumption Smoothing and the Reproduction of Inequality Under Risk and Subsistence Constraints. *Journal of Development Economics* 71 (2): 233–260.

CHAPTER 2

Occupational Diversification and Rural Transformation

INTRODUCTION

India is undergoing a much talked about and documented employment creation crisis. While the problem is often stated in terms of unemployment among educated youth in urban areas or disguised unemployment in the informal sector, the crisis appears to be more severe in the rural economy. India's rural sector faces considerable challenges, manifested most starkly in the declining employment and income shares in agriculture. The share of income emanating from the farm sector is declining continuously from 29.3 per cent of GDP in 1993–1994 to 14.7 per cent in 2011–2012. The rapidly falling income share of agriculture and allied activities in the national income is accompanied by the decline in the share of rural employment in agriculture from 79 per cent in 1993–1994 to 64 per cent in 2011–2012. The share of rural agricultural workforce declined from 79 per cent in 1993–1994 to 73.2 per cent in 2004–2005. Since then the decline has been sharper, from 73.2 per cent in 2004–2005 to 64 per cent in 2011–2012.The offshoot of this development and shift of workforce out of agriculture can been seen from the doubling of the growth rate in per worker sectoral product in agriculture (at factor cost) from 2.5 per cent per annum; between 1993–1994 to 2003–2004 to 4.6 percent per annum between 2004–2005 to 2011–2012. After 2004–2005 to 2011–2012, the real per farm income accelerated to 7.3 per cent per annum; agricultural output growth increased to 4 per cent, accompanied by reduction in the number of farmers.

© The Author(s) 2018
N. Mehta, *Rural Transformation in the Post Liberalization Period in Gujarat*, https://doi.org/10.1007/978-981-10-8962-6_2

Apparently all this augurs well for the workers engaged in this sector, but for two facts. Firstly, landlessness is increasing, and secondly the agriculture sector is progressively acquiring a small farm character. As per the population census, the share of agricultural labourers amongst the agricultural workers has increased from 45.6 to 55 per cent between 2001 and 2011. During the same period cultivators' share has declined from 54.4 per cent to 45 per cent. This process of dispossession has particularly hastened after 2001. The Agricultural Census indicates that the share of marginal holdings (less than 1 ha) rose from 50 to 65 per cent between 1970–1971 to 2004–2005. By 2010–2011, their share rose further to 67 per cent. In terms of area, the share has risen from 9 to 22 percent. In absolute terms the marginal holdings increased from 36 million in 1970–1971 to more than 92 million in 2010–2011. The continuous process of subdivision and re-distribution of landholding within the family is increasing the population pressure on arable land, with the average size of operational holding concomitantly recording a decline from 2.3 ha in 1970–1971 to only 1.16 ha in 2010–2011. Admittedly, agricultural sector in several areas faces excessive burden of labour force however, employment elasticity of agriculture sector with respect to Net Domestic Product has been falling from 1.09 (1999–2000 to 2004–2005) to −0.41 (2004–2005 to 2011–2012) (Misra and Suresh 2014). This is fuelled by the fact that employment growth in agriculture that was close to 0.85 per cent during 1999–2000 to 2004–2005, has declined to −0.90 percent during 2004–2005 to 2011–2012. The biggest challenge today is of generating livelihoods capable of providing regular, living incomes for all the households in rural areas. It may be noted that urbanization process has played a role in the pace of occupational diversification in rural areas. The poor performance of agricultural sector and increased fragmentation of holdings is accompanied by a significant shift in the rural occupational distribution away from the primary sector. The Employment-Unemployment survey of the Labour Ministry (Government of India 2016) reveals that as per National Sample Survey Office's (NSSO) 'usual principal status' definition, in 2015 58.1 percent of workers were in agriculture, followed by construction (11.6%), manufacturing (8%), and trade and repairs (7.1%). Thus the overall share of non-agricultural sector in rural employment has accelerated from 27 percent in 2005 to 42 percent in 2015. Worrying feature is that manufacturing sector has lost its share in employment in rural areas over time, while the gainers are construction and trade. Manufacturing is seen as an important factor for the revival of rural economy and hence an urgent focus on rural industrialization is required (Papola and Sahu 2012). The salient feature of the process of structural change in the country is that the changes in the gross domestic product in industry and services is accompanied by weak growth of employment in the off-farm sector.

The ongoing crisis has the added dimension of quality of livelihoods in the rural sector. Fragmentation of landholdings is making the agricultural activity un-remunerative for cultivating households and necessitates the adoption of multiple non-farm survival/livelihood strategies, including agricultural labour and migration to the nearby towns and cities and even over long distances for eking out a living. However, nearly 70 percent of the agricultural households fail to meet their consumption needs (low) even given their diverse sources of income. Basole (2017) based on data from the Situation Assessment Survey of Farmers round of NSSO shows that absolute levels of income (including net receipts from cultivation, livestock, non-farm business and wages/salary) remain lower than expenditure for agricultural households. This indicates that whether in the farm or non-farm sector, rural economy is hardly remunerative.

This obviously indicates the need for policy initiatives for emergence of an agricultural production system that accelerates growth without crossing the sustainability barrier. A recent study by Bathla et al. (2017) examined the pattern and composition of government expenditure and subsidies from 1981–1982 to 2013–2014 and estimated elasticities in order to relate to the achievement of development goals of improving agricultural production and eliminating poverty. It is a matter of concern that the share of agriculture, irrigation and flood control fell substantially in total expenditure on economic services during the period stipulated. Expenditure on education, research and development, health and energy is essential to ensure high returns and to accelerate increase in agricultural income. Clearly the path of this kind of development can be smoothened if the population pressure on land is reduced through occupational diversification. Such a process has been going on for long, with the casual workers and those with inadequate land base being increasingly attracted to part time, off season and multiple occupations in the non-farm activities. Urbanization processes and the growth of service villages/small towns are the causes and consequences of such processes leading to rural occupational diversification. In addition to increasing productivity of agriculture, and ensuring remunerative prices, robust growth in rural non-farm employment has to come particularly through livelihood generation in manufacturing sector and public services that have the ability to raise rural incomes.

This chapter deals with the nature of rural transformation and factors underlying the growth in the rural non-farm economy. Insights obtained from the published literature are highlighted in the next section. This is followed by analysis at the state level pertaining to different facets of the employment situation in India, before we proceed to establish relationship of employment and income indicators with the level of non-farm employment. The employment situation in Gujarat is seen in the context of the larger state level scenario.

OVERVIEW OF RURAL NON-FARM DIVERSIFICATION: INSIGHTS FROM LITERATURE

The design of development policies for most of the developing countries in the past including India is based on the stylised conceptual premise that countries undergo structural transformation from predominantly rural, agrarian and subsistence economies to being predominantly urban, industrial and capitalistic economies (Clark 1940; Lewis 1954; Kuznets 1966). Such theories explain that with economic growth the production structure changes in favour of industry and subsequently with the expansion of services. Changes in workforce structure follow symmetrically from agriculture to industry and services. Spatially too there will be shift in production and employment from rural to rurban and urban locations. The empirical evidences to support the structural changes in rural economy and the emergence of rural non-farm sector in the country have been discussed at length in literature (Rondinelli 1983; Vaidyanathan 1986; Basant and Kumar 1989, 1990; Basu and Kashyap 1992; Bhalla 1993a, b, 2005a, b; Saleth 1997; Unni 1998; Sen and Himanshu 2004; Himanshu et al. 2016; Nayyar and Sharma 2005; Kashyap and Mehta 2005, 2007; Kashyap 2011; Lanjouw and Murgai 2009; Jodhka 2006; Jodhka and Kumar 2017 to name a few). Various studies, following the study by Vaidyanathan (1986), tried to understand the nature of emerging non-farm sector, which is whether it was 'distress diversification' or a dynamic and viable non-agricultural sector (i.e., the relative importance of 'push' and 'pull' factors). According to Vaidyanathan the diversification phenomenon was primarily distress induced as population pressure aggravated the land constraint, and akin to urban informal sector there emerged a low wage rural residual sector. However, a pervasive phenomenon of this type was not able to explain the rise in rural real wages and falling rural poverty since the mid-seventies up to at least the eighties in most regions. The rural poverty reduction has continued since then, though the rise in rural wage rates noted from 2006 onwards is sometimes attributed to the employment guarantee programme.

Research also tried to pinpoint the factors explaining the spatial variation in the relative importance of non-agricultural sector at different levels of disaggregation—all India level, states, NSS regions, agro-climatic zones and sub-zones. Level and growth of non-farm sector was associated with various explanatory variables, such as land productivity, rural inequalities pertaining to land and assets, poverty, unemployment rates, urbanization, literacy and so on. The interaction of urban–influence, surpluses generated in the farm sector, enhanced agricultural commercialization and primary sector diversification, access to physical and social infrastructure- all explained the growth induced employment transformation with rising real wages. Size of settlement also emerged as an important factor as larger centres offer greater scope for economies of scale for sustenance of certain non-farm activities. Urban influence and locational factors also shape the work and wellbeing in rural areas (Bhalla 2005a, b). Significantly, it has also been suggested that instead of deepening of rural-urban linkages, the remote rural areas in recent times are becoming bounded spaces (Krishna and Bajpai 2011).

The research in the late 1980s and early 1990s was quite vigorous. Some micro studies were conducted that tried to understand the processes that lead to the emergence and growth of non-agricultural sector. It must, however, be stated that research in this area has been constrained by limitations of data, conceptual ambiguities and often proxy variables are substituted for want of information on relevant categories. Basant and Kumar (1989, 1990) showed that within the rural non-agricultural sector, the increase in the tertiary sector seemed to be sharper than that in the secondary sector and was explained by the increase in the proportion of casual non-agricultural (male) workers, who shifted back and forth between agricultural and non-agricultural work. Participation in non-agricultural work varied inversely with size of land owned by the households, suggesting thereby that non-farm activities attracted casual workers and/or workers with inadequate land base.

Rural occupational diversification was explained to be an extension of urban manufacturing, possibly reflecting an outflow of urban growth, which in turn, could be an outcome of negative externalities experienced in large cities and incentives given for backward area development. Bhalla

(1993a, b) noted that the sunrise industries in most of the rural and urban areas were metal and mineral based, rather than agro-based and hence argued that rural industrialization should not be treated as an adjunct to agricultural growth, but rather as a development, which needed to be fostered independently. In another study Bhalla (2005a) identified three distinct regional rural workforce development trajectories: (1) the clusters of farm income agricultural involution districts; (2) the high farm income regions depicting increasing rural non-farm work specialization and (3) the rapidly diversifying "corridor districts" spread along road and rail lines between distant urban industrial conglomerations. However, agriculturally prosperous districts and "corridor districts" were not necessarily mutually exclusive. Some districts with high rural occupational diversification, such as Surat and Baroda, and districts of UP and Haryana adjoining Delhi, showed significant agricultural prosperity.

Basu and Kashyap (1992) showed that agricultural prosperity was the prime mover of rural occupational diversification. Citing micro level studies they demonstrated that temporary migration of labour from rural to urban areas, particularly of commuting variety, accounted for a sizeable portion of workforce in various economic activities of the urban centres as well as formed a major share of off-season employment of agricultural labour and small farmers. Basant and Parathasarthy (1991) highlighted that size of village, urban access and irrigation availability rather than crop-mix and land productivity appeared more crucial in boosting non-farm sector. Irrigation provided stability to growth, and studies in Central and South Gujarat showed that irrigation induced agricultural prosperity gave boost to occupational diversification (Kashyap 1995; Mehta 2001). 'Agrarian capitalists entrepreneurs' were found to be using surpluses generated by irrigated agriculture for widespread occupational diversification (Ruttan 1995).

Character of non-farm activities and nature of household involvement was found to vary with the level of development. Even in developed regions opportunities sets often differed depending upon economic and social moorings. Bhalla (2005b) and several other studies suggested that non-farm activities could be grouped into higher-income non-farm activities (HI-NFA) and lower income non-farm activities (LI-NFA). It is noticed that "...groups with no or less land participate more in LI-NFA whereas groups with larger farms participate more in HI-NFA." (Saleth 1997:1912).

OCCUPATIONAL DIVERSIFICATION AFTER 2000

Rural non-farm sector (RNFS) shrank during the decade of structural adjustment (Bhalla 2000). The recent experience indicates an expansion. The absolute growth in urban population in India during 2001 to 2011 (91 million) was higher than growth of rural population, but the rural workers usually employed in the non-farm sector in the country increased from 33.4 to 37.2 per cent (males) and 16.7 to 20.6 per cent (females) during 2004–2005 to 2009–2010 (NSSO)– an unprecedented increase in levels of rural non-farm sector employment (4.8%). Structural transformation in India incorporated growth of rural non-farm sector and declining share of agricultural employment. The rural non-farm sector GDP grew by 70 per cent after 1993–1994 and it was the biggest source of new jobs in the Indian economy. Rural non-agricultural sector contributes 65 per cent to the rural net national product- a result of the changing rural economic structure and growing demand for non-farm services. More recent studies indicate that the expansion in RNFS is accompanied with increasing casualization and deterioration in the quality of employment (Jatav 2010; Jatav and Sen 2013; Himanshu et al. 2013). Jatav and Sen (2013) by looking at NSSO data from the 2009–10 round concluded that growth in non-farm employment was primarily distress-driven based on the inverse relationship between agricultural endowments and the probability of a household member joining the non-farm sector, and that such distress-driven labour outflows possibly result in depressing the non-farm wages. Himanshu et al. (2013) also looked at NSSO data to conclude that growth in the nonfarm sector in the country between 2004 and 2009–10 was driven by sharp increases in casual employment, and that both the wage premium of regular non-farm labour over casual non-farm labour and the wage premium of casual non-farm labour over agricultural wages, deteriorated between 2000 and 2010. However, due to the fact that the sector employs sizeable labour, its role in contributing to poverty decline through employment expansion and its linkages with agriculture, RNFS commands importance along with agriculture sector (Lanjouw and Murgai 2009).

At the all India level, the non-agricultural sector in the rural areas engage usual status (PS+SS) workers to the extent of 35.5 per cent (2011–2012), increasing from 27 per cent (2004–2005) and 23 per cent in 1999–2000. The acceleration has been more noticeable during 2004–2005 to 2011–2012. Within the non-farm sector it is the tertiary sector that has created the highest jobs- engaging 27 per cent of the workers, while manufacturing sector accounts for only 9 per cent of the usual status workforce. Between 2004–2005 and 2011–2012, construction sector witnessed the largest increase by 6.2 per cent points. Trade, hotels and transport have shown minor changes (see Tables 2.14a, 2.14b, and 2.14c). Quite apparently in the rural areas the workers exiting from the agricultural sector are being increasingly absorbed in the construction sector, during this period. It is well known that construction, including public works under the Mahatma Gandhi National Rural Employment Guarantee Act (MNREGA) has emerged as the most important source of rural non-farm employment.

The above transformation, it has also been stated, is a consequence of urban spillover to rural non-farm employment, often self-employment. It would be flawed to examine the role of urbanization in isolation of rural transformation. Urbanization in the last decade and changes in the rural economy created the demand for non-farm activities and urban wards migration. The positive-externality impact of RNFS growth for urban areas stems from non-farm sector's capacity to limit rural to urban migration, and unsustainable urban growth (Jatav and Sen 2013; Basole 2017). Needless to add the growth of rural non-farm sector shows considerable heterogeneity across space, farm environment diversity and rural-urban labour absorption process. With the operation of functional linkages across the urban spectrum, the impact of existing urban areas on the growth of rural non-farm employment also cannot be ignored. In order to understand the trajectory of development in the country it would be useful to study the functioning of the village economies and the process of their integration into urban areas.

Consistent with the distress thesis, studies (such as Saha and Verick 2016) show that it is the economically weaker sections in rural areas, mainly the marginal and small farmers and agricultural labourers who are moving to the often low productive RNFS work. In fact amongst these sections the absence of alternative sources of rural (or urban) non-farm occupational backup often constitutes the tipping point for distress and suicides (Dandekar and Bhattacharya 2017). It has been observed that often the non-farm economy is not based on modern technology, except where technology itself is a source of employment, (e.g. mobile phone repair shops, engineering/farm machinery repairs). In addition, the social organisation remains low skill-based and informal in nature, with the engagement of workers often lacking the requisite formal qualifications (Jodhka and Kumar 2017). Large farmers on the other hand, engage in highly productive non-farm jobs.

Recently a number of micro level and longitudinal studies have been undertaken and their findings provide an opportunity to understand the composition and impacts of the growth in non-farm employment and rural transformation process in the past decades. Palanpur village has been surveyed each decade after independence and the surveys have traced developments in the village across time together with the response of the village economy to changes in the economic environment. In the earliest decades, change was related to agricultural intensification, irrigation enhancement and technological changes. Following the technological change in agriculture, green revolution and enhanced rural incomes, growth-led occupational diversification led to structural changes in the village economy. After the mid-1980s change was the result of job opportunities outside the villages or agriculture sector. Labour was released due to mechanization and increased market interface. Infact this outward looking behavior aided income mobility across generations and facilitated escape from poverty. However, Himanshu et al. (2013) had found that in Palanpur in 2008, although the non-farm sector had witnessed significant expansion, access to non-farm employment was becoming more broad-based, and inequality had increased sharply due to lack of universal access to non-farm jobs with some households remaining excluded. Study of Himanshu et al. (2016), has used results of the seven surveys in Palanpur to focus on the changing role of non-farm sector and its impact on inequality and mobility across social groups. What the study revealed is not at variance from the conclusions drawn by the earlier studies cited above. The changing fortunes of the residents of Palanpur were dictated by-

1. "...their own position in the village hierarchy governed by caste and gender relations, as it is due to their ability to take advantage of the opportunities that developments outside the village opened up" (p. 44).

Himanshu et al. (2016) identify the fundamental elements of the development process in Palanpur. The evidence appears somewhat mixed:

2. "...While agriculture and limited outside jobs played a central role in income growth in earlier survey, growing non-farm and outside jobs have become more important in recent periods." (p. 45). These aspects affect the agricultural development.
3. "...there has been an intensification of farm capital in the form of mechanization that has land-augmenting as well as labour saving

attributes … it has fostered non-farm employment rather than accel-erated agricultural productivity per hectare." Furthermore, "Improvement in farms practices, more emphasis on high value crops also lend dynamism, fostering investments in non-farm employment and outside jobs". (p. 45).

The study has also highlighted role of increasing casualization of work-force due to fragmentation of agricultural holdings that makes agriculture unremunerative. Engagement as casual labour in non-farm jobs has emerged as the largest contributor to non-farm incomes. These activities are driven by growth of nearby town and cities. Urbanization attracts workers from the surrounding rural areas, leading to rise in migration and to rural to urban commuting. It has led to the expansion of manufacturing and service related jobs. The rise in casual nonfarm workers is mainly due to demand for construction within the village and also in nearby towns and villages –fuelling growth of marble polishing units and brick kilns. Nature of non- farm diversification has also taken the form of self-employment.

While research states that self-employment is a distress induced phe-nomena evidence from Palanpur points to the contrary. "The self-employment activities in Palanpur clearly indicate a process of skill and capital accumulation … as opposed to the unprofitable activities in the earlier rounds and may not necessarily be a result of distress- driven mech-anism". (p. 47).

Growth in non-farm sector and employment, leads to growth in per capital incomes but in Palanpur evidence indicates rising inequality and growing dispersion in the distribution of income. Economic mobility was widespread amongst groups that embraced non-farm sector, vis-a-vis those with affinity with cultivation. Informal and casual nature of jobs was more accessible to household at the bottom of income distribution. For more remunerative and stable non-farm jobs, access to networks and fam-ily ties were important. That the ongoing rural agrarian structural trans-formation also has implications on the rural social structure was brought out by another longitudinal study for a village in Western UP by Kumar (2016). Reiterating findings of Palanpur study the author opines:

"Diversification is reducing caste domination in general, inequalities based on caste determine the ability to different groups to move into more or less remunerative and high-status positions and improve their well-being in the new economy." (p. 62). In this, context social and cultural capital such as social network and education are key factors.

That the ownership of land is of crucial importance for the engagement in non-farm activities has also been highlighted. "Due to concentration of land ownership among a few upper caste and upper OBC households, diversification of village economy has been dramatic." (Kumar 2016: 65).

Enhanced farm mechanization in recent decades has reduced intensity of labour use in agriculture. To a large extent, the de-peaseantisation (Singh and Bhogal 2014) process or the workers moving out of agriculture into non-farm sectors is a fall out of declining labour use is agriculture, due to rising capital intensity as well as non-viability of agriculture among small and marginal farmers.

The influence of urbanism and emerging rural-urban networks impact on the socio-economic and political landscape of rural areas and also change the inter-caste relationships. While dominant landholding upper castes benefit through such influences, the involvement of asset poor sections such as marginal farmers, landless and lower caste people in informal economy and expansion of non-farm service sector has transformed class relations in the villages. The transformation in the sociality of the villages is due to rural-urban exchanges and diversification of work within groups (Kumar 2016: 70). Besides the adoption of non-farm livelihoods and de-agrarianisation, migration as a livelihood strategy and remittances are also contributing to the changes in source of income in rural areas, as can be seen from the recent study on Bihar (Datta 2016; Datta et al. 2014).

"It is the remittances that are the real lifetime of rural Bihar; one ramification of increasing migration from the states is high dependence of remittance." (Datta 2016: 87).

Majority of the households reported migrant members and 52 per cent of the households reported that remittances comprised more than half of the total income. Overall, after local non-agricultural income, remittances formed the second most important source and comprised nearly 29 per cent of overall income. Yet iniquitous access to opportunities to migrate creates income disparities. It is thus important to note that:

"...the incidence of migration is the lowest in the bottom quintile ... the poorest in rural Bihar have the lowest propensity to migrate ... owing perhaps to high initial costs of migration, there is little evidence to support the hypothesis that poverty per se is a determinant of migration from rural Bihar." (Datta 2016: 91). Thus, while migration is a game changing pathway to higher incomes, yet the very poor do not take resort to it.

Jodhka (2014) ascribes the trend of rural labourers residing in villages but commuting to small towns and cities and rising self-employment to increasing monetization of essential services and decline of "jajmani system". Out migration from rural areas is also a combination of push and pull factors. The push factors could be high levels of seasonal and disguised unemployment, search for employment and better wages. Overall imbalances arising from low levels of industrial development, pressure of population on land causing fragmentation of holdings and low investments in agriculture lead to out-migration (IIPA 2010). The lack of employment opportunities such as that faced by rural Bihar is coupled with demand for labour in other parts of the country that are developing and industrializing at a faster pace. It has been noted (Singh and Stern 2013) that variations in employment prospects and uneven level of urbanization would continue to drive out migration. The latter is the magnet or the centripetal forces that attracts or pulls migrants.

Given the population pressure and shrinking of livelihood opportunities in rural areas and to earn the higher incomes the pathways have been to shift to non-farm employment opportunities, often engagement in multiple jobs and out-migration. The major implication of growing diversification of economic activities in rural areas was the emergence of 'pluri-active' households or engagement of household members in multiple occupations for supplementing overall income (Jodhka 2006). In this context it is important to note the role played by government wage employment programmes, such as MNREGA. One of the key objectives of the wage programmes is to curb migration from rural areas. The performance of this programme has been minutely examined in the vast and varied literature. Some of the studies however, show that the role of government employment guarantee schemes in bringing about changes in the rural incomes and opportunities is at best negligible (Dutta et al. 2014; Datta 2016).

Rural and urban are often viewed as two types of social formations, representing different stages in the process of economic development and evolution of settlements. According to this framework, while traditional or premodern societies are predominantly "rural," modern societies are largely "urban," with a very small proportion of population living in rural settlements. Decline of agriculture and the move to non-farm occupations implied a process of modernisation, which tended to expand with urbanisation. Jodhka and Kumar (2017) in their field work in two locations in Bihar—one a census town and the other a village capture the possible diversities that the growth of the non-farm economy may possess and try to answer questions whether the growth of non-farm economy leads to impetus for urbanisation of a "subaltern" kind (Denis et al. 2012)? Also, whether the process has the potential of transforming a region into a modern social and economic formation? The authors reiterating distress factors surmise that decline of agriculture as a source of income/employment was the single-most important factor driving the growth of local non-farm economy. The landholdings size in the region was not a viable option of employment across communities. Agriculture was seen as stagnating work, with little hope for economic mobility. Evidence from the study however, does not seem to support the assumptions about the urbanising effects of a growing non-farm economy.

While rural transformation in relatively less developed states such as UP, Bihar etc. is orchestered by out-migration, the processes in a region such as Gujarat that receives migrants are also interesting. A country as vast as India is marked by existence of a dual economy i.e. rural/subsistence sector coexisting with urban/capitalist sector. Growth led rural nonfarm sector (RNFS) expansion accompanies urbanization, literacy and irrigation led agricultural development. Impact of urbanization on the growth of rural non-farm employment can be seen from the lens of increase in the net additions of town in Census 2011 that have not received statutory status. Such towns or the 'census towns' are large villages having defining urban characteristics, as manifested in the changing nature of economic activities, notably involvement in non-agricultural occupations. Such settlements are emerging in metropolitan peripheries and are also diffused facing autonomous growth, economically independent of metropolitan influence. In the latter case the settlements are functionally linked to the hinterland they serve. In Gujarat such towns are either concentrated near the existing industrial corridors or are in proximity to large cities and are repositories of the migrant industrial workforce. In some towns the RNFS employment growth is distress driven due to stagnation in agricultural activities and poor irrigation development. Pressure of strong rural urban linkages, proximity to urban, industrial areas and location along national highway facilitated change in rural employment structure in a few. In others, retail and service sector activities catering to undeveloped hinterland were the drivers for the rise in RNFS employment eg. in the tribal regions or districts lacking industrial growth. Some villages in agriculturally developed regions have acquired urban characteristics due to employment diversification to secondary/tertiary activities. The primary survey of the 15 towns undertaken and as described in a subsequent chapter indicates that the common feature underlying all the towns was the level of in-migration of workers in search for employment prospects, rather than outmigration. Migration was either intra-state or inter-state dictated by the location and nature of economic activities. Since rural Gujarat is not a homogenous entity, the varied economic activities led to diversity in development outcomes, sometimes hidden under the garb of apparently growing rural prosperity.

While insights from micro-studies are no doubt important in enriching policy initiatives, the macro tendencies play a far more crucial role in shaping the policy framework. In the context of the rural non-farm sector, some broad contours are highlighted:

1. There is little doubt that after the late 1990s and early part of 2000s, diversification of agriculture and its spread over newer regions resulted in demand for labour with falling labour productivity. The contribution of agriculture in rural net national product declined from 43.7 percent (1999–2000) to 34.4 percent (2004–2005) and further to 32.9 percent in 2011–2012. This led to the decline in the index of agricultural labour productivity in rural areas in most regions from 57 to 47 (1999–2000 to 2004–2005), surging again to 51 in 2011–2012 (calculated as rural NSDP from agriculture per worker/total rural output per worker). The locational factors (corridors, proximity to cities, peripheral location), at times supported by agricultural prosperity, boosted the growth of RNFS. As an outcome rural poverty underwent unprecedented decline.

2. It is now a well-established fact that in the recent years, wages in rural areas have increased at a rate higher than the inflation, contributing to increase in real wages (RBI 2012). The introduction of the Mahatma Gandhi National Rural Employment Guarantee Act (MGNREGA) has been argued to be one of the factors that has contributed to increase in wages.

3. Evidence, particularly early 2000s onwards suggests that rural growth is accompanied by poverty alleviation. The phenomenon is accompanied by:

   (a) Continuous decline in employment growth in the farm sector (as is noted earlier).
   (b) Acceleration in the employment growth in the rural non-farm activities.
   (c) Decline the share of self-employed rural males (58.1% in 2004–2005 to 54.5% in 2011–2012) and rural females (63.1% to 59.3%) (Usual principal and subsidiary status).

(d) Rise in the share of hired rural casual workers—32.9% in 2004–2005 to 35.5% in 2011–2012 for males and 32.6 to 35.1 percent for females.

(e) In early 2000s the money wage increases remained moderate leading to falling real wages during 2003–2004 to 2006–2007. There has been a significant pick-up in the pace of increase in rural real wages since 2007–2008. Impact of higher inflation and institutional factors such as MGNREGA on wages cannot be ruled out, Recent evidence also indicates that, there has been a decline in absolute number of workers employed in agriculture with construction and services segment attracting more workers out of agriculture This could have been another additional factor leading to increase in rural wages (Nadhanael 2012).

The picture has altered in recent times on almost all counts—decline in the share of self-employed and a rise for that of casual labourers, decline in employment growth in farm sector and increase in non-farm sector in rural areas, and acceleration in growth of real wage rates. Clearly, the recent happenings are quite different vis-à-vis the experience of 1970s and 1980s and even that of during 1990s (Himanshu 2007; Sundaram 2007; Unni and Raveendran 2007). The next section seeks to understand the changes highlighted above.

OVERVIEW OF MACRO TENDENCIES

Occupational diversification of the rural sector was witnessed in the 1981 census and various NSS rounds for the first time. Various studies since then have tried to unravel the nature of the emerging non-agriculture sector (distress vs. dynamic; push vs. pull; residual vs. growth led etc.). Spatial variation in the relative importance of rural non-farm growth has also been pinpointed at different levels of disaggregation. The level and growth of non-farm sector was associated with various explanatory variables as cited above (notably, land productivity, distribution of land/assets, cropping pattern, poverty and unemployment rates, urbanization and literacy etc). Despite the constraints posed by data limitations, the results from macro level and micro studies have been vigorous and enlightening.

The previous section highlighted some broad patterns emerging from empirical studies and micro level village surveys. The current section scans the data drawn from official agencies i.e., Census, NSSO and CSO. Various dimensions of employment are examined, supplemented by information on urbanization, poverty and incomes. The data on employment and estimates of RNFS are based on Employment-Unemployment surveys of NSSO (61st and 68th Rounds for 2004–2005 and 2011–2012 respectively). Sectoral income is sourced from CSO (income at factor cost at constant 2004–2005 prices). Labour productivity is derived using sectoral income and usual status (PS & SS) employment rates for major states. The overall macro features are discussed for major states to contextualize the situation prevailing for Gujarat.

The comparative static cross section (Major states) analysis of correlations of variables impinging on the process of rural transformation (led by rural employment diversification) is carried out in addition to regressing the RNFS on its purported determinants. Before proceeding to the analysis this section carries out a tabular inspection of information. Table 2.1 looks at the rural poverty for states based on head count ratio for 2004–2005 and 2011–2012 and the changes in the intervening period. The estimates are based on Tendulkar methodology, and released by Expert group to Review the Methodology for Poverty Estimates.

During this period, rural poverty declined by 16.1 percentage points (from 41.8 to 25.7 percent). The decline is sharper than that observed in urban areas (12 percentage points). The decline was sharp for Uttar Pradesh, Orissa, Maharashtra, Tamil Nadu Bihar and Andhra Pradesh. All the major state witnessed a decline in rural poverty levels. Among major states Jharkhand recorded an increase in urban poverty. Poverty decline was modest in Gujarat, Himachal Pradesh, Madhya Pradesh, Rajasthan, Punjab and West Bengal. The fall in rural poverty was very low as the case of Assam, Jammu and Kashmir, Uttarakhand, and Chhattisgarh. These states also had very high initial levels of poverty and the decline in poverty is quite slow. For some of the moderately performing states notably Punjab, Haryana, the low initial base needs to be discount for.

Rural employment situation can be reviewed from Tables 2.2 and 2.3. The labour force participating rates (LFPR) according to UPSS for the states are shown in Table 2.2. The LFPR declined for both males and females between 1993–1994 and 1999–2000. However, thereafter the LFPR increased, the rise being sharper for females by 3.1 percentage points (from 30.2 to 33.3%) while for males the gains were by 1.5 percentage points only. During the latter part of the 2000s decade, the LFPR again declined for males only marginally by 0.2 percent points, but the decline was very remarkable for females by 8 percent point (from 33.3 to 25.3%).

Table 2.1   Rural poverty levels for major states, 2004–2005 and 2011–2012 (Tendulkar methodology)

States	Head count ratio of rural poverty		Poverty change
	2004–2005	2011–2012	2004–2005 & 2011–2012
Andhra Pradesh	32.3	11.0	−21.3
Arunachal Pradesh	33.6	38.9	5.3
Assam	36.4	33.9	−2.5
Bihar	55.7	34.1	−21.6
Chhattisgarh	55.1	44.6	−10.5
Gujarat	39.1	21.5	−17.6
Haryana	24.8	11.6	−13.2
Himachal Pradesh	25.0	8.5	−16.5
Jammu & Kashmir	14.1	11.5	−2.6
Jharkhand	51.6	40.8	−10.8
Karnataka	37.5	24.5	−13.0
Kerala	20.2	9.1	−11.1
Madhya Pradesh	53.6	35.7	−17.9
Maharashtra	47.9	24.2	−23.7
Orissa	60.8	35.7	−25.1
Punjab	22.1	7.7	−14.4
Rajasthan	35.8	16.1	−19.7
Tamil Nadu	37.5	15.8	−21.7
Tripura	44.5	16.5	−28.0
Uttar Pradesh	42.7	11.6	−31.1
Uttarakhand	35.1	30.4	−4.7
West Bengal	38.2	22.5	−15.7
All India	41.8	25.7	−16.1

Source: Report of the expert group (Rangarajan) to review the methodology for measurement of poverty, GoI, planning commission, June, 2014

Table 2.2   Labour Force Participation Rates (LFPR) according to usual status (ps + ss), rural India

Year	Male	Female
1993–1994	56.1	33.1
1999–2000	54.0	30.2
2004–2005	55.5	33.3
2011–2012	55.3	25.3

Source: NSSO reports on Employment and Unemployment, Various years

Table 2.3   LFPR by usual status (ps + ss), for all persons, major states, rural, 2011–2012

States	Labour force participation rates		
	Male	Female	Persons
Andhra Pradesh	61.2	44.8	52.8
Arunachal Pradesh	49.2	28.2	38.9
Assam	56.4	12.9	35.9
Bihar	48.7	5.8	28.4
Chhattisgarh	56.3	41.6	49.0
Gujarat	60.2	27.9	44.8
Haryana	53.2	16.4	36.5
Himachal Pradesh	54.7	52.9	53.8
Jammu & Kashmir	55.9	26.3	41.5
Jharkhand	54.2	20.4	37.8
Karnataka	62.0	28.9	45.4
Kerala	58.3	25.8	41.0
Madhya Pradesh	56.4	23.9	40.7
Maharashtra	58.2	38.9	49.0
Orissa	60.6	25.1	42.7
Punjab	57.9	23.7	41.4
Rajasthan	50.0	34.9	42.7
Tamil Nadu	60.7	38.6	49.5
Tripura	59.9	28.7	44.9
Uttar Pradesh	49.6	17.8	34.1
Uttarakhand	46.5	31.5	39.0
West Bengal	60.2	19.4	40.0
All India	55.3	25.3	40.6

Source: NSSO report on Employment and Unemployment, 2011–12. No. KI 68/10

In 2011–2012, the labor force participation amongst the females is the lowest recorded since the beginning of the reforms process.

As of 2011–2012, the overall LFPRs less than the national average (40.6%) occur in Assam, Bihar, Haryana, Jharkhand, UP and Uttarakhand and can be attributed to the low LFPRs for females (Table 2.3). The employment quality can be ascertained based on the distribution of usually employed by category of rural employment for the period spanning 1993–1994 to 2011–2012., i.e. nearly two decades. In the early part of 2000s decade there was a sharp rise in the self-employment for rural females (6.4% points), for males it was slower (3.1% points). This period also registered decline in proportion of casual workers for males and females (Table 2.4).

Table 2.4   Percentage distribution of usual status (ps + ss) worker of all ages by status in employment, rural India, 1993 to 2011–2012 (ps + ss)

NSS round	Usual status (ps + ss) males			Usual status (ps + ss) females		
	Self employed	Regular employees	Casual labour	Self employed	Regular employees	Casual labour
68th (2011–2012)	54.5	10.0	35.5	59.3	5.6	35.1
61st (2004–2005)	58.1	9.0	32.9	63.7	3.7	32.6
55th (1999–2000)	55.0	8.8	36.2	57.3	3.1	39.6
50th (1993–1994)	57.7	8.5	33.8	58.6	2.7	38.7

Source: NSSO, Reports No. 515 (part 1) & KI 68/10

In the latter part of 2000s decade the employment scenario underwent significant changes. Engagement in self-employment again plummeted for males (3.6% points) and more sharply for females (4.4% points). For males the extent of self-employment at 54.5 per cent in 2011–2012 is the lowest recorded since 1993–1994. The period from 2004–2005 to 2011–2012 saw a reversal in terms of increase in workers engages in casual jobs; the change of 1.5 per cent points being equal for males and females. A notable trend is the unprecedented increase in the extent of female, regular employees showing a change by 1.8 percentage points, certainly more than that for males.

Whether there is the existence of linkages between the nature of employment and the level of consumption expenditure can be assessed from distribution of UPSS workers by status of employment for the decile classes of consumption expenditure in rural India (Table 2.5). The pattern for males is somewhat at variance from females. The percentage of self-employment rises for males up to the 9th MPCE decile class and then declines. For females self-employment rises up to the 5th decile class of MPCE. Thereafter it registered an irregular trend up to the 8th decile class. From the 8th class of MPCE onwards female self-employment showed a sharp rise. In case of males, the percentage employed as regular wage/salaried worker rises continuously with each MPCE class.

For females there is no consistently rising trend of self-employment with increasing income level. However, the highest MPCE class registered a crowding of self-employed workers. At least for females it may be summarized that self-employment offers opportunities that are heterogeneous in terms of income, though the extent of self-employment increases

Table 2.5 Distribution of usual status (ps + ss) worker by category of employment for decile classes by MPCE classes, rural India, 2011–2012

Decile classes on MPCE	Male			Female		
	Self employed	Regular salary/ wage employees	Casual labour	Self employed	Regular salary/ wage employees	Casual labour
0–10	44.5	3.5	52.0	52.3	1.8	45.9
10–20	49.1	4.2	46.7	54.8	4.1	41.2
20–30	52.4	5.0	42.6	57.6	3.5	38.9
30–40	52.9	5.9	41.3	57.9	2.9	39.2
40–50	53.9	6.2	39.9	60.6	3.9	35.5
50–60	55.2	7.9	36.9	56.7	3.8	39.5
60–70	56.8	9.8	33.3	61.8	4.1	34.1
70–80	57.2	12.2	30.4	58.5	7.6	33.9
80–90	60.5	15.9	23.6	63.9	7.3	28.8
90–100	58.3	24.8	17.0	66.3	14.7	19.0
All classes	54.5	10.0	35.5	59.3	5.6	35.1

Source: NSSO, Report No. 554

sharply only with the three highest MPCE classes. Predictably the engagement of workers in casual jobs shows the opposing trend i.e. of decline with rise in MPCE. At the lowest MPCE level clustering of casual labour occurs (52%) for males but that of self-employed (52.3%) for females. With rising income levels, such concentration of workers eases.

Between 2004–2005 and 2011–2012, the listing of states having higher than average self-employment remains largely the same (Table 2.6). As in 2004–2005, even in 2011–2012, the proportion of self-employment is higher than that for rural India (55.9%) in some of the poorest states, notably Assam (70%), Chhattisgarh (58%), Rajasthan (67.5%), Uttarakhand (74%) and UP (67%). At the other end are some of the developed states having greater than the average share of self-employed rural workers such as Gujarat (57%), Haryana (61.8%), Himachal Pradesh (71%), Jammu and Kashmir (63%). This obviously indicates the heterogeneous nature of self-employed work in rural area. Cultivators are the largest sections of rural self-employed and could be large or the resource poor farmers.

The developed regions such as Gujarat probably offer more remunerative opportunities for self-employment in the non-farm sector, while distress forces may abound in the poorer states. Most of the micro studies cited earlier also support this notion. The states which have shown a sharp

Table 2.6   Percentage distribution of employed (ps + ss) by category of employment in rural areas

States	2004–2005			2011–2012		
	Self employed	Regular employees	Casual labour	Self employed	Regular employees	Casual labour
Andhra Pradesh	47.9	7.2	45.0	46.7	8.0	45.2
Assam	71.0	9.1	19.9	70.0	11.7	18.4
Bihar	60.2	2.7	37.1	52.0	4.0	44.0
Chhattisgarh	53.9	3.9	42.2	58.2	4.1	37.9
Gujarat	53.6	7.1	39.3	57.0	10.3	32.7
Haryana	67.6	13.7	18.7	61.8	14.0	24.4
Himachal Pradesh	76.7	11.9	11.5	71.1	14.1	14.6
Jammu & Kashmir	77.4	12.5	10.1	63.0	15.3	21.7
Jharkhand	71.0	4.2	24.8	68.6	4.3	27.3
Karnataka	49.3	5.0	45.7	52.0	11.8	36.2
Kerala	45.4	16.4	38.1	38.2	17.8	44.0
Madhya Pradesh	60.5	5.2	34.3	60.0	4.9	35.1
Maharashtra	51.1	7.9	40.9	53.7	8.8	37.4
Orissa	58.4	5.6	36.0	62.4	6.7	30.9
Punjab	63.1	12.9	24.0	54.9	17.0	28.3
Rajasthan	77.4	5.4	17.2	67.5	6.8	25.5
Tamil Nadu	42.7	10.4	47.0	29.9	14.0	55.9
Uttarakhand	80.4	7.2	12.3	74.0	11.3	14.7
Uttar Pradesh	76.4	5.4	18.2	66.9	5.9	26.9
West Bengal	55.2	7.5	37.3	46.4	8.7	44.6
All India	60.2	7.1	32.8	55.9	8.8	35.3

Source: NSSO Reports No. 515, part 1 and 554

decline in rural self-employment over the period of study are Punjab, Tamil nadu, UP, Rajasthan and West Bengal. States where over 2004–2005 casual workers have increased in 2011–2012 and where the extent is more than the national average of 35.3 per cent are Bihar, MP, Tamilnadu and West Bengal. Andhra Pradesh, Chhattisgarh, Karnataka, Kerala, Maharashtra on the other hand have shown decline in casual workers over 2004–2005 but remain above the rural average.

Examination of the wage rates of casual and regular workers can be used to substantiate some of the prevailing trends. Male earnings are substantially higher than female- both for regular and casual workers as seen in Table 2.7. Also the wages rate for regular worker is more than double that of casual wage worker. There are state wise variations in wage rates of regular workers but seems not to be related to the level of development. Developed states

Table 2.7   Average wage/salary earnings per day by type of employment of age 15–59 years for states, 2011–2012, rural

States	Regular worker			Casual worker[a]		
	Male	Female	Person	Male	Female	Person
Andhra Pradesh	251.3	225.0	247.1	167.7	111.2	141.5
Arunachal Pradesh	672.7	474.9	640.1	223.4	172.9	210.0
Assam	344.0	179.7	302.9	142.6	98.4	135.7
Bihar	450.5	188.4	411.8	129.0	90.0	126.0
Chhattisgarh	266.8	162.6	243.1	89.5	75.4	83.9
Gujarat	268.7	173.1	254.4	115.8	105.0	112.8
Haryana	396.4	357.4	394.4	202.4	151.9	196.9
Himachal Pradesh	434.7	250.7	396.8	182.1	125.6	178.4
Jammu & Kashmir	453.6	222.4	426.8	209.3	219.8	209.5
Jharkhand	515.5	294.3	478.6	137.4	74.7	132.0
Karnataka	237.5	151.9	218.2	162.9	99.9	142.4
Kerala	368.4	240.5	318.1	345.1	169.6	314.9
Madhya Pradesh	270.9	108.6	245.3	107.6	97.2	105.2
Maharashtra	369.1	306.8	360.4	133.7	92.8	117.4
Orissa	245.3	223.2	242.1	123.6	87.9	117.4
Punjab	302.8	157.6	284.3	202.4	157.9	198.6
Rajasthan	328.6	177.9	305.6	167.6	118.7	159.5
Tamil Nadu	292.6	199.4	268.4	196.7	110.4	169.9
Tripura	319.6	218.7	290.2	168.0	120.0	164.2
Uttar Pradesh	296.5	171.3	276.1	136.8	95.3	133.1
Uttarakhand	457.9	392.7	450.2	179.3	123.5	174.4
West Bengal	297.4	119.8	248.0	123.9	100.5	120.9
All India	322.3	201.6	299.0	149.3	103.3	138.6

Source: NSSO, Report 515, part 1, pp. 148 & 150

[a]Engaged in works other than public works

(such as Gujarat, Karnataka, Punjab, Tamilnadu) have lower than average wage rates while less developed state (Assam, Chhattisgarh, Madhya Pradesh, Orissa, Uttar Pradesh) also belong to this group. The level of development seems to have some impact on the wages of casual workers. Less developed states (Assam, Bihar, Chhattisgarh, Jharkhand, Madhya Pradesh, Orissa) have lower than national average rural casual wage rates. Most of the developed states (Haryana, Himachal Pradesh, J&K, Karnataka, Kerala, Punjab and Tamilnadu) have higher than national average. The outliers are developed states of Gujarat and Maharasthra that have below the national average wages rates for casual workers.

On examining the overall unemployment rates (Table 2.8) it can be stated that states such as Chhatisgarh, Maharashtra, Gujarat, Madhya Pradesh and Uttar Pradesh with casual wage rates lower than national average also have lowest overall unemployment rates. Amongst the developed states unemployment rates are also lowest for Andhra Pradesh, Karnataka, and Himachal Pradesh in addition to Rajasthan. Predictably, unemployment rates are the highest for Assam, Bihar, Uttarakhand and West Bengal. What is surprising is that even the most affluent states (Haryana, Jammu & Kashmir, Kerala, Tamilnadu and Punjab) have high unemployment rates. These states depict an unusual pattern.

Table 2.8   Unemployment rates according to usual status (ps + ss), rural India, major states, 2011–2012

States	Overall			For educated persons			Among youth		
				15 and above			15 to 29		
	Male	Female	Persons	Male	Female	Persons	Male	Female	Persons
Andhra Pradesh	1.7	0.5	1.2	4.8	5.5	5.0	5.1	1.5	3.6
Assam	4.3	5.7	4.5	11.0	26.1	12.9	14.8	14.2	14.6
Bihar	2.7	8.2	3.2	3.1	22.4	4.1	8.1	19.7	9.4
Chhattisgarh	1.1	0.3	0.8	3.7	2.2	3.5	3.7	0.4	2.3
Gujarat	0.4	0.2	0.3	1.1	0.0	1.1	1.1	0.6	0.9
Haryana	2.6	1.7	2.4	4.1	8.0	4.7	6.8	6.0	6.5
Himachal Pradesh	1.1	0.8	1.0	1.9	2.2	1.9	4.2	3.0	3.6
Jammu & Kashmir	2.2	3.0	2.5	4.0	11.2	5.3	7.0	7.5	7.1
Jharkhand	1.8	2.8	2.1	3.3	26.8	6.7	5.1	9.5	6.2
Karnataka	1.2	0.4	0.9	2.8	3.0	2.9	2.7	1.9	2.4
Kerala	3.1	14.2	6.8	6.5	25.8	13.6	9.7	47.4	21.7
Madhya Pradesh	0.6	0.0	0.4	1.6	0.0	1.5	1.8	0.0	1.2
Maharashtra	0.9	0.3	0.7	2.0	2.2	2.1	2.7	1.4	2.3
Orissa	2.3	2.0	2.2	6.8	20.0	8.3	6.2	5.6	6.1
Punjab	2.2	1.3	1.9	4.0	5.4	4.3	6.4	4.2	5.8
Rajasthan	0.9	0.4	0.7	2.2	7.3	2.8	2.3	1.0	1.8
Tamil Nadu	2.1	1.9	2.0	5.2	8.6	6.0	7.6	6.3	7.2
Uttar Pradesh	1.0	0.7	0.9	1.7	3.9	1.9	2.6	1.8	2.4
Uttarakhand	2.7	2.1	2.5	5.5	11.0	6.9	13.0	7.6	10.6
West Bengal	2.8	2.4	2.7	4.6	18.3	6.6	7.7	6.2	7.3
All India	1.7	1.7	1.7	3.6	9.7	4.7	5.0	4.8	4.9

Source: NSSO, Report No. 554

The unemployment rates among educated persons and youth (15–29 years) are higher than the overall unemployment rates. Developed states of Gujarat, Himachal Pradesh, Karnataka, Maharashtra offer the largest opportunities for employment to the educated persons. Madhya Pradesh, Uttar Pradesh and Rajasthan although less developed, have the lowest educated unemployment rates. At the other end of the spectrum are developed states such as Andhra Pradesh, Jammu & Kashmir, Kerala, Tamilnadu and West Bengal and even underdeveloped ones (Assam, Jharkhand, Orissa, Uttarakhand) showing above national average rates. These are the states that require a focus on employment policy to avoid social unrest fueled by inadequate economic opportunities.

The foregoing description gives insight into the rural transformation process- there is decline in rural poverty, fall in LFPRs, decline in proportion of self-employment, variations in the wage rates across states and occurrence of high unemployment rates at both ends of the development spectrum. Clearly the situation requires a clear push for employment creation in the non-farm sectors besides support to agriculture related activities.

EMPLOYMENT AND INCOME IN ECONOMIC SECTORS

Sectoral Employment and Income Shares

The discussion on employment sets the tone for analysis of sectoral distribution of employment and incomes. The level and growth of sectoral employment and income from the period 1999–2000 and 2011–2012 are given in Table 2.9. Since the national income data from CSO for net state domestic product (NSDP) is available for rural and urban areas combined, labour productivity has been arrived at for the entire economy (i.e. by dividing sectoral product with urban plus rural workers combined). Industry wise workers are derived by using the rural UPSS percentage share of workers. The changing share of sectoral employment is annexed (Tables 2.14a, 2.14b, and 2.14c).

In 1999–2000, 87.7 per cent of the rural workers were engaged in commodity production (agriculture, mining, manufacturing, construction, electricity/gas) and the remaining in tertiary sector activities. Services over the 20 year period from 1999–2000 to 2011–2012 are engaging an increasing share of workers from 12.4 to 15.3 percent. The share of employment in commodity producing sectors has shown a decline in rural areas. Kerala is an exception and has less than 65 per cent of employment

Table 2.9   Shares of total income by economic sectors (rural + urban)

Economic activity	1999–2000	2004–2005	2011–2012
Agriculture, forestry & fishing	26.5	20.2	14.7
Mining & Quarrying	2.1	1.9	1.7
Manufacturing	12.9	13.0	13.2
Electricity, gas & water	1.5	4.9	1.0
Construction	6.2	1.1	8.3
Trade, hotel & restaurant	15.5	8.2	18.4
Transport, storage etc	6.7	15.1	10.8
Other services	28.7	35.5	31.9
All sectors	100.0	100.0	100.0

Source: CSO, National Accounts Statistics, net domestic product at factor cost (2004–2005 prices)

For 1999–2000, at 1999–2000 prices

in commodity producing sectors. In the remaining states in 2011–2012 more than 80 per cent of the rural employment was in such activities going up to 91 per cent in case of Madhya Pradesh. Non-farm activities engaged workers at a steadily rising pace during the three NSSO survey years. Rural non-farm workforce was 23.3 per cent in 1999–2000 and increased to 26.8 per cent in 2004–2005. The increase has been steeper in the period 2004–2005 to 2011–2012, from 26.8 per cent to 35.4 percent. More than a third of the rural workers are engaged in non-farm activities as per the latest estimates. There are considerable spatial variations in the extent of non-farm employment shares. In 2011–2012 it was the highest in Kerala (68%), Jammu and Kashmir (49%), Punjab, Tamilnadu (48%), West Bengal (47%) and Haryana (42%). Rural nonfarm employment (RNFE) is also high (more than 30%) in Himachal Pradesh, Orissa, Rajasthan, Uttar Pradesh, and Bihar. Rural workforce is least diversified in developed states of Maharashtra, Gujarat and Karnataka and also underdeveloped state of Madhya Pradesh.

There is considerable heterogeneity in the nature and causes for the increase in RNFS activities as can be discerned from the state level scenario. The overdependence of agriculture, fragmentation of holdings and unviable nature of primary sector could be leading to distress in rural areas. Within the RNFS, between 2004–2005 and 2011–2012, the highest increase in share of workers was registered by the construction sector (5% to 11%) and the pattern is uniform across all the states. Manufacturing, trade and transport related activities have registered marginal increase in share of workers.

An examination of income shares in the entire economy emanating from different sectors reveals that most of the income is generated in the services sector and its share is rising (Table 2.9). Share of primary sector has gone down by 11.8 percentage points and in 2011–2012 it accounted for only 14.7 per cent of the domestic product. Share of manufacturing sector has remained constant (around 13%). There as rapid expansion in income coming from transport and storage related activities in the last decade from 6.7 to 10.8 per cent- this was in fact the highest growing sector. Income from trade and hotels also expanded rapidly (by 4 percentage points) along with services (banking, financial community, services etc.). Construction activities in the earlier period saw a rapid rise in income share, but in the second period services and transportation rule the roost, showing income acceleration. Mining sector has recorded decline in income levels between 2004–2005 to 2011–2012. Electricity and gas was the other sector that witnessed decline in income shares, especially after 2004–2005.

Labour Productivity Across Sectors

Labour productivity in this section implies the per capita income earned by workers. Workers dependent in each sector can be ascertained from the Employment-Unemployment surveys of NSSO (adjusted primary and subsidiary status). For NSDP at factor cost the base is of 2004–2005 and the analysis is limited for only two comparable time points of 2004–2005 and 2011–2012. The 1999–2000 NSDP estimates are available with base of 1999–2000 but their use could have contaminated the analysis and impede strict comparability. The estimates of per worker productivity up to 2003–2004 have been attempted earlier. Since the present concern is with the rural transformation process, the rural workers' productivity would have given a truer picture. However, due to unavailability of sectoral income estimates for rural and urban areas separately and given the fact that rural and urban are not bounded spaces, the analysis is confined to the entire economy (rural + urban) and the corresponding employment and income estimates for 2004–2005 and 2011–2012.

The gap between NSDP per worker in agriculture and non-farm sector is substantial and widening. Labour productivity in the non-farm sector is in multiples of that of the farm sector (Table 2.10). The labour productivity in construction and manufacturing is more than double that of farm sector. Productivity of trade and utilities is five to six time that in farm

Table 2.10   Sectoral estimates of the income per worker (NDP at factor cost) 2004–2005 prices, 2004–2005 to 2011–2012

Economic activity	NDP per worker (Rs.)		
	2004–2005	2011–2012	CARG
Agriculture, forestry & fishing	22,050	30,156	(4.57)
Mining & quarrying	304,671	298,213	–(0.31)
Manufacturing	72,210	99,127	(4.63)
Construction	95,797	76,821	–(3.10)
Electricity, gas & water supply	266,376	187,376	–(4.90)
Trade, hotels & restaurants	111,652	158,246	(5.11)
Transport, storage etc	139,682	210,570	(6.04)
Services	205,053	270,696	(4.05)
All sectors	64,920	97,697	(6.01)

Sources: Govt of India, National Accounts Statistics, various years, CSO

Note: The income is estimated for rural and urban areas combined

For number of workers, estimates are based on NSSO, UPSS workers data, and population estimates are derived from those estimated by the NSSO for the survey years

sector. Sectors that have substantial productivity advantages are services, mining and quarrying and also transportation and communications. The latter are highly capital intensive sectors. Construction and trade are recipient sectors for the rural workers spilling out of primary activities. While the labour productivity in trade enjoyed substantial increase (at 5% per annum), that in construction faced a sharp decline. This sector has seen a steep increase in the share of workers, with a change by 6.2 percentage points between 2004–2005 to 2011–2012—in fact it is the only sector registering noticeable employment gains. Thus the engagement of workers in construction activities is at falling productivity levels.

The growth experience of per worker productivity in the other sectors show an upward trend especially in the case of manufacturing, trade, transportation and services. The trajectory of growth is at variance with the experience of early 2000s decade (Kashyap and Mehta 2007). Mining and quarrying, construction and utilities have registered negative growth in per worker productivity in the second half of 2000s decade. The pace of decline had decelerated in construction sector from 5.8 to 3 percent per annum. In the other two, the labour productivity has started declining only after 2004–2005. The pace of growth has halved in trade and hotels, while it has doubled in services and transportation sectors.

At the state level, workers in Punjab, Haryana, Kerala, Jammu and Kashmir and West Bengal have labour productivity advantage in agriculture and allied sectors (Table 2.15). Gujarat joined this group in the 2000s decade. Gains are also noticeable in Jharkhand, Madhya Pradesh, Maharashtra, Tamilnadu and Uttrakhand. In contrast Jammu and Kashmir despite having high productivity per worker has witnessed a downturn in recent years. In manufacturing, substantial gains were observed in Haryana, Himachal Pradesh, Madhya Pradesh, Uttarakhand and Maharashtra. There was a fall in labour productivity in manufacturing in Assam and Jharkhand. In the more industrialized states, such as Gujarat, Karnataka gains are smaller than the newly industrializing states possibly due to overcrowding. Utilities is the other capital intensive sector, but nearly all the states have witnessed a fall in labour productivity, with the exception of Assam, Haryana, Himachal Pradesh and Uttrakhand. Construction sector offers a far more mixed picture. Workers in Gujarat and Karnataka have income advantage and the gap between Gujarat and states like Karnataka and Maharashtra has widened. Possibly due to overcrowding of workers falling labour productivity in construction is registered in Madhya Pradesh, Jammu and Kashmir, Assam, Orissa, Rajasthan, Tamilnadu, Uttar Pradesh and West Bengal. Labour productivity in trade, transportation and other services is expanding.

CORRELATES OF RURAL NON-FARM SECTOR

Discussion in previous sections shows that construction and tertiary sector activities are leading the employment diversification process in the country. Manufacturing is facing stagnancy and agriculture sector shows declining engagement of workers. Construction is engaging workers at falling productivity levels unlike tertiary activities indicating distress and effects of overcrowding of workers. Agriculture's falling share in employment is at accelerating productivity levels. This is a welcome development and there is a need for infusion of capital in this sector along with technological advancement. A comparative static (correlation) analysis of facets of employment and economy and the emergence of rural non-farm sector for major states is expected to pinpoint the temporal changes in the nature of inter-relationships. This was carried out for three points of time coinciding with the recent NSSO rounds and the results are given in Table 2.11.

Pearson's simple correlation indicated that urbanization had a positive relation with RNFS in the early 1990s, the relation though weakened after ten years- indicating perhaps increase in the dualism between urban and

Table 2.11   Correlates of size of rural non farm sector

No.	Variable	1993–1994	2004–2005	2011–2012
1.	Urbanization	0.24	0.03	0.25
2.	Rural literacy	0.81[a]	0.75[a]	0.49[b]
3.	HCR of rural poverty	−0.28	−0.39	−0.56[b]
4.	Labour productivity (GSDP at factor cost/worker)			
	Agriculture	0.49	0.66[a]	0.61[a]
	Non agriculture	−0.15	−0.23	−0.30
5.	Land productivity (GSDPAgri/Ha NSA)	0.85[a]	0.69[a]	0.58[a]
6.	Percent of holdings			
	Marginal	0.73[a]	0.43	0.39
	Small	−0.81[b]	−0.66[a]	−0.72[a]
7.	Percent employed (UPSS)			
	Self employed	−0.30	−0.21	−0.30[a]
	Regular employed	0.86[a]	0.81[a]	0.67[a]
	Casual workers	0.09	−0.08	0.03
8.	Wages earned			
	Regular workers		0.29	0.22
	Casual workers		0.87[a]	0.86[a]
9.	Unemployment (UPSS)			
	Overall	0.74[a]	0.85[a]	0.73[a]
	Educated > 15 years	0.61[b]	0.80[a]	0.61[a]
	15–29 years	0.71[a]	0.86[a]	0.71[a]
10.	Percent indebted			
	All farmer households		0.28	0.19
	Marginal farmer households		0.31	0.58[a]
	Small farmer households		0.33	0.70[a]

Source: Based on author's computation
[a]Significant at 0.01% (2- tailed)
[b]Significant at 0.05% (2-tailed)

rural areas. In the more recent time, the strength of the relationship has increased and even though not significant indicates that rural transformation is accompanying advances in urbanization and also that rural and urban areas are not isolated spaces. That the expansion of RNFS and changes in the rural economic structure have a role in fuelling urban growth is also indicated. Education has a positive and significant effect, but the relation is progressively weakening. Over time there is a need to bring about changes in quality of education to suit requirements of changing nature of rural jobs. This could also indicate the residual nature of RNFS and preponderance of unskilled RNFS jobs, mainly in construction and services that do not require higher educational attainments. The negative relation of poverty with RNFS indicates that RNFS provides alternative livelihood opportunities for the rural poor and has a role in poverty reduction. Such a relation has further strengthened and is now statistically significant. It reiterates what others have indicated that RNFS is being employed more by the poorer sections of rural population as a supplementary measure to augment family incomes and regions where such opportunities are scarce are worse off. Amongst the productivity and income related variables, RNFS showed positive relation with labour productivity in agriculture in the early 1990s. Ten years down the line, the relationship strengthened and became significant. In the more recent past it remains statistically significant but has weakened. Labour productivity in non-farm sector predictably showed a negative albeit insignificant relation with RNFS, but the relation is strengthening. Apparently the crowding in RNFS, sometimes out of agrarian distress, brings down the wages and income. Land productivity i.e. income from agriculture per hectare of NSA was strongly correlated with RNFS in the early 1990s indicating that agricultural growth caused the employment diversification and also the existence of production and consumption linkages of non-farm with the farm sector. By 2011–2012 such linkages have weakened considerably even though the relation continues to be statistically significant. Thus it is not only the agricultural centric factors that are causing expansion in RNFS now, but growth in construction, trade and service activities in rural areas may be occurring independently. Investments that enhance agricultural productivity (irrigation etc) and forge stronger linkages between agriculture and non-farm sector (eg. roads, markets, processing facilities) have to be stepped up.

The agrarian structure was correlated with RNFS. In 1993–1994 the relation with marginal holdings was strongly positive and significant indicating that marginal holdings were not remunerative and farmers sought alternative non-farm avenues for income generation. The relation has weakened progressively and is although positive now but not significant. This reiterates the earlier contention that emergence of RNFS today is as much a result of prevailing conditions in the agriculture sector, as a more of an independent phenomena, possibly also an outcome of trickling down of urban influences. Nonetheless policy interventions for infrastructure creation and technology are imperative to make marginal farmers more profitable. In contrast to marginal holdings, the relation of RNFS with small holdings is strongly negative and significant. In the intervening years from early 1990s to early 2000s the negative relation had somewhat weakened, but by 2011–2012 it gained in strength again. This obviously indicates that unlike marginal agriculture, small holdings sustain livelihoods and have the ability to retain labour that is not forced to seek non-farm activities to augment incomes. It further indicates the fact that a minimum threshold of landholding size is essential for agriculture to remain a profitable venture and consolidation of fragmented land parcels would be make agriculture far more economical and remunerative.

In the context of agrarian structure RNFS is correlated with indebtedness of farmer households. For all the farmer households, marginal and small farmers the relation is positive. At the aggregate level the relation has though weakened with the passage of time and has lost significance. Up to 2003–2004 the relation with small and marginal farmer households was not significant either. However, in 2011–2012 the relationship has become strongly positive for small farmers and is statistically significant. Similarly for marginal farmers also, the relationship has strengthened considerably and is now significant. It implies that resource poor farm households are indebted and distress forces are taking a hold. It is a well-known fact that declining profitability in farming exacerbates rural indebtedness, compelling growing engagement of such households into alternative non-farm livelihoods for sustenance. Such households may also be using credit for non-farm activities more intensively than before. For small farming households it is of far more crucial importance.

Employment and wage aspects are examined. RNFS has a negative and currently significant relation with percent of self-employed workers. With the extent of casual workers, the relation is quite weak. However, it is with regular workers that the RNFS has a strongly positive correlation. Even though the relationship is weakening over the years, its statistical significance has been retained. The aspect of organized employment abundantly available in manufacturing and tertiary sector activities in the developed regions is captured by this. The wages of regular workers are also positively related, albeit the relationship has weakened. The wage rates of casual workers have a very strongly positive and significant relation with RNFS. This positive relation reflects the favorable impact on RNFS due to tightening of labour markets as casual wages increase.

As is expected the relationship of RNFS with overall unemployment rates, unemployment amongst the educated and unemployment rates amongst youth is positive and statistically significant. The strength of the relation had peaked during 2004–2005. In 2011–2012 it weakened considerably but is still high. The distress phenomenon at the state level is being captured in a way by these correlations. In the developed regions, higher output from land and RNFS are linked leading to a higher reservation price for labour, and causing a spill over to RNFS. In the poor regions workers are taking up any employment opportunity available and remain occupied at the going wages. However, the overcrowding in most of the non-farm economic activities in rural areas require corrective measures, as otherwise poverty may aggravate. In the transportation, communications hospitality, health, education and financial sectors, while labour productivity is accelerating in the rural areas, the requirement is of skill development so that largest benefits can accrue to rural workers that are in the process of leaving agriculture. It may be concluded that the above analysis imparts some clarity on the dynamics governing the conditions associated with the emergence of non-farm sector in the country.

DYNAMICS OF STRUCTURAL CHANGES IN RURAL ECONOMY

The discussion so far has traced the macro tendencies in the rural economic conditions and the associated employment variables. In addition to the comparative static analysis of estimating correlations between RNFS and different dimensions of rural economy, the present section measures the impact of different variables on the rural non-farm sector across the cross section of states. For this purpose a linear OLS regression was performed with employment, wage and productivity related explanatory variables. Notably, the variables are chosen in a bid to assess whether the rural structural change is under the influence of distress related factors or is growth led.

The Model: While choosing the model, it needs to be remembered that the parameters of a linear model have an interpretation as marginal effects. In contrast the parameters of the log linear model have an interpretation as elasticities. Hence the log-log or log linear model assumes a constant elasticity over all the values of the data set. Log transformation is possible when all observations of the data set are positive. A model selection approach is to estimate competing models by OLS and choose the model with the highest R squared (Gujarati 1995). However, the R squared yielded by the log-log specification is not the proportion of the variance of Y explained by the regression. It is rather the proportion of the variance of the logarithm of Y explained by the regression, as log Y is the dependent variable. The two regression models explain different sources of variations and hence the R squared are in principle incomparable (Seidman 1976), requiring adoption of corrective measures (i.e., use of antilogs of coefficients for regression). However, since there is no particular reason to assume one functional form is better than the other, the simple OLS linear regression has been adopted having the following form:

$$\gamma_i = \alpha_i + \beta_i x_i + u_i \tag{2.1}$$

A hierarchical regression analysis (block-wise entry method) is adopted, where the predictors are entered in the model in a hierarchical manner, dictated by logic of research. This form is useful if there are a large number of potential predictor variables and it allows the use of domain knowledge to capture the responses of the covariates (Gelman et al. 1995; Gelman and Hill 2007). The estimated model has the following specification:

$$\gamma_i \left(\text{RNFS} \right) = \alpha_i + \beta_1 x_{1i} \left(\text{unemployment rate} \right) + u_i \tag{2.2}$$

$$\gamma_i \left(\text{RNFS} \right) = \alpha_i + \beta_1 x_{1i} \left(\text{unemployment rate} \right) + \beta_2 x_{2i} \left(\text{casual wages} \right) + u_i \tag{2.3}$$

$$\gamma_i \left(\text{RNFS} \right) = \alpha_i + \beta_1 x_{1i} \left(\text{unemployment rate} \right) + \beta_2 x_{2i} \left(\text{casual wages} \right) \\ - \beta_3 x_{3i} \left(\text{self employed} \right) + u_i \tag{2.4}$$

$$\gamma_i \left(\text{RNFS} \right) = \alpha_i + \beta_1 x_{1i} \left(\text{unemployment rate} \right) + \beta_2 x_{2i} \left(\text{casual wages} \right) \\ - \beta_3 x_{3i} \left(\text{self employed} \right) + \beta_4 x_{4i} \left(\text{land productivity} \right) + u_i \tag{2.5}$$

The exploratory analysis in the preceding sections inferred that the extent of rural non –farm sector is associated with several distress forces, such as casualization, indebtedness, land productivity differentials, quality of employment and absence of rural employment opportunities etc., in addition to agricultural growth. Moreover non-farm sector's relationship with agricultural growth is weakening over time (agricultural prosperity led growth). On the other hand, though the rural non-farm sector is associated positively with wages earned, it is consolidating its position in the rural economy independent of the impetus provided by agriculture, including the spillover of urbanization related factors. However, since several of the variables in the correlation analysis were strongly correlated with each other, whose adoption could have resulted in the problem of multicollinearity in the regression analysis, these were dropped from the model.

In the final analysis, the percentage of employment in rural non-farm sector in a particular year (Y) was regressed on the overall rural unemployment rate (X_1), wages of casual workers (X_2), percentage of rural self-employed workers (X_3) (largely comprising of owner-cultivators) and the land productivity or the GSDP from agriculture per hectare of sown area (X_4). The 'u_i' is the random term that captures all the other factors those were not explained by the X's in Eq. 2.2. The independent variables were not a combination of other independent variables. An examination of the inter-correlations (Table 2.16) revealed that none of the independent variables were highly correlated, with the exception of wages of casual workers and unemployment rate. However, the condition index was within the accepted limits (never exceeding 15).

As was observed in the earlier discussion, it is assumed that level of non-farm sector shares a positive relation with overall *rate of open unemployment*, which is the first explanatory variable. This is the UPSS overall rural unemployment rate derived from the NSSO survey of employment and unemployment. Insufficient job opportunities in the rural areas or work in agriculture pushes the labour force into lower paying occupations such as construction, petty trading, rural transport etc., besides providing an urban ward push, hence it is expected to assume a positive sign in the regression. The variable of *wages of casual workers*, also taken from the NSSO, is expected to capture the increasing employment of casual (farm and non-farm) workers in multiple, often low-paying jobs to supplement the family incomes. Econometric estimates reveal that expansion of the non-farm sector is associated with falling poverty via two routes: a direct impact on poverty that is likely due to a pro-poor marginal incidence of non-farm employment expansion; and an indirect impact attributable to the positive effect of non-farm employment growth on agricultural wages (Lanjouw and Murgai 2009). The presence of sufficient opportunities in non-farm sector has a favorable impact as it enables the tightening of the labour markets causing the casual wages to increase. It is also expected to show a positive sign in the regression. The next variable chosen is *percentage of self-employed workers* (NSSO) in the rural economy. The other categories of workers are 'casual workers' and 'regular or salaried workers'. This variable has consistently depicted a weakly negative relationship with the extent of rural non-farm sector. Since a large section of the rural workers are cultivators in own farms, the magnitude of non-farm sector is expected to be low where returns from agriculture are sufficient and subsistence is not threatened. On the other hand, there are increasing instances of exit of small peasants from cultivation related activities with the declining size of holdings or land fragmentation and engagement in casual wage work or self-employment in non-farm jobs. Thus this variable is expected to show a negative sign. The variable of *land productivity per hectare* is obtained by dividing the net state domestic product from agriculture by the net sown area in a state. It captures the nature of agriculture, cropping pattern, as well as the profitability aspects. This variable is also related to the push forces and the engagement of landless labourers, marginal and small farming families into alternative employment avenues to supplement family incomes when the agricultural earnings are meagre. On the other hand, non-farm sector is expected to be vibrant when it is led by agricultural prosperity and production and consumption linkages are strong. Also the richer sections of the farming community diversify into more remunerative non-farm activities. This variable is expected to have a positive relation with both distress and prosperity led RNFS job creation.

Results: A four-stage hierarchical multiple regression was conducted with extent of rural non-farm sector employment as the dependent variable for three points of time, 1993–1994, 2004–2005 and 2011–2012 to observe the dynamics in ground conditions. Table 2.12 gives the summary of the variables and Table 2.13 shows the detailed description of the regressand (dependent variable) and the regressors (explanatory variables), as estimated from the model. All the coefficients showed the expected signs. Unemployment rate was entered at the first stage to

Table 2.12 Descriptive statistics

	Mean			Std. deviation		
	93–94	*04–05*	*11–12*	*93–94*	*04–05*	*11–12*
RNFS (%)	22.4	28.1	37.2	7.9	9.5	11.6
Total Unemployment (%)	1.4	2.0	2.0	1.5	2.4	1.6
Casual wages (Rs/person)	38.5	58.3	153.5	11.7	22.3	50.9
Self-employed (%)	60.2	61.9	57.7	13.4	12.0	11.4
Land Productivity (Rs/ha)	18,534	55,005	71,993	7761	28,876	32,348

Source: Based on author's computation

Table 2.13 Hierarchical regression analysis for determinants of rural non-farm sector employment

Model	Unstandardized β coefficients						
	Unemployment rate	Wages of casual workers	Self employed	Land productivity	Adjusted R^2	Δ Adj R^2	F statistic
1993–1994							
1	3.63* (3.78)				0.45		14.32*
2	2.24*** (1.98)	0.29*** (1.94)			0.54	0.09	10.36*
3	1.84 (1.33)	0.32*** (1.95)	−0.07 (−0.53)		0.51	−0.03	6.65*
4	1.74 (1.45)	0.11 (0.61)	−0.07 (−0.64)	0.000** (2.30)	0.64	0.13	7.96*
2004–2005							
1	3.23* (5.62)				0.62		31.6*
2	2.05* (3.34)	0.20* (3.03)			0.74	0.12	27.6*
3	1.63** (2.25)	0.24* (3.14)	−0.12 (−1.08)		0.74	0.00	18.9*
4	1.71* (2.5)	0.14 *** (1.45)	−0.13 (−1.24)	0.001*** (1.77)	0.77	0.03	16.9*
2011–2012							
1	5.52* (4.7)				0.53		22.1*
2	2.30*** (2.06)	0.15* (4.31)			0.76	0.23	31.2*
3	2.22*** (1.93)	0.15* (4.15)	−0.07 (−0.62)		0.75	−0.01	20.1*
4	1.97*** (1.82)	0.12* (3.48)	−0.13 (−1.1)	0.000*** (1.79)	0.78	0.03	18.0*

Source: Based on author's computation
Notes: Figures in brackets are t-values. N = 17 (1993–1994), 20 (2004–2005 and 2011–2012)
*$p < 0.01$, **$p < 0.05$, ***$p < 0.10$

control for distress push into non-farm activities, wages of casual workers was entered sequentially in the second stage, percent of self-employed at stage three and productivity of land per hectare at stage four. The analysis revealed that in all the years overall unemployment rate contributed significantly to the regression model (F = 14.3, $p < 0.01$). In 1993–1994 it caused for an increase in 3.6 percent in RNFS and accounted for 45 percent of the variation in non-farm sector employment. In the first half of 2000 decade, its explanatory power increased to 62 percent, even though the coefficient remained unchanged. In 2011–2012 its coefficient increased to 5.5, though it explained 53 percent of the variation. The declining role of farm based incomes, open unemployment in agriculture along with disguised unemployment necessitates enhanced engagement in non-farm sector. Moreover, rural non-farm sector continues to attract skilled labour and provide employment for youth, women and other workers in the rural areas. The involvement especially amongst resource poor farmers and farm labourers in multiple jobs (self- employment in non-farm sector, migration earnings) is an important driver of rural non-farm employment, considering the fact that non-farm activities are far more remunerative than agricultural earnings.

Introducing the casual wages variable in the second equation explained an additional 9 percent of the variation in rural non-farm sector in 1993–1994 and the change in the R square was significant ($F = 10.4$, $p < 0.01$). In 2004–2005 and 2011–2012, the incremental contribution of casual wage variable in explaining variation in RNFS was much more, increasing progressively by 12 and 23 percent respectively and the model was also significant as shown by the statistically significant F values, even though after 1993–1994 the value of coefficient of casual wages declined to 0.20 and 0.15 from 0.29. Clearly the unique effect of casual rural wages on the magnitude of non-farm employment is strengthening over time. The growth of certain non-farm sub-sectors is strongly associated with higher agricultural wage rates, notably construction. Direct contribution of the nonfarm sector to poverty reduction is possibly quite muted as the poor often lack assets. Nonetheless policy efforts seeking to maximize the impact of an expanding non-farm sector on rural poverty, need to focus on removing the barriers to the entry of the poor into the non-farm sector (Lanjouw and Shariff 2004). The overall explanatory power of this model increased quite substantially (74 and 76 percent) after 1993–1994. This signifies that non-farm sector development in rural areas is an important co-variate of wage increase, and has a positive impact on rural livelihoods and poverty reduction. The employment guarantee programme, no doubt has also enacted a significant role in pushing up the casual wages, and the increased engagement in the latter along with non-farm jobs have possibly given an upward push to wages in the states.

In the third model, the inclusion of the self-employment variable led to a decline in the explanatory power of the model by 3 percent in 1993–1994. However, there was nearly no change in the explanatory power of the model in the subsequent years, even though this model in all the three years remained significant. The coefficient of self-employment variable showed the expected negative sign, implying that a decline in self-employment (self-cultivation, with rise in wage work or labour) is also accompanied with increase in the incidence of rural non-farm employment. However, the coefficient was not statistically significant in all the three years.

Finally, with the addition of the land productivity variable to the model explained an incremental 13 percent of the variation in rural non-farm employment in 1993–1994 and this change in R square was significant ($F = 7.96$, $p < 0.01$). This was the largest incremental contribution by any predictor to explain the variation in RNFS in 1993–1994. Such behavior reiterates the importance of agricultural development in explaining the linkages and emergence of the non-farm sector. Non-farm activity also affects the performance of agriculture by providing farmers with cash to invest in productivity-enhancing inputs. Development of RNFS (including agro-processing, distribution and the provision of farm inputs) increases the profitability of farming by increasing access to inputs and markets, that in turn, increases rural incomes. Dynamism in agriculture enables growth of the RNF sector, particularly when farm output is amenable for processing and distribution. Higher agricultural incomes in turn raise the demand for non-agricultural goods and services impacting on their employment growth. On the other hand, push factor such as inadequate farm output and risks in farming also induce households to diversify income options. It can be seen that with the addition of all four variables in the fourth stage, except for land productivity variable neither unemployment rate, casual wages earned or self-employment were significant predictors of rural non-farm employment. Together the four independent variables accounted for 64 percent of the variance in RNFS during the period coinciding with the beginning of economic reforms.

The last model in 2004–2005 and 2011–2012 showed somewhat different results. In 2004–2005 and 2011–2012 land productivity variable explained only around 3 percent of the incremental variation in RNFS, but unemployment rate and casual wages earned turned significant predictors of rural non-farm sector employment, along with land productivity

(Self-employment continued to be insignificant factor for determining the non-farm sector). The results indicate the weakening of agricultural led growth in the non-farm sector after 1993–1994, and prominence of other factors in explaining the emergence of non-farm sector.

Lastly, the explanatory power of the model when all four independent variables were included in the analysis increased over time substantially from 64 percent in 1993–1994 to 77 percent (2004–2005) and 78 percent (2011–2012). While it may be there were excluded variables that are important, it can be safely concluded that the model adopted has given a fair indication of the determinants of rural non-farm sector in the country along with the dynamics involved in the process.

Concluding Remarks

The rural non-farm sector (RNFS) sector after decades of stagnancy had emerged in 2004–2005. In the period following 2004–2005, RNFS is demonstrating accelerated employment generation. Labour absorption in the farm sector continues to show negative growth (1% per annum). The heartening development is that for workers dependent on agriculture and allied activities, labour productivity shows a high growth (4.6% per annum) that has had an impact on rising rural wages. There is also evidence of accelerated urban growth having a trickledown effect on the rural economy. Unlike the experience of the last decade, the rapid developments in the urban sector are deepening the rural-urban linkages and the rural areas are no more isolated or bounded spaces.

The pace of rural poverty decline has accelerated in all the major states. In the latter part of 2000s decade self-employment has declined and is accompanied by forging ahead of casual wage employment. However, there seem to be overcrowding in construction activities as can be visualized from the declining per worker productivity in this sector. All the other non-farm sectors i.e. manufacturing, utilities, trade, transportation and services are absorbing workers at rising productivity levels. The RNFS sector has grown in all the states reflecting the reversal of earlier prevalent dualism and existence of a rural and urban divide. Together with rising farm productivity levels, the rural areas are showing indications of greater integration with the rest of the economy. The access to non-farm jobs within and outside the rural areas has eased the pressure of population on land and agriculture to some extent. Even though land owned is getting fragmented, the land productivity has seen substantial improvements. Land is also getting monetized with increased demand for it for urban uses.

As noted by Himanshu et al. (2016), experience of micro study over longer time reveals that the increase in non-farm employment opportunities has meant that the labour market is no longer dependent overwhelmingly on agriculture. Mechanization and technical change are leading to a relative decline in labour demand in agriculture. Wages continue to increase, that may be linked to closer integration with outside labour market. (p. 50). What is also important is that "the flow of urban ethos, aspirations and tastes through the rural urban material and cultural exchanges has integrated the rural and the urban more intimately than before". (Kumar 2016: 70).

Econometric analysis indicates that raising labour productivity and correcting labour market imperfections is crucial to structural transformation of the rural economy. Policies and institutional arrangements are required to increase labour productivity, wages in rural areas and employment opportunities in the rural sector. The existence of linkages between wages, real incomes, labour productivity particularly within agriculture for poverty reduction are well known (De Janvry and Sadoulet 2010). Raising agricultural output and productivity is an important precursor for bringing about structural changes in the rural economy. However, of late the disconnect between agricultural growth and employment diversification is growing and possibly distress or push forces may be playing an active role in spurring the growth of employment in non-farm activities as well as the urban ward migration.

From the viewpoint of policy it is important to note that the agrarian economy is moving towards a market-based system, with enhanced rural to urban migration and tightening of labour markets. Such trends, no doubt, indicate the need to step up the creation of social and economic infrastructure in villages. Rural education and skill development is also essential to improve rural employability. These findings pave the way for an in depth look into the nature of urbanization and rural transformation process underway in Gujarat. The next chapter looks at the employment situation in greater details both at the country level and for the state of Gujarat, along with analysis of changing nature of economic activities in terms of their size and location.

ANNEXURE

Table 2.14a Percentage distribution of usually working persons (ps + ss) by broad industry division, rural areas, 2011–2012

S. No	States	Agriculture, mining & quarrying	Manufacturing, electricity & water	Construction	Trade, hotels etc	Transport etc	Other services	Rural NFS
1	AP	70.3	8.0	6.7	6.1	3.5	5.4	29.7
2	Bihar	67.7	4.8	10.4	8.3	2.6	6.3	32.3
3	Gujarat	75.1	8.3	4.3	5.3	2.8	4.2	24.9
4	Haryana	58.0	10.0	14.3	6.8	6.8	4.2	42.0
5	HP	63.4	5.5	15.3	4.2	3.6	8.0	36.7
6	Karnataka	70.5	9.6	4.3	6.2	3.3	6.1	29.5
7	Kerala	32.1	12.8	18.5	13.6	8.6	14.4	67.9
8	MP	72.7	4.9	12.9	4.2	1.4	3.9	27.3
9	Maharashtra	77.2	6.0	5.2	4.9	2.0	4.8	22.8
10	Orissa	62.8	9.8	12.3	7.1	2.5	5.6	37.3
11	Punjab	52.4	12.3	16.2	5.8	3.8	9.5	47.6
12	Rajasthan	61.8	5.4	20.3	4.8	3.6	4.1	38.2
13	Tamil Nadu	51.7	15.2	15.5	6.8	4.0	6.8	48.3
14	UP	64.1	8.8	13.4	6.1	2.7	4.9	35.9
15	WestBengal	53.5	19.5	8.4	7.4	3.6	7.5	46.5
16	All India	64.6	8.9	11.1	6.5	3.0	6.0	35.4

Source: NSSO, Report No. 554

Table 2.14b Percentage distribution of usually working persons (ps + ss) by broad industry division, rural areas, 2004–2005

S. No	States	Agriculture, mining & quarrying	Manufacturing, electricity & water	Construction	Trade, hotels etc	Transport etc	Other services	Rural NFS
1	AP	73.0	8.7	3.3	6.6	2.6	5.8	27.0
2	Bihar	78.0	5.8	2.5	7.5	2.2	3.9	21.9
3	Gujarat	77.8	7.9	3.0	4.7	2.7	4.0	22.3
4	Haryana	64.2	9.4	8.3	7.5	4.0	6.5	35.7
5	HP	69.7	6.3	9.8	4.3	3.2	6.6	30.2
6	Karnataka	81.4	6.2	2.1	4.5	2.0	3.7	18.5
7	Kerala	43.3	13.9	10.6	12.2	7.0	13.0	56.7
8	MP	83.2	5.1	3.6	4.0	0.7	3.4	16.8
9	Maharashtra	80.3	5.7	2.9	4.7	2.3	4.2	19.8
10	Orissa	69.8	11.2	5.5	6.7	2.0	4.9	30.3
11	Punjab	67.0	8.1	8.8	6.4	3.5	6.1	32.9
12	Rajasthan	74.1	6.0	9.6	4.1	2.1	4.1	25.9
13	Tamil Nadu	65.7	14.1	5.7	6.4	2.8	5.5	34.5
14	UP	73.0	9.0	5.3	6.2	2.1	4.5	27.1
15	WestBengal	62.9	13.6	3.9	9.5	3.6	6.4	37.0
16	All India	73.2	8.3	4.9	6.1	2.5	5.0	26.8

Source: NSSO, Report No. 515, part 1, p. 142

Table 2.14c Percentage distribution of usually working persons (ps + ss) by broad industry division, rural areas, 1999–2000

S. No	States	Agriculture, mining & quarrying	Manufacturing, electricity & water	Construction	Trade, hotels etc	Transport etc	Other services	Rural NFS
1	AP	79.6	5.7	2.2	4.6	1.7	6.2	20.4
2	Bihar	81.1	6.2	2.2	4.5	1.4	4.6	18.9
3	Gujarat	80.2	7.1	2.7	3.9	2.4	3.7	19.8
4	Haryana	68.9	8.2	6.5	6.0	3.3	7.0	31.0
5	HP	73.6	5.1	9.2	3.4	2.3	6.4	26.4
6	Karnataka	82.9	5.4	1.5	4.5	1.5	4.2	17.1
7	Kerala	50.0	12.8	9.4	11.9	6.2	9.9	50.2
8	MP	87.5	4.1	1.8	2.7	0.7	3.2	12.5
9	Maharashtra	82.7	5.1	2.3	3.8	1.8	4.2	17.2
10	Orissa	78.6	8.3	3.2	4.6	1.1	4.2	21.4
11	Punjab	72.6	6.7	5.3	5.8	3.8	5.8	27.4
12	Rajasthan	79.1	4.5	7.9	3.5	1.7	3.3	20.9
13	Tamil Nadu	68.4	14.1	4.0	5.6	2.6	5.3	31.6
14	Uttar Pradesh	76.3	7.9	3.3	5.4	2.1	4.9	23.6
15	West Bengal	63.9	16.7	2.2	8.5	3.3	5.4	36.1
16	All India	76.8	7.6	3.3	5.1	2.1	5.2	23.3

Source: NSSO, Report No. 458, part 1, p. 120

Table 2.15   State Domestic Product (SDP) per worker for states

	Agriculture & allied		Mining & quarrying		Manufacturing		Electricity, gas & water	
	2004–2005	2011–2012	2004–2005	2011–2012	2004–2005	2011–2012	2004–2005	2011–2012
Andhra Pradesh	18,672	24,586	36,979	92,560	39,509	68,080	746,458	311,279
Assam	20,937	28,651	106,954	428,324	161,435	94,332	326,647	1,096,572
Bihar	15,086	19,006	14,560	36,917	32,015	41,027	478,939	302,241
Chattisgadh	12,449	18,670	705,846	469,854	205,600	198,639	1,180,523	777,958
Gujarat	25,329	42,495	400,217	428,163	159,541	198,691	1,128,544	380,919
Haryana	49,278	82,378	152,323	63,345	183,550	267,797	316,401	615,356
HP	29,932	33,316	191,598	360,079	154,950	319,227	377,626	644,269
J&K	54,653	44,492	37,946	183,041	50,585	62,946	491,867	281,815
Jharkhand	14,981	27,392	288,997	354,051	231,817	184,523	382,145	140,830
Karnataka	20,595	34,254	177,302	81,382	128,317	149,723	573,170	472,086
Kerala	48,170	77,483	28,537	94,734	59,475	87,217	744,922	321,855
Madhya Pradesh	17,322	27,853	189,421	344,060	61,884	113,278	663,393	607,187
Maharashtra	18,881	26,571	157,737	466,609	170,329	258,047	698,133	647,264
Orissa	18,070	23,442	369,304	500,785	51,471	106,694	982,395	445,567
Punjab	64,844	91,238	25,644	19,597	117,794	167,098	329,196	257,496
Rajasthan	22,110	35,425	85,432	257,202	73,675	154,885	398,396	242,572
Tamil Nadu	19,438	34,068	149,035	78,490	81,759	131,765	727,175	78,966
Uttarakhand	24,203	38,313	NA	NA	183,726	454,800	275,713	389,098
Uttar Pradesh	21,191	27,339	209,537	45,053	47,579	63,580	349,439	160,067
West Bengal	34,956	43,014	194,062	103,980	45,295	39,329	683,881	421,606

Source: Computed from net state domestic product data (various years) from Central Statistical Organisation and employment-unemployment data from National Sample Survey Office (various years), as in text

Construction		Trade, hotels etc		Transportation etc		Services		NSDP/worker	
2004–2005	2011–2012	2004–2005	2011–2012	2004–2005	2011–2012	2004–2005	2011–2012	2004–2005	2011–2012
52,372	44,701	49,378	77,050	59,354	85,285	96,157	119,803	33,455	47,889
130,658	83,591	72,780	59,205	85,516	138,682	125,490	161,584	49,561	62,081
81,084	66,773	76,302	98,422	67,868	123,013	162,060	137,319	31,645	44,803
76,880	152,063	68,290	97,923	108,690	248,139	165,330	195,589	39,431	57,921
150,229	244,281	149,223	224,680	135,767	275,385	214,001	277,555	77,712	130,746
136,056	128,522	152,189	388,789	167,992	183,175	196,614	360,097	99,999	179,664
135,839	117,148	117,195	213,410	93,160	169,787	180,246	260,571	66,825	93,934
201,087	54,409	78,528	52,388	73,670	77,131	241,579	196,373	88,475	68,931
37,737	34,871	84,728	76,487	102,458	156,394	167,807	221,918	55,603	68,419
150,998	170,988	94,853	110,157	118,633	109,745	224,689	272,157	62,169	95,216
111,528	123,049	132,590	150,819	108,280	231,101	171,674	238,650	87,479	140,195
83,678	57,414	72,549	86,745	118,548	141,335	129,500	188,446	38,462	60,065
126,213	180,514	141,263	197,138	147,318	226,485	272,904	382,772	86,709	141,897
84,204	69,463	59,627	98,434	116,068	159,891	148,947	201,293	42,580	59,417
79,054	75,607	93,532	133,258	109,498	144,788	186,593	231,713	88,087	124,683
66,956	45,078	92,258	134,498	82,841	116,485	153,074	196,028	46,927	72,850
117,826	82,883	114,241	162,088	142,786	188,878	204,481	464,972	71,597	120,347
132,966	114,828	138,292	283,436	139,077	204,012	164,574	264,178	64,576	144,043
56,659	39,576	55,650	74,652	85,605	152,186	145,231	207,251	38,829	54,025
110,806	66,292	82,531	115,274	102,808	153,053	159,220	218,746	63,191	79,747

Table 2.16   Correlation matrix

	Unemployment	Casual wages	Self-employment	Land productivity
1993–1994				
Unemployment	1.000	0.630	−0.402	0.457
Casual wages		1.000	0.027	0.692
Self-employment			1.000	0.010
Land productivity				1.000
2004–2005				
Unemployment	1.000	0.631	−0.243	0.434
Casual wages		1.000	0.255	0.772
Self-employment			1.000	0.262
Land productivity				1.000
2011–2012				
Unemployment	1.000	0.666	−0.243	0.387
Casual wages		1.000	−0.235	0.487
Self-employment			1.000	0.081
Land productivity				1.000

Source: Based on author's computation

REFERENCES

Basant, Rakesh, and B.L. Kumar. 1989. *Rural Non-Agricultural Activities in India: A Review of Available Evidence.* Working Paper No 20. Ahmedabad: Gujarat Institute of Area Planning.

———. 1990. *Non-Agricultural Employment in Rural Gujarat—A Review of Evidence.* Working Paper No 28. Ahmedabad: Gujarat Institute of Area Planning.

Basant, R., and R. Parathasarathy. 1991. *Inter-Regional Variations in Rural Non-Agricultural Employment in Gujarat, 1961–81.* Working Paper No 36. Ahmedabad: The Gujarat Institute of Area Planning.

Basole, Amit. 2017. What Does the Rural Economy Need. *Economic and Political Weekly* 52 (9).

Basu, D.N., and S.P. Kashyap. 1992. Rural Non-Agricultural Employment in India: Role of Development Process and Rural-Urban Employment Linkages. *Economic and Political Weekly* 27 (51/52): A178–A189.

Bathla, Seema, Thorat Sukhadeo, P.K. Joshi, and Bingxin Yu. 2017. Where to Invest to Accelerate Agricultural Growth and Poverty Reduction. *Economic and Political Weekly* 52 (39): 10.

Bhalla, Sheila. 1993a. Tests of Some Prepositions About the Dynamics of Change in the Rural Workforce Structure. *The Indian Journal of Labour Economics* 36 (3): 428–439.

————. 1993b. Patterns of Employment Generation in India. *The Indian Journal of Labour of Economics* 36 (4).

————. 2000. *Behind Poverty: The Qualitative Deterioration of Employment Prospects for Rural Indians.* IHD Working Paper Series 7. New Delhi: Institute of Human Development.

————. 2005a. *India's Rural Economy: Issues and Evidence.* Working Paper Series No 25. New Delhi: Institute of Human Development.

————. 2005b. Rural Workforce Diversification and Performance of Unorganized Sector Enterprises. In *Rural Transformation in India: The Role of Non-Farm Sector*, ed. Rohini Nayyar and Alakh N. Sharma. New Delhi: Institute for Human Development.

Clark, Colin. 1940. *The Conditions of Economic Progress.* Macmillan and Co. Ltd.

Dandekar, Ajay, and Sreedeep Bhattacharya. 2017. Lives in Debt: Narratives of Agrarian Distress and Farmer Suicides. *Economic and Political Weekly* 52 (21): 77–84.

Datta, Amrita. 2016. Migration, Remittances and Changing Sources of Income in Rural Bihar (1999–2011): Some Findings from a Longitudinal Study. *Economic and Political Weekly* 51 (31).

Datta, Amrita, Gerry Rodgers, Janine Rodgers, and B.K.N. Singh. 2014. Contrasts in Development in Bihar: A Tale of Two Villages. *Journal of Development Studies* 50 (9).

de Janvry, Alain, and Elisabeth Sadoulet. 2010. Agricultural Growth and Poverty Reduction: Additional Evidence. *World Bank Research Observer* 25: 1–20.

Denis, Eric, P. Mukhopadhyay, and Marie-Helene Zerah. 2012. Subaltern Urbanization in India. *Economic and Political Weekly* 47 (30): 52–62.

Dutta, Puja, Rinku Murgai, Martin Ravallion, and Dominique van de Walle. 2014. *Right to Work? Assessing India's Employment Guarantee Scheme in Bihar.* Equity and Development, Washington, DC: World Bank.

Gelman, Andrew, and Jennifer Hill. 2007. *Data Analysis Using Regression and Multilevel/Hierarchical Models.* Cambridge: Cambridge University Press.

Gelman, A., J.B. Carlin, H.S. Stern, and D.B. Rubin. 1995. *Bayesian Data Analysis.* Chapman and Hall.

Government of India, Labour Bureau. 2016. *Report on Fifth Annual Employment – Unemployment Survey (2015–16)*, Volume 1. Chandigarh.

Gujarati, D.N. 1995. *Basic Econometrics.* 3rd ed. New York: McGraw-Hill, Inc.

Himanshu. 2007. Recent Trends in Poverty and Inequality: Some Preliminary Results. *Economic and Political Weekly* 42 (6).

Himanshu, Bhavna Joshi, and Peter Lanjouw. 2016. Non-Farm Diversification, Inequality and Mobility in Palanpur. *Economic and Political Weekly* 51 (26 & 27): 43–51.

Himanshu, Peter Lanjouw, Rinku Murgai, and Nicholas Stern. 2013. Non-Farm Diversification, Poverty, Economic Mobility and Income Inequality: A Case Study in Village India. *Agricultural Economics* 44: 461–473.

IIPA. 2010. *A Study of Bihari Migrant Labourers: Incidence, Causes and Remedies.* Indian Institute of Public Administration. Sponsored by Department of Labour Resources, Govt of Bihar.

Jatav, Manoj. 2010. Casualisation of Workforce in Rural Non-Farm Sector of India: A Regional Level Analysis Across Industries. *The Indian Journal of Labour Economics* 53 (3): 501–516.

Jatav, Manoj, and S. Sen. 2013. Drivers of Non-Farm Employment in Rural India. *Economic and Political Weekly* 48: 26–27.

Jodhka, Surinder. 2006. Caste and Democracy: Assertion and Identity Among the Dalit of Rural Punjab. *Sociological Bulletin* 55 (1): 4–23.

———. 2014. Emergent Ruralities: Revisiting Village Life and Agrarian Change in Haryana. *Economic & Political Weekly* 49 (26&27): 5–17.

Jodhka, Surinder, and Adarsh Kumar. 2017. Non-Farm Economy in Madhubani, Bihar: Social Dynamics and Exclusionary Rural Transformations. *Economic and Political Weekly* 52 (25&26).

Kashyap, S.P. 1995. Irrigation Induced Agricultural Growth, Occupational Diversification and Poverty Alleviation: Experience of a Prosperous District in Gujarat. In *Growth, Employment and Poverty: Change and Continuity in Rural India*, ed. G.K. Chaddha and Alakh N. Sharma. New Delhi: Indian Society of Labour Economics, Vikas Publishing House Pvt Ltd.

———. 2011. Emerging Tendencies in Rural Non-Farm Enterprise Sector: Role of Policy. *Sampada* 67 (9).

Kashyap, S.P., and Niti Mehta. 2005. Rural Non-Farm Sector in Gujarat: Growth and Emerging Nature. In *Rural Transformation in India: The Role of Non-Farm Sector*, ed. Rohini Nayyar and Alakh N. Sharma. New Delhi: Institute for Human development.

———. 2007. Non-Farm Sector in India: Temporal & Spatial Aspects. *Indian Journal of Labour Economics* 50 (4): 611–632.

Krishna, Anirudh, and Devendra Bajpai. 2011. Lineal Spread and Radial Dissipation: Experiencing Growth in Rural India, 1993–2005. *Economic and Political Weekly* 46 (38): 44–51.

Kumar, Satendra. 2016. Agrarian Transformation and the New Rurality in Western Uttar Pradesh. *Economic & Political Weekly* 51 (26&27): 61–71.

Kuznets, S. 1966. *Modern Economic Growth: Rate, Structure and Spread.* New Haven: Yale University Press.

Lanjouw, Peter, and Abusaleh Shariff. 2004. Rural Non-Farm Employment in India: Access, Incomes and Poverty Impact. *Economic and Political Weekly* 39 (40).

Lanjouw, P., and R. Murgai. 2009. *Poverty Decline, Agricultural Wages, and Non-Farm Employment in India: 1983–2004.* Policy Research Working Paper No 4858. Washington, DC: World Bank.

Lewis, W.A. 1954. Economic Development with Unlimited Supplies of Labour. *The Manchester School* 22 (2): 139–191.

Mehta, Niti. 2001. *Development Process and Occupational Diversification: A Case of Kheda*, Ph.D. Thesis. Ahmedabad: Gujarat University.

Misra, Sangita, and Anoop K. Suresh. 2014. *Estimating Employment Elasticity of Growth for the Indian Economy*. RBI WPS (DEPR): 06/2014. Mumbai: Reserve Bank of India.

Nadhanael, G.V. 2012. Recent Trends in Rural Wages: An Analysis of Inflationary Implications. *Reserve Bank of India Occasional Papers* 33 (1&2).

Nayyar, Rohini, and Alakh N. Sharma, eds. 2005. *Rural Transformation in India – The Role of Non-Farm Sector, Institute of Human Development*. New Delhi: Manohar Publishers & Distributors.

Papola, T.S., and P.P. Sahu. 2012. *Employment Growth and Structure: Policies, Performance and Prospects*. (Mimeo). New Delhi: Institute for Studies in Industrial Development.

Reserve Bank of India. 2012. *RBI Releases Time Series Data on Average Daily Wage Rates in Rural India for Men*. Press Release-2012-2013/465, September 18.

Rondinelli, D.A. 1983. Towns and Small Cities in Developing Countries. *Geographical Review* 73 (4): 379–395.

Ruttan, Mario. 1995. *Farms and Factories: Social Profile of Large Farmers & Rural Industrialists in West India*. Delhi: Oxford University Press.

Saha, Partha, and Sher Verick. 2016. *State of Rural Labour Markets in India*. ILO Asia-Pacific Working Paper Series, May.

Saleth, Maria R. 1997. Occupational Diversification Among Rural Groups: A Case Study of Rural Transformation in Tamil Nadu. *Economic and Political Weekly* 26: 1908–1916.

Seidman, David. 1976. On Choosing Between Linear and Log-Linear Models. *Journal of Politics* 38: 461–466.

Sen, Abhijit, and Himanshu. 2004. Poverty and Inequality in India, Parts I and II. *Economic and Political Weekly* 39 (38): 4247–4263.

Singh, Sukhpal, and Shruti Bhogal. 2014. Depeasantization in Punjab: Status of Farmers Who Left Farming. *Current Science* 106 (10): 1364–1368.

Singh, N.K., and Nicholas Stern. 2013. *The New Bihar, Rekindling Governance and Development*. New Delhi: HarperCollins.

Sundaram, K. 2007. Employment and Poverty in India, 2000–2005. *Economic and Political Weekly* 42 (30): 3121–3131.

Unni, Jeemol. 1998. Non-Agricultural Employment and Poverty in India: A Review of Evidence. *Economic and Political Weekly* 33: 36–44.

Unni, Jeemol, and G. Raveendran. 2007. Growth of Employment (1993–94 to 2004–05): Illusion of Inclusiveness? *Economic and Political Weekly* 42: 196–199.

Vaidyanathan, A. 1986. Labour Use in Rural India – A Study of Spatial and Temporal Variations. *Economic and Political Weekly* 21 (52): 130–146.

CHAPTER 3

Changes in the Employment Scenario in Gujarat

INTRODUCTION

The previous chapter had an in-depth discussion on the rural transformation process, including trends in employment pattern and output in the country, growth of rural non-farm sector and the associated variables. Econometric analysis captured the magnitude of impact of the causal variables and dynamics over time. The present chapter uses the available secondary information to examine the shifts in the overall employment situation in Gujarat and changes in the sectoral activity pattern. It has been established beyond doubt that urbanisation processes influence the nature of economic activity in rural areas. Moreover, the inter- and intra-state worker mobility is reflected in the locational shift of economic activities from rural to urban or vice versa, in addition to the changes in scale of operations of economic activities. For policy response it is important to identify the activities that are absorbing the workers released from the shrinking agriculture. This chapter examines some of these issues.

Gujarat economy is witnessing structural change as depicted by trend in the gross domestic product and the share of non-agricultural income and employment. This is also accompanied by noticeable shifts in the rural and

An earlier version of this chapter was presented in the 57th Annual Conference of the Indian Society of Labour Economics (ISLE), held at Srinagar, J&K. As a summary of the paper was published in the Conference Proceedings, the permission of the Editor of Indian Journal of Labour Economics has been taken.

urban composition of workforce. The annual growth rate of non-farm employment has shown significant acceleration since 1990s. An examination of the sectoral workforce estimates derived from the National Sample Survey Office's (NSSO) work participation rates (UPSS definition) shows that non-farm employment share in the total economy has shown a steady rise, from 36 per cent (1993–1994) to 52.5 per cent (2011–2012). In rural areas the increase has been from 19.8 per cent to 25 per cent. The annual growth rate of non-farm employment for the entire economy showed a significant acceleration in 2000s decade (from 0.9 per cent in the 1990s decade) to 3.8 per cent (1999–2000 to 2004–2005) and nearly 5.6 per cent from 2004–2005 to 2011–2012. Given the limited share of employment in the organised sector, it is obvious that the unorganised sector plays a major role in sustaining this growth. It is thus imperative to assess the relative resilience of employment generation in the non-farm unorganised sector activities in the state.

The unorganised, non-agricultural economic activities are likely to show regional contrasts in performance as these are rooted in the locational resource endowments. Such activities are fluid in nature and subject to rapid changes, due to high mobility or morbidity of smaller units and also on account of birth of new units. There are spatial variations in the magnitude of job losses in certain industries and gains by others. Moreover, given the recent, fast pace of urbanisation in Gujarat, it is possible that several industries have experienced locational shifts and are undergoing changes related to their size.

Growth in economic activity is usually ascertained on the basis of labour productivity, output levels or employment. The non-agricultural sector includes both rural and urban non-agricultural activities, and in the present discussion non-agriculture sub-sector is disaggregated into rural and urban areas. Information available from the Economic Census is used to examine the extent of employment in economic activities and changes in them. Economic Census (EC) is the complete count of all establishments (i.e. units engaged in production and/or distribution of goods and services not for the purpose of sole consumption) located within the geographical boundaries of the country. The EC enumerates all establishments engaged in various agricultural and non-agricultural activities excluding crop production, plantation, public administration, defence etc. The basic purpose of conducting the EC is to prepare a framework for the follow up enterprise surveys intended to collect more detailed sector specific information between two economic censuses. In view of the rapid changes in unorganized sectors of non-agricultural economy due to high mobility of smaller units, the scheme of conducting the economic census is introduced periodically by Central Statistical Organisation (CSO), Government of India for updating the frame from time to time (DES, GoG 2017).

Based on the share of employment derived from EC of 1990, 1998, 2005 and 2012, the dynamic economic sectors (at 1-digit NIC classification) are identified for Gujarat. It needs clarification at this juncture that with the launch of the EC, information on workers available from the decennial population census became highly aggregated as the non-farm workers were clubbed under "other workers". The census worker classification currently does not include a category of "allied agricultural activity", as this is included in the "other workers" category. The information from the population census "household industry workers" category also does not tell much about the nature of jobs. The activity wise details of employment from the NSSO do not throw light on size of enterprises, magnitude of hired workers and other techno-economic characteristics with state and sectoral disaggregation. Such information on enterprises is available from the EC and the follow up Enterprise Surveys. However, in the EC the numbers of workers engaged in non-agricultural enterprises at the aggregate level are nearly 29 per cent less than that enumerated by the Population Census. This difference is enormous and could be because the EC excludes home based workers.

The next section deals with the stylised employment accounting for Gujarat state. In the subsequent sections attempt is made to identify the economic activities that:(1) have an important share in the total non-agricultural employment, and have experienced growth over time, (2) are experiencing locational shifts (between rural and urban areas) and (3). are experiencing size substitution. The share of activity groups in the net domestic product is ascertained together with the changes over time. The last section draws conclusions and policy inferences.

Overall Scenario

The secondary data sources reveal the following aggregate insights with regard to the employment situation in Gujarat:

1. Gujarat has recorded a falling share of the primary sector in the Net State Domestic Product (NSDP) from 23.7 per cent in 1993–1994 to 14.7 per cent in 2013–2014 (CSO, various years). The non-primary sectors have recorded high growth rates from 1980–1981 onwards. These developments have led to a growth accelerating impact on the state economy.

2. Within the secondary sector, specifically manufacturing and construction, output levels have shown positive and significant growth
acceleration in the 2000s decade (at 12 and 14 per cent per annum
respectively). Transport and trade sectors within the tertiary sector
have also shown growth acceleration.

3. High growth of non-primary sectors, unlike in the previous decade,
has led to the commensurate high level of urbanisation (42.5%) in
Gujarat, with urban population showing a percentage change of 36
per cent. From 2001 to 2011 although the concentration of urban
population in class 1 cities has risen from 68 to 72 per cent, the
smaller towns (classes 6, 5, and 4) are growing at faster annual rates
(5.1, 9.8 and 5.3 per cent respectively).

4. The other notable feature of Gujarat economy during this period
has been that unlike the scenario in the last decade, growth of workforce (1.5 per cent per annum) has been lower than the population
growth rate (1.8 per cent per annum). This is possibly reflected in
the state's performance in rural poverty reduction (by 17.6 per cent
points from 2004–2005 to 2011–2012), that is marginally better
than the national average (16.7 per cent points). However, the
reduction in urban poverty is slower (by 10 percentage points), and
lower than the national figure (12 percentage point reduction).

5. As in other urbanised states, in Gujarat also a large number of rural
residents commute for work to urban areas and are working primarily in manufacturing, construction and trade related activities. From
NSSO (2009–2010) employment data, it can be seen that in Gujarat
10.3 per cent of rural residents report urban as their place of work
(Chandrasekhar 2011).

The scenario presented above is mixed and throws several challenges in
the nature of generating adequate livelihood opportunities for the workers
in the rural areas. The growing importance of smaller settlements demands
timely action to ensure delivery of services and jobs for the workers diversifying out of the primary sector. For crystallizing the nature of economic
transition, the changes in workforce composition are examined.

WORKFORCE COMPOSITION

The trends in employment based on the census population tables for 2001 and 2011 establish certain notable features. In the last decade the rural areas in the state witnessed a falling share in the total workforce. The dramatic shift in the rural and urban composition of workers is undoubtedly associated with urbanisation, industrialisation and a robust agriculture. The participation of marginal workers in rural areas declined from 12 to 10.6 per cent. The proportion of main workers in rural areas declined more steeply (65 to 58%), resulting in the fall in the total workers (by 8% points), that was also quite noteworthy (change from 3.4% point recorded in last decade). The urban ward shift of workforce is rather stark from the fact that while in absolute terms a total of 0.6 million workers were added in rural areas (all in the category of main workers, as the rural marginal workers declined), in urban areas the increase was by 3 million. The urban marginal work participation rates (WPR) doubled from 1.8 to 2.8 per cent, leading to a doubling in the share of urban marginal workers over that in 2001. In absolute terms in urban areas the additions were more pronounced in the category of main workers (by 2.6 million), i.e. 88 per cent of the incremental workers in urban areas were main workers (Table 3.1).

At the country level Chand and Srivastava (2014) using NSSO data, show that rural workforce participation rates at the all India level for both males and females declined between 1993–1994 to 2009–2010, more steeply for females (by 6.7 percentage points). In contrast using census (2001, 2011) data Kasturi (2015) shows that in rural areas WPR declined for both males and females but increased in urban areas, quite significantly

Table 3.1 Changes in workforce composition, Gujarat, 2001 and 2011 (in thousand)

Particulars	Rural		Urban		Total	
	2001	2011	2001	2011	2001	2011
Main workers	11,114	11,878	5904	8487	17,018	20,365
% to total	(65.3)	(58.3)	(34.7)	(41.7)	(100.0)	(100.0)
Marginal Workers	3879	3692	348	710	4227	4402
% to total	(91.8)	(83.9)	(8.2)	(16.1)	(100.0)	(100.0)
All Workers	14,993	15,570	6252	9197	21,245	24,767
% to total	(70.6)	(62.9)	(29.4)	(37.1)	(100.0)	(100.0)

Source: Census of India, 2001 and 2011

for urban females. In Gujarat such patterns find a reflection. The work participation rates for the rural male main workers in the state did not reveal much change (increase by 1.1 percentage point). In urban areas however it nearly doubled (1.6 to 3%), together with a steep increase in the urban male participation rate (54 to 57%). The work participation rates for rural female, both main and marginal declined; the latter more steeply. Urban female participation rates in both categories increased in Gujarat (Table 3.2).

Some broad inferences about the industrial composition of (main) workers over the twenty year period from 1991 to 2011 can be made from census classification of workers (Table 3.3). By census definition of "main workers" is meant "those who had worked for the major part of the year preceding the date of enumeration i.e., those who were engaged in any economically productive activity for 183 days (or six months) or more during the year". It is observed that the share of agricultural workers declined from 77 per cent to 68 per cent in 2001 and then showed a sharp rise in 2011 to 74 per cent. While the share of cultivators decreased by 7.6 percentage points over the twenty year period, in the last decade there was a decline by only 3 percentage points, indicating near stagnation. On the other hand, agricultural labourers in the 2001–2011 period swelled by 9.1 percentage points, indicating rising landlessness and sharp proletarianiza-

Table 3.2 Worker participation rates, Gujarat, 2001 and 2011 (per cent)

Particulars	2001			2011		
	Male	Female	Total	Male	Female	Total
Main worker						
Rural	50.3	18.8	35.0	51.4	16.2	34.2
Urban	52.3	7.1	31.2	54.2	8.8	33.0
Total	51.1	14.6	33.6	52.6	13.1	33.7
Marginal worker						
Rural	5.1	19.7	12.2	5.8	15.8	10.6
Urban	1.6	2.2	1.8	2.9	2.5	2.8
Total	3.8	13.3	8.3	4.6	10.3	7.3
Total worker						
Rural	55.5	38.5	47.2	57.1	32.0	44.9
Urban	53.9	9.3	33.0	57.2	11.3	35.7
Total	54.9	27.9	41.9	57.2	23.4	41.0

Source: Census of India, 2001 and 2011

Table 3.3 Distribution of rural (main) workforce by activities in Gujarat (1991–2011) (per cent)

Category	1991	2001	2011
Cultivators	46.1	41.5	38.5
Agricultural labourers	30.7	26.3	35.4
Activities allied to Agri.	3.6		
Household industry	1.4	1.6	0.98
Other worker	18.2	30.5	25.1
Total	100.0	100.0	100.0

Source: Census of India

tion of Gujarat's rural areas. In fact that the number of "marginal cultivators", (working for less than six months a year), rose very sharply, by nearly 57 per cent, suggesting a sharp marginalization of the workforce in Gujarat's farm sector, possibly also depressing the agricultural wages in the state (Shah 2013).

The category of 'other workers' nearly doubled over 1991–2001, though recorded a decline by 5.4 percentage points during 2001–2011 period. It is noted that this category comprises of allied sector workers, non-household based manufacturing and tertiary workers. Employment in rural household industries sector, already miniscule has recorded further decline. Evidence thus points to the inability of the rural industry to "absorb" the workforce released in the agrarian sector. Table 3.3 however, points towards rural occupational diversification within the primary sector. Although detailed breakup of occupational categories is not given in the census after 1991, evidence provided by the EC (2005, 2012) suggests that employment in allied activities (or agricultural establishments i.e., livestock, forestry, hunting, fisheries etc. excluding the crop sector) recorded gains by nearly 2 million workers in rural Gujarat. Despite the under-enumeration of workers in the EC, in 2012 there were apparently 3.3 million workers in the allied sectors that comprise around 21 per cent of the total rural (census) workers.

Industry-wise non-farm data generated by various rounds of NSSO Employment and Unemployment surveys (UPSS) is far more substantive (Table 3.4). In rural Gujarat up to 1999–2000 the relative importance of the primary sector increased. Industries sector witnessed a reduction by nearly 2.5 percentage points, even though tertiary activities, mainly trade, transport, storage etc. recorded enhanced share of workers. Between

Table 3.4 Percentage distribution of employed (UPSS) by broad industry divisions, rural Gujarat

Category	1999–2000 55th round	2004–2005 61st round	2011–2012 68th round
Agriculture, allied, mining & quarrying	80.2	77.8	75.1
Manufacturing, electricity& water	7.1	7.9	8.3
Construction	2.7	3.0	4.3
Wholesale & retail trade, hotels etc.	3.9	4.7	5.3
Transport, storage, communications	2.4	2.7	2.8
Other services	3.7	4.0	4.2
Rural non-farm sector	19.8	22.3	24.9
Total	100.0	100.0	100.0

Source: Computed from NSSO employment-unemployment surveys, various years

1999–2000 and 2011–2012, the share of primary sector in the workforce declined, though it continued to engage three-fourths of the workforce. Rural occupational diversification, at least at the aggregate level gained vigour. Non-primary sectors that gained in terms of share of workers in the 2000s decade were largely construction, trade and hotels. Manufacturing and other services depicted weak gains. Transport and communication sector at the aggregate level remained unchanged. Thus in Gujarat, two sets of emerging sectors can be identified; one belonging to the primary sector and the other to the non-farm sectors. Allied agricultural activities represent the promising activities in the rural primary sector. It would be useful to examine and identify the non-primary sectors and the activities that are gaining in importance. In the subsequent sections we deal with the emerging activities belonging to the non-primary sector.

NON-AGRICULTURAL EMPLOYMENT: A DISAGGREGATED VIEW

Emerging non-agricultural activities are identified on the basis of labour productivity, output and employment growth. This section attempts to identify non-farm economic activities that are gaining on the basis of their shares in employment and growth performance, as well as those that are experiencing shift in location. A comparison is done using data from the Economic Census for 1990 (Third EC), 1998 (Fourth EC), 2005 (Fifth EC) and 2012 (Sixth EC). In the EC while the crop and plantation sector is excluded, information is available on allied agricultural enterprises, besides the non-agricultural activities. The EC defines an "Establishment" as an enterprise having at least one hired worker on a fairly regular basis. An "Own Account Enterprise" (OAE) is one that is normally run by household members and does not engage any hired worker on a regular basis.

Size Structure of Enterprises

The information on size structure of non-agricultural activities in terms of their numbers and employment therein and their rural-urban composition is shown in Table 3.5. Between 1998 and 2012 in the state the share of rural areas in all the non-agricultural enterprises taken together declined in numbers as well as employment, while the urban areas recorded gains in the share of number of all enterprises and employment therein. There was a higher concentration of non-agricultural establishments (with hired workers) in urban areas, both with regard to their numbers and workers employed. As compared to establishments, larger sections of OAEs are located in rural areas. However, in the period under consideration (1998–2012), the rural share of numbers of OAEs and employment therein was declining, while gains were accruing in the urban areas. Annual growth of employment in urban non-agricultural OAEs accelerated at 4.6 per cent.

Table 3.5   Size structure of non-farm employment and rural-urban composition (percentage of rural + urban)

Size	Rural			Urban		
	1998	2005	2012	1998	2005	2012
OAE						
Numbers	41.4	44.0	36.3	58.6	56.0	63.7
Employment	41.0	44.0 (0.6)	36.2 (−0.2)	59.0	56.7 (−1.2)	63.8 (4.6)
Establishments						
Numbers	33.5	34.8	28.1	66.5	65.2	71.9
Employment	26.6	29.3 (4.2)	27.5 (3.5)	73.4	70.7 (2.2)	72.5 (4.8)
All enterprises						
Numbers	39.0	40.0	32.6	61.0	60.0	67.4
Employment	31.2	33.3 (2.8)	29.7 (2.3)	68.8	66.7 (1.3)	70.3 (4.8)

Source: Reports of the fourth, fifth and sixth Economic Census, DES (2000, 2006, 2015), Government of Gujarat, Gandhinagar

Note: Figures in brackets are the annual growth rates

The annual rate of increase for workers in all the non-agricultural enterprises was higher in urban (4.8%) than in rural areas (2.3%) during 2005 to 2012, showing a reversal of trend witnessed during 1998 to 2005. In urban areas the high growth was contributed by the increase in employment in both own account enterprises and establishments with hired workers. In the earlier period, the former had registered a decline (−1.2%). In the rural areas of late the entire growth of employment in enterprises is only because of employment growth in establishments hiring workers (at 3.5%, though lower than 4.2% recorded in 1998 to 2005). Rural own account enterprises growth is nearly stagnant.

It would also be interesting to observe changes in the scalar aspects of individual activity. Viability of activities increases with the size of operations, through the employment of hired workers. On the other hand several activities are emerging where self-employment is the norm. Table 3.6 depicts the size substitution for economic activities during the period 2005 to 2012.

Mining and quarrying, manufacturing, electricity, gas and water, communication, construction, and all services are activities that function dominantly in enterprises with hired workers. In the rural areas, self-employment (own account work) has risen only in the construction, transport and storage activities. Own account retail trade continues to be dominant in the rural areas. All other rural based activities are depicting a rising trend of unorganised enterprises functioning with hired/casual workers, particularly those related to manufacturing, wholesale trade, communication and other service activities. In the urban areas, changes in size composition are obvious in case of both wholesale and retail trade, communication sector, financial/business, real estate sectors in favour of enterprises that hire workers. Urban self-employment in 2012 increased remarkably in utilities sector, construction, hospitality/food services, all the service sector activities excluding financial/business services. Non-agricultural sector in rural areas in entirety is veering towards enterprises that hire casual workers.

Rural–Urban Distribution of Employment in Non-Farm Enterprises

The activity wise rural-urban distribution of non-agricultural employment is shown in Tables 3.7a, 3.7b, and 3.7c. Considering the share of employment in all enterprises (OAEs and Establishments), it can be observed that urban areas depict a dominant and increasing share in 2012, after facing a

Table 3.6   Changes in size of enterprises by activity & location, 2005 to 2012

Industry	Size	Rural		Urban	
		2005	2012	2005	2012
Mining & quarrying	% OAE	14.4	8.3	17.6	8.9
	% Estb.	85.7	91.7	82.4	91.1
Manufacturing	% OAE	24.6	19.2	11.2	12.7
	% Estb.	75.4	80.8	88.8	87.3
Electricity, gas & water	% OAE	9.7	8.3	4.9	15.5
	% Estb.	90.3	91.7	95.1	84.5
Construction	% OAE	21.6	39.8	22.6	44.0
	% Estb.	78.4	60.2	77.4	56.0
Wholesale trade	% OAE	30.0	17.1	26.8	16.5
	% Estb.	70.1	82.9	73.2	83.5
Retail trade	% OAE	60.0	59.5	41.9	36.1
	% Estb.	40.0	40.5	58.1	63.9
Restaurants & hotels	% OAE	32.6	32.0	18.4	23.8
	% Estb.	67.4	68.0	81.6	76.2
Transport & storage	% OAE	56.0	54.1	38.1	39.3
	% Estb.	44.0	45.9	61.9	60.7
Communication	% OAE	33.1	29.4	31.4	13.6
	% Estb.	66.9	70.6	68.6	86.4
FIRE & bus. services	% OAE	29.7	24.0	15.9	11.9
	% Estb.	70.3	76.0	84.1	88.1
All other services	% OAE	19.7	18.8	12.8	22.6
	% Estb.	80.3	81.2	87.2	77.4
Total non-agricultural	% OAE	36.0	30.3	22.8	22.6
	% Estb.	64.0	69.7	77.2	77.4

Source: Reports of the fourth, fifth and sixth Economic Census, DES, Government of Gujarat, Gandhinagar

dip in 2005. During 1998 mining & quarrying, and construction followed by electricity, gas and water were concentrated in rural areas. By 2012, within the secondary sector, urban locations are employing more workers in the manufacturing enterprises. Employment in construction activities in urban areas showed a significant jump in 2005, but by 2012 it reduced in share, though it is dominant over rural areas (60%). Employment in enterprises belonging to wholesale and retail trade, communications and hospitality sectors is predominantly urban based and continued to record an increasing share here. In contrast, service sector employment seen in isolation though dominantly urban, was shifting to rural areas by 2012 as compared to 1998. Shift towards rural areas was steeper for com-

Table 3.7a   Change in rural–urban distribution of non-agricultural employment in all enterprises (1998–2012) (percentage of rural + urban)

Location/industry group	1998		2005		2012	
	Rural	Urban	Rural	Urban	Rural	Urban
Mining & quarrying	89.3	10.7	78.2	21.8	77.9	22.1
Manufacturing	32.2	67.8	28.1	71.9	27.9	72.1
Electricity, gas & water	42.3	57.8	41.6	58.4	26.7	73.3
Construction	51.7	48.3	29.8	70.2	40.2	59.8
Wholesale trade	20.2	79.8	25.6	74.4	17.6	82.4
Retail trade	31.0	69.0	34.5	65.5	26.6	73.4
Restaurants & hotels	24.1	75.9	27.0	73.0	23.6	76.4
Transport	32.6	67.4	47.3	52.7	32.9	67.1
Communication	19.4	80.6	25.4	74.6	11.9	88.1
FIRE & business services	10.5	89.3	16.4	83.6	14.5	85.5
Community etc. services	31.7	68.4	41.4	58.6	42.5	57.5
Other activities	12.5	87.5	24.4	75.6	35.7	64.3
Total non-agricultural	31.2	68.8	33.3	66.7	29.7	70.3

Source: Reports of the fourth, fifth and sixth economic census (1998, 2005, 2012), DES, GoG, Gandhinagar

Table 3.7b   Change in rural–urban distribution of non-agricultural employment in OAEs (1998–2012) (percentage of rural + urban)

Location/industry group	1998		2005		2012	
	Rural	Urban	Rural	Urban	Rural	Urban
Mining & quarrying	83.2	16.8	74.5	25.5	76.7	23.3
Manufacturing	51.5	48.5	46.2	53.8	36.9	63.1
Electricity, gas & water	72.2	27.8	58.5	41.5	16.3	83.7
Construction	48.0	52.0	28.8	71.2	37.8	62.2
Wholesale trade	21.9	79.0	27.8	72.2	18.1	81.9
Retail trade	37.8	62.2	42.9	57.1	37.4	62.6
Restaurants & hotels	35.0	65.0	39.5	60.5	29.3	70.7
Transport & storage	46.4	53.6	56.9	43.1	40.3	59.7
Communication	15.0	85.0	26.5	73.6	22.6	77.4
FIRE & business services	12.4	87.6	26.1	73.2	25.4	74.6
Community etc. services	42.3	57.7	52.1	47.9	23.4	76.6
Other activities	30.4	69.6	32.6	67.4	38.2	61.8
Total non-agricultural	41.0	59.0	44.0	56.0	36.2	63.8

Source: Reports of the fourth, fifth and sixth economic census (1998, 2005, 2012), DES, GoG, Gandhinagar

Table 3.7c Change in rural–urban distribution of non-agricultural employment in establishments (1998–2005) (percentage of rural + urban)

Location/industry group	1998		2005		2012	
	Rural	Urban	Rural	Urban	Rural	Urban
Mining & quarrying	89.8	10.2	78.9	21.1	78.0	22.0
Manufacturing	28.0	72.0	24.9	75.1	26.3	73.7
Electricity, gas & water	41.0	59.0	40.4	59.6	28.3	71.7
Construction	53.7	46.3	30.1	69.9	42.0	58.0
Wholesale trade	19.8	80.2	24.8	75.2	17.5	82.5
Retail trade	19.0	81.0	26.8	73.2	18.7	81.3
Restaurants & hotels	19.7	80.3	23.4	76.6	21.6	78.4
Transport & storage	23.6	76.3	39.0	61.0	27.1	72.9
Communication	20.7	79.3	24.9	75.1	10.0	90.0
FIRE & business services	10.2	89.8	14.1	85.9	12.7	87.3
Community etc. services	28.2	71.8	39.4	60.6	43.9	56.1
Other activities	6.8	93.2	21.8	78.2	34.0	66.0
Total non-agricultural	28.7	71.3	29.3	70.7	27.5	72.5

Source: Reports of the fourth, fifth and sixth economic census (1998, 2005, 2012), DES, GoG, Gandhinagar

munity, personal and other services than financial and business services (Table 3.6).

In the period 1998 to 2012 the urban ward shift of own account workers is noticeable for secondary sector activities including construction, as well as hospitality and transport/storage sectors. Engagement of own account workers in wholesale and retail trade does not show much change and continue to predominate in urban areas. Within the tertiary sector, own account workers engaged in communication, business, financial services and real estate have increasingly shifted to rural areas, despite urban dominance, though reverse was the case with community/personal services (Table 3.6). With regard to the employment in unorganised establishments (hiring workers), except mining and quarrying all other activities have an urban base. For the period under consideration (1998 to 2012), manufacturing activities, retail trade, and financial and business services retained the status quo with urban dominance. Substantial shift towards rural areas is visible in the case of community and personal services, other services, as also hospitality sector, transport and storage sectors. Utilities, construction and wholesale trade in urban areas are engaging more and more workers.

At least from the information provided by the Economic Census it can be observed that non-agricultural enterprises and employment in them (both with or without hired workers) are showing a spatial shift from rural to urban locations. In rural areas the dominant non-agricultural enterprises apart from mining and quarrying are those relating to construction and transportation sector. Petty trading enterprises and artisanal own account manufacturing also dominate in rural areas. Education, health and personal/community services are the activities that hire workers in rural Gujarat as revealed by the recent information.

Share of Activities in Total Non-Agricultural Employment

There have been absolute employment gains by nearly 31 per cent in secondary and tertiary activities between 2005 and 2012 in Gujarat, the additions being far higher (38.7%) in urban areas than rural (17%). In addition to identifying the changes in location of non-agricultural activities across space, there is also the need to ascertain changes in their shares in overall employment. The sectors where employment gains are substantial require adequate policy support. Further the base of the demand driven non-farm activities needs strengthening, given the increased trend of relocation of enterprises to the urban areas. Gujarat is facing enhanced degree of agricultural commercialisation that has been an important contributor to the overall growth. Census (2011) results show that connectivity to rural areas has improved and many villages are showing urban characteristics. Possibly the rural-urban divide is becoming rather thin, and a large share of villages have satisfied the census criteria of urban designation or are on the threshold. Further given the problems experienced by bigger urban centres in the nature of over-congestion, pollution and other externalities, the rural areas have to develop as receptacles of non-farm activities. This section focuses on activity wise shares of employment and changes over the three points of time (1998, 2005 and 2012) as shown in Tables 3.8a, 3.8b, and 3.8c.

1998 to 2005: An initial scanning of the employment shares in all enterprises (OAE and Establishments) in the overall economy shows that during 1998 to 2005 the share of workers engaged in unorganised manufacturing, community, social and personal services declined noticeably. The most important emerging employment generators were wholesale and retail trade and communication related activities, as far as the aggregate economy is concerned. In rural areas seen separately manufacturing showed a steep decline in share of employment, while gainers were retail

Table 3.8a Employment share of activities in all non-agricultural enterprises (OAE + Establishment), 1998–2012 (% share to total employment)

Location/industry group	1998			2005			2012		
	Rural	Urban	Combined	Rural	Urban	Combined	Rural	Urban	Combined
Mining & quarrying	1.6	0.1	0.6	1.1	0.2	0.5	1.7	0.2	0.6
Manufacturing	35.6	33.9	34.4	26.3	33.6	31.2	35.5	38.8	37.9
Elect, gas & water	0.8	0.5	0.6	0.8	0.6	0.6	1.0	1.2	1.2
Construction	2.8	1.2	1.7	0.5	0.5	0.5	3.2	2.0	2.3
Wholesale trade	2.2	3.9	3.4	4.4	6.3	5.7	2.2	4.4	3.8
Retail trade	22.1	22.2	22.2	30.3	28.7	29.3	20.9	24.3	23.3
Restaurants & hotels	1.6	2.2	2.0	1.6	2.1	1.9	3.0	4.1	3.8
Transport & storage	4.1	3.8	3.9	5.6	3.1	3.9	5.9	5.1	5.3
Communication	0.6	1.1	0.9	0.9	1.4	1.3	0.3	1.0	0.8
FIRE etc. services	1.0	4.0	3.1	1.8	4.6	3.7	1.1	2.7	2.2
Community & other services	27.8	27.1	27.3	21.9	18.8	21.5	25.2	16.2	18.9
Total non-agricultural	100	100	100	100	100	100	100	100	100

Source: Reports of the Third, Fourth and Fifth Economic Census (1990, 1998, 2005), GoG, Gandhinagar

Note: FIRE—Financial, insurance, real estate & business services

Table 3.8b Employment share of activities in non-agricultural OAEs, 1998–2012 (percentage share to total employment)

Location/industry group	1998			2005			2012		
	Rural	Urban	Combined	Rural	Urban	Combined	Rural	Urban	Combined
Mining & quarrying	0.28	0.04	0.14	0.44	0.12	0.26	0.5	0.1	0.2
Manufacturing	24.68	16.18	19.67	17.98	16.49	17.15	22.5	21.8	22.0
Electricity, gas & water	0.12	0.03	0.07	0.22	0.12	0.16	0.3	0.8	0.6
Construction	2.15	1.62	1.83	0.27	0.53	0.42	4.2	3.9	4.0
Wholesale trade	1.70	4.44	3.32	3.64	7.44	5.77	1.3	3.2	2.5
Retail trade	41.03	46.95	44.52	50.30	52.67	51.63	40.9	38.9	39.6
Restaurants & hotels	1.57	2.03	1.84	1.41	1.70	1.57	3.2	4.3	3.9
Transport & storage	5.50	4.42	4.86	8.73	5.21	6.76	10.5	8.8	9.4
Communication	0.25	0.97	0.67	0.88	1.93	1.47	0.3	0.6	0.5
FIRE & business services	0.45	2.18	1.47	1.49	3.20	2.45	0.8	1.4	1.2
Community & other services	22.28	21.14	21.61	14.62	10.59	12.36	15.6	16.3	16.0
Total non-agricultural	100	100	100	100	100	100	100	100	100

Source: Reports of the Third, Fourth and Fifth Economic Census (1990, 1998, 2005), GoG, Gandhinagar

Table 3.8c Employment share of activities in non-agricultural establishments, 1998–2012 (percentage share to total employment)

Location/industry group	1998			2005			2012		
	Rural	Urban	Combined	Rural	Urban	Combined	Rural	Urban	Combined
Mining & quarrying	2.48	0.10	0.73	1.49	0.17	0.55	2.2	0.2	0.8
Manufacturing	43.42	40.50	41.28	31.00	38.69	36.43	41.2	43.8	43.1
Electricity, gas & water	1.22	0.64	0.79	1.14	0.70	0.83	1.4	1.3	1.3
Construction	3.21	1.00	1.59	0.55	0.53	0.54	2.7	1.4	1.8
Wholesale trade	2.53	3.71	3.40	4.78	6.00	5.65	2.6	4.7	4.2
Retail trade	8.42	12.98	11.77	19.09	21.63	20.88	12.1	20.1	17.9
Restaurants & hotels	1.54	2.27	2.08	1.64	2.23	2.05	2.9	4.0	3.7
Transport & storage	3.11	3.63	3.49	3.86	2.51	2.90	3.9	4.0	4.0
Communication	0.84	1.16	1.08	1.00	1.25	1.18	0.3	1.1	0.9
FIRE & business services	1.47	4.69	3.84	1.98	5.00	4.11	1.2	3.0	2.5
Community & other services	31.75	29.30	29.95	33.46	21.28	24.86	29.4	16.3	19.8
Total non-agricultural	100	100	100	100	100	100	100	100	100

Source: Reports of the Third, Fourth and Fifth Economic Census (1990, 1998, 2005), GoG, Gandhinagar

and wholesale trade, transportation and storage. Urban areas were also depicting increasing prominence of the trading sector, while a third of the urban workers continued to be engaged in manufacturing. Share of urban workers in services, except financial and business sectors declined sharply.

Insight by types of enterprises show that in the period under consideration, within larger non-agricultural establishments (using hired labour), employment share in manufacturing though dominant was declining across the economy. Trade, financial and business services recorded a rise. Employment shares in these activities increased sharply both in rural and urban areas seen separately. Employment share in retail trade in urban areas increased from 13 to 22 per cent, even though in rural areas it doubled to 19 per cent in 2005. The distribution of own account workers also showed a similar trend. Petty (own account) retail trade was the largest employer and recorded increase in share both in rural and urban areas. Share of own account workers in transport segment also increased, though services (except financial and business services) the next big employment provider within own account enterprises showed a sharp decline. Decline in the share of own account workers engaged in rural manufacturing was also quite drastic in rural areas.

2005–2012: The more recent period shows reversal of some of the earlier trends. It can be observed that for the entire economy and taking all the enterprises into consideration, manufacturing sector has faced a revival and increased employment shares. Persons employed in manufacturing in rural areas increased from 26 to 36 per cent, the gains being more than that in urban areas, where also manufacturing enterprises in 2012 engaged nearly 39 per cent of all non-agricultural workers. Unlike the earlier period employment share in trade shows changes. For the entire economy employment share of wholesale and retail trade fell from 36 to 27 per cent. The loss in share was higher in rural (35 to 23%) than urban (35 to 29%) areas. Employment in construction sector increased for both rural and urban areas. Job increases in transportation/storage sector were more noticeable in urban areas. In rural areas on the other hand unlike urban Gujarat, community and personal services registered growth.

Amongst establishments, employment gains were substantial for manufacturing, and this trend was prevalent across rural and urban areas. Employment creation in construction and transportation enterprises, albeit constituting a minor share (2 to 4%) also witnessed an upswing. In the entire economy share of employment in trading enterprises that hired workers recorded a steep fall (27 to 18.4%) in the period under consideration. Both the rural and urban areas mirrored this trend. There was sharp erosion in employment share in all service related establishments (from 29 to 22%) across the economy.

During the period under consideration, trends in the employment of own account workers are not different than enterprises that function with hired workers. Own account workers engaged in manufacturing have recorded a rising share and comprise a fifth of the non-agricultural employment (22%). Workers in construction sector have recorded a sharp increase (around 4%), while own account workers engaged in petty retail trade have declined very sharply from constituting more than half of the workforce in 2005 to around 40 per cent in 2012. Only in rural areas own account workers have gained modest share in transport, storage and communication activities. On the other hand, only in urban areas own account workers are finding livelihood in community and personal and other services; rural areas face a diminishing share.

It is quite clear from the above discussion that while between 1998 to 2005, tertiary activities created more jobs, in the more recent period secondary sector shows resurgence across space and size of enterprises. There is large scale, unreported, short-term migration from rural to urban areas for work in the non-farm sector. Most of such migrants earn higher cash income (than agriculture) for short periods in urban areas, mostly in construction and manufacturing. A large number of rural residents are commuting to work in the urban areas; especially for jobs in the construction sector, manufacturing as well as trade, repairs and related activities.

Share of Industry Groups in the Net State Domestic Product

On examining the net state domestic product (Table 3.9) emanating from the non-agricultural sectors, the following can be observed. The share of agriculture in the Gujarat's output is declining, far more sharply after 2004–2005. Manufacturing sector output depicts a more volatile trend. Output share emanating from the secondary sector has remained unchanged though of late there is some improvement in job creation in manufacturing. The share of employment in manufacturing activities increased from 34 to 38 per cent between 2005 and 2012. Share of output from manufacturing sector dipped to the lowest in 2004–2005 but recovered to 27 per cent in 2010–2011. After 2010–2011, its share

Table 3.9   Output share of industry groups in NSDP (2004–2005 prices) (per cent)

No.	Industry group	1999–2000[a]	2004–2005	2009–2010	2012–2013
1	Agriculture, forestry, logging, fishing, mining & quarrying	20.1	21.1	14.4	12.8
1.1	Of which agriculture & animal husbandry	17.4	14.4	10.3	9.6
2	Manufacturing, electricity, gas & water, construction	35.2	32.2	38.1	34.9
2.1	Of which manufacturing	26.5	23.4	27.3	25.2
3	Trade, hotels & restaurants, transport, storage and communications	19.2	25.5	28.3	32.7
4	Banking, insurance, real estate, business services	13.7	12.8	11.9	12.8
5	Public administration & other services	11.7	8.4	7.3	6.9
	Tertiary	44.6	46.7	47.6	52.3

Source: Socio-economic review of Gujarat state, Bureau of Economics & Statistics, GoG, 2013–2014
[a]At 1999–2000 prices

declined again. But there was a significant rise in the output coming from trade, hotels, transport, and communications. The combined net state domestic product emanating from these sectors increased from 19 per cent to 33 per cent between 1999 and 2013. Growth in trade is related to the increasing income levels and enhanced spending on a variety of goods and services. Liberalisation of the economy has also bestowed maximum benefit to modern sectors like communications, transport, hospitality sector, financial services and real estate, causing faster growth in these sectors.

It is also useful to examine the per capita productivity and changes across the industry groups (Table 3.10). Even though rural and urban per capita output for the states has been ascertained by other scholars, for the purpose of the analysis we have estimated it using workforce as derived from the Economic Census (i.e. employment in all enterprises in rural and urban areas combined), The net state domestic product (NSDP) is at constant (1999–2000 and 2004–2005 prices).

The per capita NSDP for each subsector for Gujarat shows interesting pattern. It is observed that in the first period (1998 to 2005) annual growth in per capita output was the highest for construction, followed by

Table 3.10   Per capita sectoral NSDP and annual growth, Gujarat

Industry group	Per capita income (Rs.)				CAGR	
	1998	2005	2005	2012	1998–2005	2005–2012
	(1999–2000 base)		(2004–05 base)			
Mining & quarrying	971.8	1078.9	2628.7	1399.9	1.5	−8.6
Manufacturing	171.0	225.5	274.2	339.3	4.0	3.1
Electricity, gas & water	823.5	633.3	861.1	1160.1	−3.7	4.3
Construction	889.2	3098.3	5259.2	1972.3	19.5	−13.1
Trade, restaurants & hotels	113.6	131.2	185.1	375.3	2.1	10.6
Transport, storage & communications	262.7	280.8	482.7	809.7	1.0	7.7
FIRE & business services	991.7	915.4	1280.9	3054.5	−1.1	13.2
Other services	95.7	117.5	142.6	197.5	3.0	4.8
Total non-agricultural	183.2	217.0	301.1	466.5	2.4	6.5

Source: As explained in text

manufacturing. Per capita income from construction sector turned negative between 2005 to 2012, possibly due to overcrowding in this sector. Total workers in this sector had witnessed a decline by 14 per cent per annum in the first period under consideration. However, from a low in 2005, the employment growth accelerated to 29 per cent in the later period. During 2005–2012 per capita income growth accelerated in trade and restaurants sector, financial and business services as well as transport and communication sector. Overcrowding of workers in the manufacturing sector does not bode well as seen from the declining productivity levels. Trade (retail and wholesale) seemed to be the last resort for the workers spilling out from the primary activities earlier but lately the acceleration in per capita productivity levels (by more than 10% annual increase) indicate that employment increase in trade and hospitality sectors has stalled. The communications revolution is causing the growth in transportation sector- both formal and informal, engaging workers at increasing productivity levels. Of late the financial and real estate sector in rural Gujarat is expanding very fast. However tertiary sector requires skilled manpower to sustain its growth momentum.

A flourishing agriculture sector in the 2000s decade fuelled the growth in the secondary and service activities. The process was helped by rural to urban migration of workers not finding adequate livelihood opportunities in the rural areas; nearly 3 million workers were added in urban areas. While 88 per cent of the incremental workers in urban areas were main workers, share of marginal urban workers also doubled. The labour absorbing capacity of agriculture is limited. Labour saving cropping pattern adjustments and increasing mechanisation of field crop operations need to be introduced. Livestock and animal husbandry in Gujarat threw up additional work in rural areas that has lent momentum to the diversification of primary sector- a healthy development for the state economy.

EMERGING ECONOMIC ACTIVITIES IN GUJARAT

The analysis in the previous sections enables comparison of the emerging economic sectors in Gujarat. Table 3.11 classifies enterprises on the basis of their growth experience in employment between 1998–2005 and 2005–2012 (in descending order). The activities that were creating employment opportunities in the non-agricultural sector in rural areas during 1998–2005 were retail and whole sale trade, transport, storage, financial/business services and communication related activities. Rural manufacturing activities reported a large decline in importance (−9.3 per cent points), besides community, personal and other services and construction related jobs. Urban areas during this period did not show a much disparate picture. Gains for retail and whole sale trade (by 6.5 and 2.4 per cent points) were quite significant, followed to a much lesser degree by financial/business services (0.6 per cent point change). Urban areas registered a much larger scale of decline in the importance of other services (nearly 8 per cent point change).

The subsequent period (2005–2012), depicts a turnaround in terms of employment shares. In rural areas manufacturing witnessed a massive increase in engagement of workers (more than 9 per cent points), followed by other services, construction and the food and hotels sector. In contrast to earlier period, a downslide in ability to provide employment was recorded by trading activities, retail more than wholesale trade (−9.2 and −2.2 per cent points). Urban areas mirrored this pattern. Manufacturing sector recorded acceleration in employment generation by 5.2 per cent. Other sectors gaining importance in urban Gujarat during this period were hotels, restaurants, transport, storage sectors, along with construction. Trade and all services registered a fall in engagement of workers in urban areas of Gujarat.

Table 3.11   Classification of non-agricultural activities (Employment in establishments and OAEs) by their relative growth experience, 1998–2012

Urban		Rural	
Increase in share	*Decline in share*	*Increase in share*	*Decline in share*
Growth in employment share (percentage change), 1998–2005			
Retail trade (6.5)	Other services (−8.3)	Retail Trade (8.2)	Manufacturing (−9.3)
Wholesale trade (2.4)	Construction (−0.7)	Wholesale Trade (2.2)	Other services (−5.9)
FIRE (0.6)	Transport & Storage (−0.7)	Transport & Storage (1.5)	Construction (−2.3)
Communication (0.3)	Manufacturing (−0.3)	FIRE (0.8)	Mining (−0.5)
Mining (0.1)	Restaurants (−0.1)	Communication (0.3)	
Utilities (0.1)			
Growth in employment share (percentage change), 2005–2012			
Manufacturing (5.2)	Retail trade (−4.4)	Manufacturing (9.2)	Retail trade (−9.4)
Restaurants (2.0)	Other services (−2.6)	Other services (3.3)	Wholesale trade (−2.2)
Transport & storage (2.0)	Wholesale trade (−1.9)	Construction (2.7)	FIRE (−0.7)
Construction (1.5)	FIRE (−1.9)	Restaurants (1.4)	Communication (−0.6)
Utilities (0.6)	Communication (−0.4)	Mining (0.6)	
		Transport & Storage (0.3)	
		Utilities (0.2)	

Source: Tables 3.8a, 3.8b, and 3.8c

Note: Figures in brackets are the percentage point change in employment share of each activity to total employment in respective period

FIRE: Financial, insurance, real estate & business services

Other services: Community, social, personal and other services; Utilities: Electricity, gas and water

In rural Gujarat, along with commercialisation of agriculture, diversification within the primary sector as seen through the increased employment in allied activities such as, forestry, fishing, animal husbandry etc. is an on-going process. Analysis also indicates that in the more recent period (2005–2012) in rural areas of Gujarat the activities in the non-primary sector that were experiencing growth in terms of creation of job prospects were manufacturing, other services, construction related activities, restaurants/hotels. Retail and wholesale trading, financial and business services were losing importance in rural areas, unlike in the earlier period (1998–2005). Community, personal and other services are shifting towards rural areas. It is imperative that the manufacturing sector witnesses technological up-gradation to increase productivity. Household based industry in addition also requires support in the nature of easy access to raw materials, credit, training, power and machinery etc. Lack of adequate and timely policy support in these areas may have detrimental impact on technological up-gradation and adversely affect the competitive edge of the state in the manufacturing sector.

Manufacturing and utilities sector engaged around eight per cent of the total workers and contributed to 26 per cent of the NSDP. Annual per capita NSDP growth in manufacturing declined from four to three per cent. Construction sector contributing to around four per cent of workers and 8.5 per cent of the NSDP has witnessed a paid decline in per capita NSDP growth (13% per annum). The share of trade, hotels and restaurants, storage and communication in total employment in 2012 was also around eight per cent, and their share in NSDP was 21 per cent. However, the per capita NSDP from these activities has been accelerating at between 11 to 8 per cent per annum. Rising per capita productivity indicates that shift towards these activities may not be distress induced. Possibly the entry of organised chain retailing and foreign investments has had a positive impact on the economy. The communications revolution and transportation both formal and informal is another welcome development, engaging workers at increasing productivity levels.

Per capita NSDP from financial, business and real estate services accelerated at more than 13 per cent per annum, followed by all other services at five per cent per annum. Some of these activities are concentrated in the self- employment. Nonetheless some of these activities, notably manufacturing, construction, services other business and financial services are operating as depositories of surplus labour and where the surplus rural labour is finding a space. It remains for the state to create an environment where these activities become productive and viable and get integrated with the mainstream economic sectors. Needless to add that service activities require skilled manpower to remain a sustainable driver of economic growth. At the aggregate level, unlike the decline observed in between 1998–2005, the pictured altered after 2005. Share of urban employment in establishments hiring workers and self-employment both showed improvement vis-à-vis rural areas. Analysis earlier had brought out that this was the result of large scale shift of the tertiary activities to urban locations.

In Gujarat it is quite evident that the rural economy seems to be enmeshed with the rest of the economy as can be observed from the rather uniform pattern of employment growth. In several major state economies, the structure of employment in the rural and urban areas is converging after liberalisation, but Dholakia et al. (2014) also indicate that in the states of Gujarat and Maharashtra, the structural pattern of urban and rural areas has remained almost constant over time. It is not that the employment pattern in these economies has remained stagnant over time, but the changes have been of similar dimension across space. That the rural and urban are no more bounded spaces and that rural areas are marked by trickle down of growth impulses, flow of information and employment opportunities is a precursor to the changes visible in the rural settlement pattern of the state. The rural transformation process is visible in the nature of economic activities as well as the behaviour of settlements in terms of size and characteristics. This is dealt with in a detailed fashion in the subsequent chapters.

REFERENCES

Chand, Ramesh, and S.K. Srivastava. 2014. Changes in the Rural Labour Market and Their Implications for Agriculture. *Economic and Political Weekly* 49 (10): 47–54.
Chandrasekhar, S. 2011. Workers Commuting Between the Rural and Urban: Estimates from NSSO Data. *Economic and Political Weekly* 46 (46): 22–25.
Dholakia, Ravindra H., Manish B. Pandya, and Payal M. Pateriya. 2014. *Urban-Rural Income Differential in Major States: Contribution of Structural Factors.* Ahmedabad: Indian Institute of Management.
Directorate of Economic and Statistics. 2000. *Report on Fourth Economic Census, 1998, Gujarat.* Gandhinagar: Government of Gujarat.
———. 2006. *Report on Fifth Economic Census, 2005, Gujarat.* Gandhinagar: Government of Gujarat.
———. 2015. *Socio-Economic Review of Gujarat State, 2013–14.* Gandhinagar: Government of Gujarat.
———. 2017. *Report on Sixth Economic Census, 2012, Gujarat.* Gandhinagar: Government of Gujarat.

Kasturi, Kannan. 2015. Comparing Census and NSS Data on Employment and Unemployment. *Economic and Political Weekly* 50 (22): 16–19.

Shah, Rajiv. 2013. *Rural Proletarianization: Census 2011 Data Suggest Sharper Rise in Agricultural Workforce in Gujarat than Most of India,* May 2. Counterview.org.

CHAPTER 4

Structural Changes and Implications for Urbanization

INTRODUCTION

An examination of output and employment trends have indicated that after 2004–2005, in the rural areas the real per farmer income in the country accelerated to 7.3 percent/annum (Chand et al. 2015), owning to the reduction in the number of cultivators. As noted earlier, during this period not only did the agricultural output growth increase to four per cent, but farm families also diversified to non-agricultural occupations. A rise in rural wage rates was also noted from 2006 onwards (sometimes attributed to the employment guarantee programme). In the rural areas workers employed in non-farm sector increased from 33.4 to 37.2 percent (males) and 16.7 to 20.6 percent (females) between 2004–2005 and 2009–2010 (see annexure Table 4.8). According to the NSSO there was an almost unprecedented increase in the level of rural non-farm sector employment.

Structural transformation embodies the growth in output and the share of non-agricultural employment, whereby labour moves away from the subsistence sector to the modern sectors also increasing the wage rates and overall productivity (Lewis 1954). However, in India there exists a dual economy with a rural-subsistence sector coexisting with urban/capitalist

An earlier version of the work in this chapter has appeared in an edited volume (Role of Public Policy in Development Process, New Delhi: Academic Foundation). The present chapter comprises of a more comprehensive analysis and is included with the permission of Academic Foundation, New Delhi.

© The Author(s) 2018
N. Mehta, *Rural Transformation in the Post Liberalization Period in Gujarat*, https://doi.org/10.1007/978-981-10-8962-6_4

99

sector, albeit with a near stagnancy in the growth of manufacturing sector. The standard definition of structural transformation equates with growth of non-agricultural employment in urban areas, but in the Indian case it incorporates the growth of rural non-farm sector or declining share of agricultural employment. The rural non-farm sector (RNFS) GDP grew at seven percent after 1993 and it was the biggest source of new jobs in the Indian economy. Contribution of non-agricultural sector to the rural net national product is now 65 per cent. Rising rural incomes and growing demand for non-farm services has also played its role in bringing about the growth of RNFS. Scholars also argue that structural transformation is a consequence of urban spillover to rural non-farm 'self-employment' activities (Misra 2013). It has been noted that the positive externality impact of RNFS growth stems from its capacity to limit rural to urban migration and unsustainable growth in the already overburdened cities (Jatav and Sen 2013). However, urbanization and changes in rural economic structure have created the demand for non-farm goods and services and also urban ward migration. Thus both processes reinforce each other.

The land constraint exacerbates decline in agricultural employment. Increasing fragmentation of land holdings due to population pressure and the dispossession of land based livelihoods due to decline in self-cultivation has enhanced casualization in both farm and non-farm sectors (Dixit 2009). The standard discourse in literature pertains to the growth led RNFS expansion causing buoyancy in the rural wage rates, while distress driven process is believed to have a dampening effect on the wages. The indicators for former are urbanization, literacy, irrigation development, on the other hand, economic distress is indicated by population pressure, landlessness, unemployment and enhanced dependency ratio. Irrespective of the factors leading to growth in non-farm employment, which are diverse, increasing share of non-farm employment is often accompanied with the growth of population in large villages and their transition to small towns and service centres.

Small towns are defined by the UN Human Settlements Program (2006) as 'first-tier markets and service providers for rural enterprises and development'. They function as intermediaries between the rural areas and higher levels of the urban hierarchy. Urban growth is the outcome of concentration of the population in response to the availability of diverse amenities and facilities. Subsequently, an urban hierarchy emerges, whereby the urban population is distributed among settlements of varying sizes (Alam and Choudhury 2016). Small towns in most cases originate as villages and due to the increasing agglomeration economies, develop over time as urban centers due to the functions they perform and services they deliver (Verma 2006; Ali and Varshney 2013). Often, small and intermediate towns evolve as a consequence of crowding in large towns, in addition to the growth in the surrounding rural economy. Data from the decennial census shows that in India the small towns (less than 20,000) accounted for 12.8 percent of the share of urban population in 2011. These towns also depicted a rising decadal growth rate in their population during 1981–1991, and accounted for the largest share in the number of settlements as compared to other size class towns.

That the impact of existing urban areas on the growth of non-farm economy and town growth cannot be ignored is quite evident. The positive externalities of agglomeration of existing towns such as access to capital, labour, technology and input and market access increase the non-farm employment opportunities and result in urban growth in the hinterland (Marshall 1920; Perroux 1955; Cadène and Holmström 1998). Economic development and urbanization are related, there is nonetheless a lack of inter-relationship between relative economic development and city size distribution (or morphology). Cities as a part of urban hierachy provide a network for the diffusion of social and technical change over the regional space economy. Urban primacy has been identified as an important variable in the determination of some economic activities, notably industrial location in a state (Wadhwa and Kashyap 1985). In the location of industrial activity, the urban structure and decentralized urban growth in the form of multiple lakh plus cities, also have a positive impact. However, Berry (1961) showed that countries having the lowest degree of primacy but with city size distribution showed considerable industrialization and a history of urbanization.

Their function as providers of education and health services as well as financial amenities to their hinterlands also determines the growth of small towns in India. In fact most of the non-farm activities and services across the spectrum of urban hierarchy are functionally organized. Misra (2013) argues that due to such functional linkages, the rural towns/large villages even though assuming urban characteristics; remain tightly linked to the surrounding rural hinterland. Functional differentiation of a hierarchy of settlements and the degree of interaction among activities distributed in space is an important criteria for measuring the maturity of the urban structure. It is also well known that agricultural innovations and development coupled with the growth of transportation networks have traditionally led to the growth of urban centres (Freidmann 1961; Krugman 1991), and urbanization is the natural corollary to economic growth. Spatial determinants, notably, location and accessibility, also play a pivotal role in the growth of small towns (Alam and Choudhury 2016). Accessibility is highly linked with transportation networks. Transportation is essentially a spatial service that enables various entities to execute activities in separate locations (Rehman 2008).

The intermediate towns function as base for the collection and bulk reducing primary processing as well as the subsequent distribution of agricultural products of the surrounding region (Misra 2013). The agriculture related functions link the smaller urban settlements with the rural areas. In addition, along with the nearby cities the small market towns serve as the centers of administration, finance, trade and commerce, and provide access to institutions related to health, and education. While the urban centers with a population less than 20,000 are categorized as 'small towns', the Census of India also includes criteria other than population in the definition of a town, notably 75 per cent of the male working population being engaged in non-agricultural sector apart from the density criterion.

The above discussion sets the tone for an in-depth analysis of the situation of large village and town growth in Gujarat, this being the subject of the study. The subsequent sections deal with the nature of urbanization process in India with particular reference to Gujarat. The relationship between emergence of census towns and preexisting metropolitan areas is explored. Section "Constituents of Urban Growth in Gujarat" attempts at understanding the determinants of urban growth in Gujarat. Later the challenges of urban growth process and aspects related to identification of urban centres are discussed. The last section provides a summary of discussion and highlights issues critical for policy support.

RURAL ECONOMIC CHANGES AND NATURE OF URBANIZATION

At present the positive role of urbanization in overall development has been recognized, as the urban areas contribute nearly a third (62 percent) of the gross domestic product (GDP) (Bhagat 2012). The 11th Five Year Plan realized that attainment of 9–10 percent annual GDP growth is contingent upon a vibrant urban sector (Planning Commission 2008). The considerable inducement of funds for the expansion in urban infrastructure and services was therefore to ease the urban transition process in the country (Kundu and Samanta 2011). The definition of 'urban' varies from country to country. The Registrar General of India defines a settlement as an urban area if it satisfies certain demographic and economic criteria, i.e. the population exceeding 5000, density of 400 persons per sq. km and 75 percent of male workers engaged in non-agricultural sector. Such settlements are termed 'census towns'. The state government grants municipal status to a settlement (corporation, municipal council, notified area committee or *nagar panchayat*). Such settlements are designated as 'statutory/municipal towns' in the census definition of urban areas. Between 2001 and 2011, contrary to expectations (Kundu 2011b), the country's urban population grew at 2.8 percent per annum to 377 million, with the level of urbanization increasing from 27.7 to 31.1 percent. Hence between 2001 and 2011, there was an increment of 91 million in urban population- the largest since independence, and was higher than 90.5 million recorded in the rural population. This was commensurate to an increase in the growth of the Indian economy at 8 percent in the decade of 2000s (up from 6% per annum in 1990s).

Table 4.1 shows the trends in urbanization for India and Gujarat. The disparity in the rural-urban population growth is critical to the process of urbanization which had increased to 1.61 percent per annum during 2001 to 2011. According to Bhagat (2012), the urban-rural natural increase growth differential remained constant (4 per 1000 population) during the 1990s and 2000s decades indicating that it was the rural-urban classification and rural to urban migration that contributed to higher urban-rural

Table 4.1   Trends in urbanisation (1961–2011)

	Year	Rural population (million)	Annual GR (%)	Urban population (million)	Annual GR (%)	Rural-urban growth differential
India	1961	360		79		
	1971	439	2.00	109	3.23	1.23
	1981	524	1.79	160	3.79	2.00
	1991	629	1.84	218	3.09	1.25
	2001	743	1.68	286	2.75	1.07
	2011	833	1.15	377	2.76	1.61
Gujarat	1961	15		5		
	1971	19	2.39	8	4.81	2.42
	1981	24	2.36	11	3.24	0.87
	1991	27	1.18	14	2.44	1.26
	2001	32	1.71	19	3.10	1.39
	2011	35	0.90	26	3.19	2.29

Source: Census of India

growth differentials during 2001–2011. Reclassification and migration led to the emergence of a large number of new towns in 2011- increasing from 5161 in 2001 to 7935 (net addition of 2774 town; 2532 census towns and 242 statutory towns). Census towns (CTs) are not merely over-grown villages but have defining urban characteristics, as manifested in the changing nature of economic activities, notably more than 75 per cent of male workers involved in the non-agricultural occupations. That urbaniza-tion is happening outside the administrative framework is reflected in the unprecedented growth of such settlements. These are often emerging in a diffused manner, beyond the metropolitan peripheries and are possibly autonomous, often being economically independent of metropolitan influence.

Urbanization level in Gujarat (42% in 2011) was higher than the national average (31%) and the rural-urban growth differential between 2001 and 2011 at 2.3 percent/annum was also larger than the national average. The growth rate of rural population halved in 2000s decade, showing unprecedented deceleration, (Table 4.1) indicating the enhanced role of net rural-urban migration and rural-urban classification in the state's urban growth. Gujarat belongs to the group of states (including Kerala, Andhra Pradesh, Karnataka, West Bengal, Bihar, Jharkhand, Chhattisgarh and Uttarakhand) that have recorded an increase in urban population growth rate during 2001 to 2011.

The urban hierarchy or the distribution of towns (census and statutory) by size classes is shown in Table 4.2. The skewed nature of population concentration is visible from the fact that nearly 72 percent of all the urban

Table 4.2 Distribution of towns by categories in Gujarat, 2011

Class size	Statutory towns		Census towns		All towns		Percentage (All towns)	
	Pop	No.	Pop	No.	Pop	No.	Pop	No.
Class 6	26,388	20	44,834	11	71,222	31	0.3	8.9
Class 5	25,161	4	459,275	62	484,436	66	1.9	19.0
Class 4	504,249	29	963,272	70	1,467,521	99	5.7	28.5
Class 3	2,434,157	77	245,584	9	2,679,741	86	10.3	24.8
Class 2	2,301,895	32	53,794	1	2,355,689	33	9.1	9.5
Class 1	18,867,615	32			18,867,615	32	72.8	9.2
Total	48,107,783	194	1,766,759	153	25,926,224	347	100.0	100.0

Source: Town directory, Census of India, 2011, Registrar General of India

areas are small in size (classes 3 to 5), yet a similar proportion of the urban population (73 percent) resides in the Class 1 cities or urban centres alone having population greater than 1,00,000. The compound annual growth rate of urban centers in Gujarat is shown in Table 4.3a. It can be observed that the drivers of urbanization in Gujarat lately have been the smaller towns, notably, classes 6 (industrial townships, university towns, port town etc.), 5 (5 to 10,000) and 4 (10 to 20,000) towns/UAs that were growing at the rates of 5.1, 9.8 and 5.3 percent annually respectively, thereby increasing in size at a faster rate than the bigger towns/UAs. These three town categories accounted for nearly eight percent of the urban population residing in 56 percent of urban areas (an increase from 6% population residing in 41% of towns in 2001). The decline in growth rate of metropolitan centers (either state or national capital) has been noted for the country too (Kundu 2011b).

Table 4.3a   Share and growth in size class of towns in Gujarat, 1991 to 2011

		1991	2001	2011	CARG	
					1991 to 2001	2001 to 2011
UA/Towns	No.	264	242	347		
	Total Urban Population	14,246,061	18,930,250	25,715,077	2.88	3.11
(Class 6) < 5000	Pop.	34,774 (0.2)	43,373 (0.2)	71,222 (0.3)	2.23	5.08
(Class 5) 5000–9999	Pop.	401,032 (2.8)	188,937 (1.0)	484,436 (1.9)	−7.25	9.87
(Class 4) 10,000–19,999	Pop.	1,339,892 (9.4)	872,061 (4.6)	1,467,521 (5.7)	−4.20	5.34
(Class 3) 20,000–49,999	Pop.	1,723,974 (12.1)	2,445,667 (12.9)	2,679,741 (10.4)	3.56	0.92
(Class 2) 50,000–99,999	Pop.	2,206,874 (15.5)	2,461,131 (13.0)	2,355,689 (9.2)	1.10	−0.44
(Class 1) 100,000 & Above	Pop.	8,539,515 (60.0)	12,919,081 (68.2)	18,867,615 (73.4)	4.23	3.86

Source: Town directory, Census of India, 2011, Registrar General of India

Note: Figures in brackets are percent share to urban population

It is quite clear that of late the smaller sized towns in settlement hierarchy of the state, as in India, are garnering momentum, while the larger category of towns are witnessing either stagnation or deceleration. The annual growth rate of population in class 1 cities (>1 lakh) hovered around 4 percent, even though the concentration of urban population in them has risen from 68 to 72 percent. Such a gain has been on account of the loss in the share of population in class 3 and 2 towns, in addition to increase in the size of million plus cities. In 2001, nearly 68 percent of urban population was residing in 11 percent of class 1 urban centers. This ratio by 2011, changed to 73.4 percent and nine percent respectively.

In terms of creating work opportunities, the larger cities continue to be dominant (Table 4.3b). Overall, the metropolitan centres in Gujarat, provided (urban) employment to the tune of 47.4 percent of the urban workers in 2011–2012 (30.4% in India) gaining from 43.4 percent in 2004–2005 (27.6% in India) (NSSO, 2007 & 2015). An examination of the data on employment in towns and cities from National Sample Survey Office (NSSO) corroborates that the employment growth between 2004–2005 to 2011–2012 was faster in 'other urban areas' or the NSSO defined class 2 (50,000 to 1 million) and 3 (<50,000) towns, than the metro cities (million plus) in activities such as utilities, construction, trade and repairs, and the traditional services (financial and business services, real estate). Moreover, the growth rate of employment in these activities is higher in

Table 4.3b   Annual growth in employment by industry, 2004–2005 to 2011–2012

	Gujarat		India	
	Metro	Other urban	Metro	Other urban
Agriculture	13.2	−0.7	−3.3	−0.6
Mining	6.8	−5.5	−5.3	3.7
Manufacturing	9.1	3.0	3.7	2.0
Utilities	−0.7	47.9	4.5	14.4
Construction	−0.9	8.1	3.9	5.7
Trade, hotels & repairs	6.9	4.4	3.3	2.1
Transport & communications	3.8	−0.6	1.9	0.4
Traditional services (NIC 65–93)	6.6	6.8	7.9	4.7
Personal/HH services (NIC 95)	−6.1	−9.4	4.9	−5.2
Total	6.8	4.4	4.5	2.5

Source: Author's calculations based on data from NSSO, employment & unemployment situation in towns and cities of India, various rounds

the smaller class 3 towns than the class 2 towns. In contrast manufacturing, trade, transport and communication sectors continue to be dominant in metros. Construction is perceived to be the starting point of the shift from agriculture to non-agriculture for rural workers, and provides employment to migrant or commuting workers. In fact from the NSSO information for employment for Gujarat it is evident that 10.3 percent (2009–2010) of the rural residents were commuters reporting urban centers as their place of work.

Up to 2001 number of census towns increased slowly and their share in total urban population was only 7.4 percent. Their sudden rise in numbers in 2011 led some researchers (Kundu 2011a) to assign their emergence to census activism. Others, notably Bhagat (2012) and Pradhan (2013) ruled out this possibility as most of the CTs met the eligibility criteria including that of 'sectoral diversification' much earlier, even though there causes of emergence were not defined. The notion of census activism is ruled out also by the contention of Registrar General of India that for identification of places which would be classified as urban in 2011 those villages had to be considered that satisfied the three demographic criteria in 2001 census. There is thus a clear gap of a decade between the actual transformation of the village and it being identified as CT in 2011 (Guin and Das 2015). Even though some of these CTs could attain statutory status, they opted to remain as villages. Amongst the incentives to remain rural besides larger number of rural schemes, are lower taxation rates, cheaper power, absence of urban-by laws and regulations (for building/construction). The absence/laxity in enforcing urban regulations gives freedom to develop land in and around rural areas and large sale conversion to non-agricultural uses (mostly residential), albeit without adequate development of public amenities/services. According to Denis et al. (2012):

> "…it is perhaps not a coincidence that Kerala and West Bengal the two states with the largest number of census towns should also be those with agreeably the most empowered Panchayats. It is possible that given the limited devolution of powers to the urban local bodies and the relatively large number of schemes focused on rural areas it is more advantageous for a settlement to remain rural at least in some states." (p. 58)

The use of census data sets is not adequate to understand the transformation process and the various factors active in the countryside. Besides the use of spatial and socio-economic data from census and NSSO, field observation is therefore essential, particularly to recognize the linkages (rural to urban and urban to urban). Several researchers have taken recourse to field studies in order to unravel the processes of emergence of the smaller towns and the relationship that these settlements share with their hinterlands and even the larger urban centres located in proximity. Amongst such studies noteworthy are by Raman (2014); Coelho and Vijayabaskar (2014); Samanta (2014). These studies show that while the endogamous forces (infrastructure, entrepreneurial activity, growth of market based agriculture etc.) are significant forces in shaping the development of a town's economy, the transformation is also shaped by supra-local capital and labour flows from the region or even from afar. Given such developments, the subsequent sections are exploratory for Gujarat and the impact of metropolitan expansion and emergence of census towns is examined foremost.

Relation Between Census Towns and Metropolitan Areas (Diffused vs. Metropolitan Growth)

The emergence of an unprecedented number of census towns calls for in-depth exploration of the processes associated with 'dispersed' or diffused urban growth and 'subaltern' urbanization vis-a-vis 'concentration'. The process of subaltern urbanization indicates inter-connectedness of the urban and rural. It may occur even in peripheral settlements, where rural-urban linkages are important as a process. Further it also focuses on settlements away from the large cities that have the ability to grow and interact autonomously with other settlements (Raman 2014). Thus subaltern urbanization results in "...smaller settlements outside the metropolitan shadow indicating a pattern of urbanization that is extensive, widespread, economically vital and autonomous" (Denis et al. 2012: 53).

The issues of economic and social transformation and governance are crucial. In the midterm appraisal of the Eleventh Plan, Planning Commission (2011) believed that the pace of urbanization in India is slower than the other developing countries. It was believed that urbanization at 32 percent was concentrated in developed regions and larger cites, with backward areas and smaller towns facing stagnation. Nijman (2012) on the other hand, after examining census 2011 results inferred that in smaller towns rural to urban migration was significant and was due to the poor agricultural performance in the surrounding countryside even though not so much by the pull exerted by industrialization in the cities. Pradhan (2013) dwelling deeper into the extent of urbanization outside recognized urban local bodies, showed that only 34 percent of the urban population fell in the periphery of towns above 1 lakh; thereby indicating that much of the census towns emerged outside the spatial influence of existing large towns. Apparently the census towns are widely spread out and not only concentrated close to the metros, indicating the process of spontaneous transformation of settlements. Such non-metropolitan urban areas are marked by diversified economic activities, comprising a mix of manufacturing, traditional services and construction.

In another study, Denis and Marius-Gnanou (2011) on the basis of contiguous built up area discerned through satellite imagery, identify "settlement agglomerations (SA)" (housing cut off level of 10,000 population), located less than 200 meters apart from each other. Such SAs consist of multiple census settlements. It was observed that unlike towns having at least 10,000 inhabitants that housed 26.6 percent of population (2011), such contiguous SAs contained 37.5 percent of the population in the country. By following such a methodology, most of the states appear far more urbanized than declared by the census. It is apparent that large settlements often fail to meet the official criteria of 75 percent of male non-agricultural workforce. This is an uncommon definition internationally and may account for India's low level of urbanization, and which could be higher if this filter is relaxed. Further, Mukhopadhyay and Pradhan (2012) after examining the location of high growth districts in relation to capital city noted that in states such as Jharkhand, Kerala, Gujarat, Rajasthan and West Bengal, districts other than with the capital or located in its periphery were growing significantly faster than the rest of the state. In the other states district housing the capital city was either the only high growing district or one of them.

Denis et al. (2012) note that many of today's large towns were relatively small in the past indicating their economic dynamism, e.g. Surat, Vapi, Bhiwandi, Aurangabad, Dhanbad to name a few. Considerable urban growth in India is located outside the metros; examination of the growth factors of newly transformed villages/census towns is deemed important in this context. Such towns satisfy the criteria of subaltern and autonomous urbanization, giving credence to the claim that urban system in India is a system of diversified cities with growth occurring across the urban spectrum. It also needs to be underscored that small urban centers play an important role in the creation of rural-urban linkages, besides contributing to a balance network of urban centers (Ramachandran 1989; Rondinelli 1983), and due to their function as service centers. As service towns these locate the factors or agencies which are important forces of transformation.

Some of them are not only connected locally or national, but may even have global connectivity (especially in case of those housing specialized clusters), even though not located in the metropolitan periphery.

In the case of a developed and urbanized state as Gujarat, an enquiry in to the reasons for emergence of new CTs would be quite revealing and have significance for devising policy response. A large number of the CTs in the state are concentrated near the developed and industrial corridor (DMIC) starting from Vapi in southern Gujarat to Ahmedabad and Baroda (see Map). Some of such towns also have a diffused location (e.g. those in Saurashtra, tribal areas etc.) and are possibly large service villages that are important for the surrounding areas for social and economic reasons (most act as market centres, or are hubs for education, health, financial and business services for their hinterlands) or are the *taluka* headquarters. The latter even though not located in the vicinity of large cities have grown in size over time and have acquired urban features.

It is believed that location of a settlement in close proximity to a class 1 city contributes to its faster growth. Sridhar (2010) concluded that proximity to cities with population of a lakh or more encourages other settlements within a certain distance to grow. The growth accelerates as there is a shift from agriculture toward service activities and manufacturing. In order to see the effect of proximity to large cities, the number of CTs (old and new in 2011) falling within a certain radius road distance of class 1 cities is calculated.[1] Adopting a similar way as Pradhan (2013) had for India to ascertain metropolitan influence, the nearest class 1 city to each census town in Gujarat has been considered in order to gauge the influence of larger settlement on the emergence of census towns. All the towns having population of more than one lakh (class 1 town) in 2011 were disaggregated into four groups on the basis of population, viz., one to five lakh, five to ten lakh, ten to forty lakh and more than forty lakhs. Distances of ten km for one to five lakh town, fifteen km for five to ten lakh town, twenty km for ten to forty lakh towns and twenty-five km for towns with more than forty lakh population were identified to ascertain the number of census towns (both old and new) falling within the earmarked region. Even though a census town was located afar from a one lakh and above city, it could be in the vicinity of a tier two or tier three town.

[1] The census provides the distance of each settlement with the nearest class 1 towns; both the nearest city having population of 1 lakh and the second having 5 lakh and above. This information has been used for the present computations, and not the radial distance of each class 1 town based on GIS mapping.

Table 4.4   Distribution of CTs in Gujarat in proximity to class sizes of towns, 2011

Size class of towns	All CTs				New CTS in 2011			
	Number		Population		Number		Population	
1 to 5 lakh	33	52%	436,987	52%	30	65%	399,381	66%
5 to 10 lakh	4	6%	37,381	4%	3	7%	26,027	4%
10 to 40 lakh	12	19%	162,440	19%	7	15%	125,654	21%
More than 40 lakh	15	23%	202,881	24%	6	13%	51,331	9%
Total in proximity to large towns	64	42%	839,689	48%	46	44%	602,393	51%
Not in proximity to large towns	89	58%	921,650	52%	59	56%	587,508	49%

Source: As cited in text

Note: Percentages are the share of each category in the total census towns (numbers and population)

Table 4.4 indicates the distribution of census towns in the proximity of large towns for Gujarat. Overall 44 percent of the newly recognized CTs in 2011 accounting for 51 percent of the population were located near tier 1 towns. The table further shows that amongst the CTs near class 1 towns, 65 percent comprising 66 percent of the population were proximate to urban areas with population under five lakhs. Nearly seven percent of the CTs comprising four percent of the population were located in the influence area of urban centres of five to ten lakhs. It can be seen that even amongst the CTs located close to class 1 towns, only about 28 percent totaling 30 percent of their population were located near the million plus cities in Gujarat. Thus even though a considerable number of census towns were located in the periphery of class 1 towns, several others were not around the mega cities. What is noteworthy is that nearly 56 percent of the CTs comprising a population of 49 percent emerged in a dispersed manner across the countryside as revealed by 2011 census data. Quite evidently, several transformative processes are functional in the state fuelling the formation of small towns. On account of such changes, a distinct set of challenges for urban governance are likely to arise in the state.

It is also important to note that about twenty-four settlements that were CTs in 2001 were upgraded or merged with existing urban agglomerations in 2011. Nearly forty-seven CTs in 2011 were located within the UAs and maintained a CT status. Thus while population growth in class 1 cities in the state (as in India) showed a downward trend (from CAGR of 1.1 to 0.4%) in the last decade, the peripheries have depicted higher growth and could be due to growth of CTs (Pradhan 2013). Our primary observations in the field have shown that often such growth has been in the absence of any planning mechanism or implementation of building by-laws and regulations. But since, as the earlier analysis has revealed, a larger share of population of CTs is not around large towns; their characteristics could be at variance with those having nearness to large cities/towns. The relationship of the latter group of settlements with their surrounding rural areas would also differ considerably.

CONSTITUENTS OF URBAN GROWTH IN GUJARAT

Census towns (CT) emerge due to the reclassification of villages and urban out growths (OG).[2] CTs can also be (though rarely) de-notified into villages, if these cease to satisfy the economic/demographic criteria of an urban settlement. CTs can also be amalgamated into or reclassified into statutory towns (ST). For the country as a whole, 2553 villages were reclassified as CTs, while 141 other settlements (OG or ST) were reclassified as CTs (Pradhan 2013). As many as 144 CTs of 2001 were identified as independent STs or merged with existing STs in 2011, and 55 CTs were de-notified as villages. Thus 90 percent of the new CTs were erstwhile villages and very few existing CTs in 2001 were recognized as STs or merged with existing STs. Such a trend indicates that only a small share of urban settlements is governed as urban areas (Ibid.). It was also shown that 29.5 percent of the urban growth between 2001 and 2011 at the India level was due to reclassification of rural areas into CTs, although there were considerable regional variations in this share.

In Gujarat as against 74 CTs in 2001, census 2011 identified 153 CTs (an increase by 107%). Since the number of CTs in the state has more than doubled, it would be important to ascertain their contribution to the total urban growth during the 2000s decade. A substantial part of the additional urbanization in the state could be accounted by the CTs—the correlation coefficient between urban growth and new census towns (across districts) being 0.70.

In Table 4.5 the components of urban growth in Gujarat are arrived at from the information available in the primary census abstract of the town and village directory. Overall the share of CTs in total urban population in Gujarat in 2011 was 9.3 percent (3.8% in 2001). Of the 75 CTs in 2001,

[2] As per the census of India out growths are settlements located adjacent to but outside the limit of statutory towns. These are however not independent units, but dependent on the neighboring larger city.

Table 4.5   Constituents of urban growth in Gujarat

No.	Item	2001	2011
1	Urban population	18,930,250	25,715,077
2	Urban population change (2001–2011)		6,784,827
3	Urban population growth (%)		35.8
4	a. New CTs that were OG		23
	b. New CTs that were villages		81
	c. Existing CTs		49
	d. Total CTs	74	153
	e. Population in CTs	975,196	1,766,759
	f. Share of CTs in urban population	3.8 (7.4)[a]	9.3 (14.5)[a]
5	Villages population that became CTs	625,654	819,491
6	CTs in 2001 that became STs in 2011		9
	Population	142,141	206,310
7	Villages that became STs in 2011		31
	Population	417,144	474,517
8	Urban growth due to reclassification of villages to STs (%)		6.2
9	Urban growth due to reclassification of villages to CTs (%)		12.1
10	Urban growth due to migration or expansion of boundaries (Residual)%		17.5
11	In situ urbanization (%) (col 8 + 9)		18.3

Source: Computed from Town & Village directory, Primary Census Abstract 2001 & 2011, Registrar General of India. (Following, Pradhan 2013)
[a]Figures in brackets are for India

1 (Vadia) was re-designated as a village, 49 CTs in 2001 continued to remain CTs in 2011 and did not acquire statutory status, nor did they merge with the existing STs. Of the remaining (24 CTs), 20 CTs of 2001 were merged with the existing UAs.[3] Three CTs in 2001 (Damnagar, Sikka and Gandevi) acquired ST status in 2011.

In the case of Gujarat, the urban growth of 35.8 percent can be disaggregated into its constituents. Urban growth can be ascribed partly to the reclassification of rural areas to CTs. This growth occurred without significant migration between settlements and can be designated as 'in situ urbanization'. Zhu (2000) analyses the trend of urban development in China highlighting the transformation of rural areas without migration

---

[3]6 in Ahmedabad UA, 3 in Okha UA, 1 each with Jamnagar UA, Navsari and Kanavav, 4 with Surat UA, 2 each with Valsad and Vapi towns. The process of merging of census towns with the larger city is ongoing.

but increasingly driven by the development of small town and village enterprises. The author uses the expression "in situ urbanization" to describe this process. This is contrary to what is usually perceived to constitute the process of urbanization. By estimating the contribution of growth of CTs to the urban population growth 'the residual' can be ascertained which is the contribution of migration and natural increase to growth. As per Pradhan (2013, 2017), residual can be ascertained after subtracting the contribution of net reclassification of settlements (into CTs, STs) and expansion of boundaries of towns by incorporation of villages. The author believes that between 2001 and 2011, 44 percent of India's urban growth could be ascribed to natural growth, while the rest can be attributed to reclassification.

By comparing the constituent settlements from census 2001 and 2011, it can be ascertained that in Gujarat 12.1 per cent of urban growth can be attributed to reclassification of rural areas (81 villages) to CTs (Table 4.5). Nearly 31 villages were reclassified as statutory towns contributing to 6.2 percent of the total urban growth (these settlements had a population of 474,517, increasing from 417,144 in 2001). This also entails the incorporation of settlements into existing STs through boundary expansion. Thus overall 18.3 percent of urban growth of 35.8 percent in the state could be due to reclassification of rural settlements.[4] On comparing 2001 and 2011 data on STs, it can be seen that in Gujarat all the STs in 2001 (154) remained as STs in 2011. In addition, 9 CTs of 2001 became STs in 2011, besides the 31 rural areas that were reclassified as STs. Hence the remaining 17.5 percent of the urban growth would be due to migration and expansion of boundaries. Surprisingly there were no STs in 2001 that were merged or declassified in 2011, although 40 settlements (CTs & villages) that were categorized as STs merged in exiting towns/UAs.

Looking at the extent of migration and contribution of new CTs, it can be seen that the increase in urbanization owing to change in classification of settlements was more than that due to migration or natural increase. This is indicative of a shift in pattern namely, an increasing share of urban areas administered by rural institutions. This has already been reported for India per se (Pradhan 2013). Gujarat being a highly industrialized and urbanized

---

[4] Quite obviously merging of STs and reclassification of other urban settlements into ST will not have an effect on the urban population.

state, such trends are likely to be even more dominant, as rural areas are undergoing significant degree of transformation. Gujarat adopted a policy of integrated townships in 2007, whereby settlements are classified as technology parks, education based townships, healthcare townships, tourism, logistic parks and residential townships. In 2011, there were 20 such (class 6) towns in Gujarat comprising a population of 26,388, designated as industrial notified areas. This marked an increase from only 10 such notified areas in 2001 (class 6 towns have population of less than 5000).

It is noteworthy that in Gujarat within the 153 CTs listed in 2011, amongst the 81 villages of 2001 that were reclassified to CTs, 62 satisfied the population criteria of being an urban area in 2001 itself, while 76 qualified the workforce condition. It is also interesting to note that 56 villages in 2001 itself possessed both the demographic and workforce attributes to be classified as urban areas. Similarly from amongst the outgrowths, 23 that became CTs in 2011, 21 qualified to be a CT in 2001, having the required population and workforce characteristics to be classified as urban centers. Moreover, if we relax the population criteria to 4000 it can be seen that all the new CTs (villages or out growths) in 2011 had already fulfilled the required criteria in 2001. Thus the fact that all the new CTs in 2011 had already met the criteria in 2001 and awaited recognition, points out that there would be more such settlements in 2011. The above discussion quite clearly brings forth the fact that extent of urbanization in the state (as in the country at large) is underestimated and if the population figures of these villages were added to the urban population of 18.9 million in 2001, the urbanization rate would be upgraded even further.

Determining Factors for Emergence of Census Towns

In order to validate the earlier discussion and to impart rigour to the analysis, the present section examines the relationship between census towns with the regional (district) characteristics through a regression analysis. Factors aiding the process of town growth are explained in the current section. The number of census towns increases as the urbanization rate increases and is also defined by other characteristics crucial to the definition of urban in India. The method adopted was a simple OLS (multivariate) regression equation used in earlier studies to analyze the variables participating in urban growth processes (Pradhan 2013; Bhowmick et al. 2009).

The following equation depicts the relationship between the dependent and the independent variables:

$$Y_i = \alpha + \beta_1 \left(X_1 \right)_i + \beta_n \left(X_n \right)_i + \gamma_i + e_i \quad \text{for district } I \qquad (4.1)$$

Where Y is the dependent variable, X_n are the independent variables and e is the error term. The functional model can be explained in the following form:

$$
\begin{aligned}
\left(\text{No.of New CTs in 2011} \right) Y_i &= \alpha \, \text{Constant} + \beta_1 \left(\text{No.of Existing CTs in 2001} \right)_i \\
&+ \beta n \left(\text{Other district Characteristics} \right)_i \qquad (4.2) \\
&+ \gamma \left(\text{district dummy} \right)_i + e_i
\end{aligned}
$$

While examining the relationship between the regional characteristics and new CTs, Pradhan (2013) considered the level of urbanization for districts in India; however given the fact that rate of growth of urban population determines the level and share of urban population, this variable is considered in the specification that looks at the situation in districts of Gujarat. The dependent variable is the number of newly recognized census towns in a district during 2011. The independent variables also merit some explanation. The level of urbanization in a district, nature of economic activity and concentration of non-farm employment play a role in the transformation of villages in to towns. With increasing *levels of urbanization* (x_1), the employment pattern in a region diversifies to non-farm activities, and if it crosses a certain limit in a village, it satisfies one of the basic conditions for becoming a CT. In order to verify the association between urbanization and new CTs, we have included the urbanization rate of a district in the base year. The emergence of unrecognized large villages as towns is also related to the *growth rate of urban population* (x_2), as growth rate itself determines the magnitude or size of urban population. In Gujarat even the less urbanized districts have experienced a fast rate of growth in urban population in the 2000s decade on account of large scale movement of people from small to large villages and to towns. Rural transformation is also manifest in the increase in the non-farm employment and incomes in the countryside. On the other hand, as we have seen earlier, the emergence of census towns in the metropolitan peripheries has significantly fueled the growth of urban population, even though the metro areas per se are witnessing stagnation.

Whenever industrial or service activity in a rural area employs the speci-fied share of male labour force, one of the conditions for identification of urban area is satisfied, hence in the analysis the extent of *male nonagricul-tural workforce* (x_3) is included as an independent variable. *Number of existing CTs* (x_4) was also used in the specification by Bhowmick et al. (2009) on new firms in an area. The number of existing CTs would have a bearing on new ones. In a way this variable reflects the policy scenario and the perhaps the states' reluctance to recognize large rural settlements possessing urban characteristics, as statutory towns. Variable defining *vil-lages with more than 4000 population* (x_5) is also included as presence of such settlements on the threshold will possibly lead to some of them growing into census towns in due course of time. Often *taluka* headquar-ters and large villages act as service/market centres for the nearby smaller rural settlements and are attractive destinations for employment opportu-nities, spurring migration and natural increase in population.

Besides the rate of urban growth, proportion of large villages in a dis-trict, and share of male non-agricultural workers that will define the emer-gence of new CTs, proximity is indicated by presence of *major urban center/metropolitan region* (x_6) in a district. The geographical location of small towns plays an important role in their existing and future influence including the spread effects emanating from large urban centers (Owusu 2008; Vaishar 2004). A large urban centre exerts centripetal or pull force, attracting migrants/commuters who reside in the surrounding peripheries (in outgrowths or villages) and commute to the nearby large centres for jobs. As has already been discussed earlier, nearly 28 percent of the new CTs are in the proximity of million plus cities, hence this is a district dummy used in the model. All the variables are expected to show a posi-tive relation with the dependent variable.

The results of the simple ordinary least squares (OLS) regression with the extent of new CTs for districts in Gujarat as dependent variable are shown in Table 4.6. In the first model, urban population growth was con-sidered as the independent variable. The regression result indicated that the urban population growth rate during the decade had a statistically significant positive relation with emergence of new CTs. Emergence of new CTs and districts' urban growth were highly correlated as reported in the earlier section. Since the explanatory power (0.45 adjusted R square) was moderate, in the second model magnitude of existing CTs and large villages were also considered in the regression equation. The model's overall explanatory power improved (0.52) with the addition of these

Table 4.6   Relationship of new CTs in Gujarat and district characteristics: result of the regression analysis

Independent variables	I	II	III
No. of existing CTs in 2001		0.422***	0.357 (1.224)
		(1.597)	
Urbanisation rate (2001)			−0.205**
			(−2.214)
Urban population growth	0.142*	0.131*	0.089**
(2001–2011)	(4.657)	(4.009)	(2.442)
No. of large villages		−0.018	−0.013
(Population > 4000)		(−1.357)	(−0.779)
Share of male non agricultural			0.200**
workforce (2001)			(2.091)
District with million plus city			3.038 (1.609)
Constant	−0.456	0.288 (0.235)	−2.969
	(−0.417)		(−1.286)
N	26	26	26
Adjusted R^2	0.45	0.52	0.55
F Statistics	21.7*	10.0*	6.1*

Source: Based on author's computation

Significance of t *$p < 0.01$, **$p < 0.05$, and ***$p < 0.10$

Figures in brackets are t values

variables. The number of existing CTs showed a positive and statistically significant coefficient. The significance of urban population growth variable was also maintained, even though its explanatory power declined. Existing large villages (having population of more than 4000) showed a negative coefficient and possibly points towards the reluctance in the identification of populous settlements as urban areas.

Finally in the last model we also included the base (2001) level of urbanization in the districts, share of male non-agricultural workers in the base year and dummy variable depicting location of million plus city in the district. The overall explanatory power of the equation improved to 0.55. The statistical significance of existing CTs in the third model was lost with the inclusion of other variables. Urbanisation level in 2001 showed a negative (significant) coefficient, hinting at the co-existence of diffused nature of urban growth, far from metropolitan influence and in some less urbanized regions of Gujarat. Urban population growth rate continued to depict a positive and statistical significant relation. Positive association with male non-agricultural workforce was quite predictable and also showed statistical significance. Emergence of new CTs showed a positive association with existence of metro city (district dummy) though the coefficient was not significant. This reiterates the fact that majority of the census towns are emerging in the peripheries of existing large urban agglomerations. That the urban growth in an area is produced mostly by the expansion of existing urban areas which spread out in an irregular and dispersed way has been concluded by others too, for instance by Garcia et al. (2016) in studying emergence of new residential areas in Spain. The variable showing large villages (>4000 population) maintained its negative relation in the third model too, though it is statistically insignificant.

It may be tentatively concluded from the above results that even though census towns are related to pace of urban growth and the urbanization levels in a region, the emergence of urban centers is spread out in a dispersed fashion, underscoring the 'subaltern urbanization' hypothesis in some parts of the state. Notable areas are Saurashtra, North Gujarat and even tribal areas that are less urbanized in comparison to south and middle Gujarat. The results of the regression analysis also reflect the state policy and reluctance to give a statutory status to the CTs. Even though CTs are becoming constituents of existing urban agglomerations in an ongoing process, a large number of rural settlements are on the threshold and await recognition as urban centers. Furthermore, growth of CTs is occurring both in the proximity of large urban centers, along industrial and urban corridors, but also in a dispersed manner. This can also be seen visually in the map of the location of new CTs in the state. However, it needs adding here that the nature of interaction of both types of towns with their surrounding areas is quite different. The dual urbanization process consistent with growth of new CTs in proximity to major centers of urbanization as well as in a dispersed manner has been reported for all India level by scholars (Denis et al. 2012; Pradhan 2013).

The above analysis aids in acquiring deeper insights into the expansion processes of small towns and re-designation of rural settlements to urban, which can be extrapolated to other regions too. The discussion also highlights the increasing concerns regarding governance and the role of *Panchayat* vs. *Nagar Panchayat*/Municipalities, especially in those settlements that are transforming rapidly.[5] The definition of a *Nagar Panchayat*

---

[5]A Nagar Panchayat or Notified Area Council (NAC) or City Council is a settlement in transition from rural to urban. The determination of such areas is left to the states taking into account some criteria like total population, density of population, non-agricultural employment, annual revenue generation, etc. A lot of variation exists amongst the states. The Constitution (74th Amendment) Act, 1992 had specified a population range of 10 to 20,000 for a Nagar Panchayat.

is varied and the interpretation of population and other criteria are often casual. As a result, municipalisation of urban areas is resisted. There are also considerations like lower tax liability, availability of more grants in the case of rural areas, etc., which act as disincentives to re-designation to urban status even though it may be justified. Often areas already given municipal status are denotified and made into *Panchayats*.

The related issue is of the provision of equal standards of public goods and services to all spatial entities, especially at the lower levels of settlement hierarchy. While better transport connectivity has enabled greater integration of larger villages with urban centres, the question of development and service provision is left to be tackled or is inadequately addressed in this reluctance to acknowledge hidden urbanization. The PURA (Provision of Urban amenities in Rural Areas) and RURBAN schemes propose to benefit non-municipal *taluka* headquarters and the CTs along with rural growth centres. Furthermore, since nearly half of the population of the new CTs is in proximity of class 1 town these are likely to fall under the city jurisdiction in future. The ones located within the UAs could be incorporated in cities by the process of boundary expansion.[6] A large section of the CTs away from major urban centres and governed by rural administrative systems, have different economic characteristics from villages. These also possess potential for future growth and require adequate state recognition and acknowledgment.

MAGNITUDE OF THE FUTURE URBANIZATION CHALLENGE

The magnitude of future development challenge faced due to unrecognized urbanization is ascertained by looking at the status of large villages that are on the threshold of being defined as urban. The eligible villages in 2001 have been identified based on two criteria viz., villages having male non-agricultural work force of more than 75 per cent and with population in excess of 5000.[7] The census worker classification does not provide for the category of allied agricultural activity and it is included in "other workers". In order to identify non-agricultural workforce the agricultural workers have been simply subtracted from total workers. The estimates of non-agricultural workers in the analysis thus also include those engaged in

---

[6] As we proceeded for our primary survey of CTs in Gujarat, we encountered that this has in fact already happened with a number of CTs in the periphery of UAs.

[7] The density criteria could not be calculated due to absence of readily available data from the primary census abstract of the villages.

forestry, fishing, plantation and related activities. Due to this anomaly the list of numbers of eligible villages may show some discrepancies.[8] A phenomenal increase in urban population was registered in the tribal dominated districts of Valsad, Sabarkantha, Banaskantha and also Kutch, underlying the fact that urbanization in Gujarat is a quite widespread (DNA 2011). As stated earlier, the momentum of urban growth is fuelled by classes 4 to 6 towns. Over a decade, growth of population in class 1 cities is by 44 percent while it is by 73, 156 and 64 percent in classes 6, 5 and 4 towns, as stated earlier. Urbanization process and transformation of villages into small towns is an ongoing process, even though their statutory status remains unclear. In this context, the contents of Table 4.7 are somewhat revealing. If the population criterion is relaxed, it may be observed that in 2001, 31 percent of the rural population resided in 1468 villages having population of more than 4000- these were the settlements on the threshold of acquiring urban characteristics. Out of these villages, 957 had population in excess of 5000, accounting for nearly 12 percent of the rural population.

Table 4.7 Villages eligible for town status, Gujarat

Item	2001	2011	Implied urbanization in 2011
(A) With population > 4000	1468 (30.6%)	1821 (33.5%)	61.8%
(B) With population > 5000	957 (12.0%)	1129 (24.8%)	56.8%
(C) Population > 4000 + MNFW > 75%	157	111	44.0%
(D) Population 4000 to 5000 + MNFW > 75%	35[a]	30	42.8%
(E) Population > 5000 + MNFW > 75%	122[b]	81	43.8%
(F) Population > 4000 + MNFW > 50%	446	359	47.2%

Source: Computed from Primary Census Abstract of Gujarat, 2001 and 2011, Registrar General of India

Note: MNFW- male non-farm worker

Percentages in brackets in row 2, 3 are share of rural population

[a]76 villages with 50–75% MNFW

[b]213 villages with 50–75% MNFW

[8] In 1991, when the detailed breakup of workers was last available, it was shown that only 3.6 percent of the main workers were engaged in allied sectors, with Kutch, Mehsana and Kheda having the highest share (ranging between 6 to 8 percent of main workers).

In 2001, villages having a population greater than 4000 and with male non-agricultural workforce more than 75 percent (by following the criteria mentioned earlier) numbered 157 (Table 4.7). There were 35 villages having population between 4000 and 5000 and with more than 75 percent male non-agricultural workers in 2001. On comparing the settlement wise data it was found that out of this list, 19 were granted CT status in 2011. In addition, 122 villages could be identified that had population in excess of 5000 with more than 75 percent male non-agricultural workers. It was ascertained that from this list only 62 were recognized as CTs in 2011. Thus only 81 out of the eligible villages in 2001 were designated as CTs in 2011.

Further, from amongst the eligible villages, 25 were classified as statutory towns in 2011. A few viz., 6 statutory towns in 2011 were converted from villages, but did not possess eligibility. These possibly were designated as industrial notified areas. Thus what is interesting is 76 eligible villages (in 2001) have not received town status in 2011 and have been kept as villages—an indication of under estimation of the urban population in the state. On the other hand, there were nearly 26 new CTs in 2011 which did not qualify the prescribed requirement of population size in 2001 when they were villages. Thus the extent of mismatch is quite noticeable. If we consider the list of eligible villages based on population criteria, but relax the employment qualification to between 50 to 75 percent, a further 213 villages were on the threshold of acquiring urban status in 2001 itself.

Examination of the urbanization potential as seen from 2011 census village listing is quite revealing (Table 4.7). Unlike 2001, in 2011 nearly 34 percent of the total rural population in Gujarat resided in 1821 large villages (>4000 population). Of these 1129 had population of more than 5000, comprising 25 percent of the rural population. Census data shows that overall, 4528 villages had male non-agricultural workers between 50 to 75 percent, but did not fulfill the population criterion. If we relax the employment criterion amongst only the large villages (>4000), 359 villages had more than 50 percent of male workers engaged in non-farm sector. Out of these, 111 had more than 75 percent of male workers engaged in non-farm activities. Of these 111 villages, 81 villages had population greater than 5000 and 30 with population between 4000 and 5000. These are the villages that are clearly eligible for a town status immediately. The remaining 248 villages satisfy the population criteria but with the relaxed employment criteria (50–75% male non-farm workers). It is interesting to note that the urbanization levels in Gujarat during 2011 would have been higher (ranging from 43% to 62% instead of 42%) if population of these eligible villages under the various scenarios mentioned in Table 4.7 is added to the existing urban population. Possibly, a large number of currently ineligible villages may also achieve the required eligibility by the time the 2021 census is conducted.

When we compare the list of eligible villages of 2001 and 2011, drawn on the basis of the population and employment criteria, it can be seen that 32 eligible villages of 2001 have appeared again in 2011, and have been left as villages. In addition to these 32 villages in 2011, there are 47 new eligible villages that have developed the town characteristics. In other words, 79 villages can be considered as towns if they meet the density criteria. Thus coupled with the backlog of already eligible villages of 2001 and the ones whose recognition is imminent, Gujarat's level of urbanization appears to be significantly under estimated. The analysis so far suggests that in Gujarat the villages have undergone a pervasive change in their economic structure (as in India), due to diversification of their workforce. Even though changes in population and density criteria can be attained easily, what is remarkable is that a large number of villages in the state are on the way to satisfy the census workforce criteria to be eligible for town status. Thus evidence indicates that the impact of work force diversification on small town development is irrefutable in the last decade.

Agricultural growth in the state could have prompted this occupational diversification. It is well known that despite long term declining share of agricultural sector and severe output and income fluctuations, 2000s was a period of high agricultural growth in Gujarat, with most of the crop groups showing significant output acceleration. Substantive changes in the cropping pattern have taken place in the state in the post liberalization phase (Mehta 2012a). Food grain production accelerated from 2.6 to 9.0 percent per annum from 1990s to 2000s decade. Oilseeds output also accelerated from 5 to 6.1 percent per annum. Cotton has gained considerable prominence- its output growth accelerated from 10 to 25 percent annually, contributed by yield gains and diversion of area from pulses and coarse cereals. The higher value crops, notably fruits, vegetables and spices as a group also acquired importance in 2000s decade and their combined output growth accelerated from 5.7 to 12 percent per annum. These crops occupy nearly one-fifth of the cropped area in the state. Significantly, most of the crops now dominant in the states cropping pattern (wheat, oilseeds notably castor, groundnut, cotton, spices fruits, vegetables, floricultural and medicinal plants) provide better returns and promote value added agribusiness enterprises. Some even have a global demand (for instance, castor, spices, and medicinal plants like *isabgol*).

It has been noted (Gaiha 2016) that agricultural commercialisation inherently provides higher returns per unit of land, resulting in higher incomes and create pathways for employment generation in rural areas. These include creation of value chains for agricultural commodities, remunerative non-farm opportunities for labourers, smallholders and those self-employed in non-agricultural activities. Modernization of agriculture is also tied to greater demand for marketed commodities such as chemical fertilizers, pesticides, machinery, seeds and other inputs which strengthens linkages with non-agricultural production and services. Growth in rural incomes creates demand for processed foods/goods that spurs local production, thereby generating employment. Declining food prices provides food security and overall poverty reduction, while also lowering the real product wage in the non-agricultural sector, raising profitability and investment (Ibid.). With income expansion, the nature of agriculture also changes from subsistence-oriented farming to commercialised and market oriented farming having closer linkages with the non-agricultural sector.

The industrial distribution of workforce showed that between 1999–2000 and 2011–2012, the share of primary sector in the workforce declined and occupational diversification gained vigour. Agricultural commercialization was accompanied by increased employment in allied activities (forestry, fishing, animal husbandry), and the shift of workers from rural to urban areas. Rural main workers declined from 65 to 58 percent and in absolute terms while only 0.6 million main workers were added in rural areas, in urban area the increase was by 3 million. Thus the generation of economic momentum in the countryside with a vibrant agricultural sector spurred the process of urban growth.

Concluding Remarks

Analysis and discussion so far indicate that for smoothening the rural transformation process and urban growth requires concerted focus of policy, that can be summarized here. Rural employment structure is changing and is manifested in the growth of the villages into towns, in addition to the in-situ population growth, and migration. It also appears that the rural and urban are no longer disjointed entities. Urbanisation in the state is the result of diffused growth of smaller towns, emergence of towns along the transport/industrial corridors as well as in the metropolitan peripheries. Smaller towns are growing faster than larger towns and the activity base of smaller towns is also undergoing rapid change, that often functions as pull forces for rural migrants and commuters. Nearly a third of the rural population in the state is on the threshold of acquiring urban character. Recognition of the statutory status of a census town or urban village involves complex decisions at the village level. The mapping of the development schemes of the government over urban/rural areas is a crucial factor in the reluctance of villages to acquire urban status. Further complexity is lent by the often casual and imperfect implementation of crucial regulations that ushers in indiscriminate changes in land use. Increase in the number of census towns indicates underestimation of the urban areas and population. Increase in the rural administered urban areas indicate that even villages acquiring urban characteristics are not declared as urban. The reluctance to give statutory status to the CTs is a reflection of the state's policy. This is also indicated by the regression analysis, as preexisting large villages show negative relation with emergence of census towns. Results of the regression analysis also indicate that the emergence of towns depends on the level of urbanization in a region, growth rate of urban population, besides the non-agricultural male workforce. Proximity to larger urban settlement influences growth of small towns and plays a positive role in the provision of physical infrastructure, particularly road networks and accessibility to market and service centers.

With the relaxation of census urban definition, it is indicated that urbanisation levels in the state could be much higher, as a large number of villages are undergoing rapid structural changes seen through the lens of workforce and population criteria. Nearly a third of the rural population is on the threshold of acquiring urban nature. This has a bearing on the provision of equal standards of public goods and services to all settlements. Growth of rural administered urban areas leads to under provision and neglect of basic amenities available for healthy, productive and sustainable urban living.

It is apparent that issue of villages undergoing structural transformation should require focus of development. Such villages occurring in dispersed locations or in the vicinity of larger cities, demand urban facilities (paved roads, drainage, piped water, educational, health amenities etc.). Peripheral villages or those along transportation axes also face the issue of agricultural land being acquired for urban uses. That the increase in the urban characteristics in rural areas would have an impact on the food habits, nutritional aspects, besides the crucial human development indicators is the added dimension. Lag in the development process and distribution of gains needs to be viewed with caution, as it may have adverse human development and social outcomes. The smaller urban settlements or larger villages are providing avenues for economic advancement and non-farm jobs even though these may be unrecognized as towns. These are also bearers of social emancipation and fulfill functions of cities. Often these forge linkages with larger settlements, or at other times, in autonomous capacity as 'subaltern urbanization' these provide growth avenues to the hinterlands, forcing the discourse to move away from metro-centricity (Mukhopadhyay and Maringati 2014). Gujarat being a forerunner in this aspect needs to lead through policy focus for attaining sustainable urbanization goals. With the exception of a few census towns in the industrial belts are large number are undergoing expansion in a haphazard and unplanned growth. There is a dire need for devising local level plans to minimize the negative externalities and even for utilizing the funds available under various schemes, (notably PURA, RURBAN) in a far more judicious manner.

It is obvious that the way ahead involves addressing the challenges of urbanisation with the adoption of a multi-pronged approach that focuses on the following aspects:

- Investment to provide adequate urban (economic and social) infrastructure in smaller urban areas, census towns and large villages.
- Reforming institutions and governance structures, and building capacity of local government bodies to analyse, assess and implement urban interventions. There is a crying need to do a rethink on area based schematic mapping.
- Providing basic amenities and opportunities especially to vulnerable and deprived economic sections have to be expedited.
- Education, health interventions and skill development in the new cities/towns are required these settlements are to lead Gujarat's manufacturing and service sector growth.

Lastly as argued by scholars (e.g. Gaiha 2016) prioritizing public investment would spur rural transformation due to access to technology, credit and markets. Strengthening of extension services and rural infrastructure enhances agricultural commercialization. Given this, skill formation of rural workers is likely to increase productivity and living standards thereby arresting distress induced rural to urban migration. Analysis indicates that creating more remunerative opportunities in rural areas deserves greater attention of policy.

ANNEXURE

Table 4.8 Percentage of rural workers usually employed in non-farm sector, India, 1983 to 2009–2010

Years	Male	% change	Female	% change	Persons	% change
1983	22.2	–	12.2	–	18.4	–
1993–1994	25.9	3.7	13.8	1.6	21.6	3.2
1999–2000	28.6	2.7	14.6	0.8	23.7	2.1
2004–2005	33.4	4.8	16.7	2.1	27.3	3.6
2009–2010	37.2	3.8	20.6	3.9	32.1	4.8

Source: NSSO, employment and unemployment surveys, various years

REFERENCES

Alam, Ashfaque, and Binayak Choudhury. 2016. Spatio-Functional Determinants of Small Towns: A Case Study of Selected Indian Small Towns. *Review of Urban and Regional Development Studies* 28 (2): 75–88.

Ali, Md. Julfikar, and Deepika Varshney. 2013. Spatial Modelling of Urban Growth and Urban Influence. *Environment and Urbanization ASIA* 3 (2): 255–275.

Berry, B.J.L. 1961. City Size Distributions and Economic Development. *Economic Development and Cultural Change* 9 (4): 573–588.

Bhagat, R.B. 2012. Emerging Pattern of Urbanization in India. *Economic and Political Weekly* 46 (34): 10–12.

Bhowmick, S.K., Shubhashis Gangopadhyay, and Shagun Krishnan. 2009. Reforms and Entry: Some Evidence from the Indian Manufacturing Sector. *Review of Development Economics* 13 (4): 658–672.

Cadène, Philippe, and Mark Holmström, eds. 1998. *Decentralized Production in India: Industrial Districts, Flexible Specialization and Employment.* New Delhi and London: Sage.

Chand, Ramesh, R. Saxena, and S. Rana. 2015. Estimates and Analysis of Farm Income in India, 1983–84 to 2011–12. *Economic and Political Weekly* 50 (2): 139–145.

Coelho, K., and M. Vijayabaskar. 2014. On the Charts, Off the Tracks. *Economic and Political Weekly* 49: 49–79.

Denis, E., and K. Marius-Gnanou. 2011. Toward a Better Appraisal of Urbanisation in India. *Cybergeo: European Journal of Geography* 569.

Denis, Eric, P. Mukhopadhyay, and Marie-Helene Zerah. 2012. Subaltern Urbanization in India. *Economic and Political Weekly* 47 (30): 52–62.

Dixit, A. 2009. Growth and Non-Farm Employment: The Case of Gujarat. *The Indian Journal of Labour Economics* 52 (3).

DNA (Daily News & Analysis) (2011). Urbanisation Has Touched Even Tribal Areas in Gujarat, October 17 Issue.

Freidmann, John. 1961. Cities in Social Transformation. *Comparative Studies in Society and History* 4 (1): 86–103.

Gaiha, Raghav. 2016. The Overrated Urban Spinoff. *The Indian Express*, November 2.

Garcia-López, Miquel-Àngel, Camille Hémet, and Elisabet Viladecans-Marsal. 2016. *Next Train to the Polycentric City: The Effect of Railroads on Subcenter Formation*. Working Paper 2016/14, Institut d'Economia de Barcelona.

Guin, Debarshi, and D.N. Das. 2015. New Census Towns in West Bengal – 'Census Activism' or Sectoral Diversification. *Economic and Political Weekly* 50 (14): 68–72.

Jatav, Manoj, and S. Sen. 2013. Drivers of Non-Farm Employment in Rural India. *Economic and Political Weekly* 48: 26–27.

Krugman, Paul. 1991. Increasing Returns and Economic Geography. *The Journal of Political Economy* 99 (3): 483–499.

Kundu, Amitabh. 2011a. Politics and Economics of Urban Growth. *Economic and Political Weekly* 46 (20).

———. 2011b. Method in Madness: Urban Data from 2011 Census. *Economic and Political Weekly* 46 (40): 13–16.

Kundu, Debolina, and D. Samanta. 2011. Redefining the Inclusive Urban Agenda in India. *Economic and Political Weekly* 46 (5): 55–63.

Lewis, W.A. 1954. Economic Development with Unlimited Supplies of Labour. *The Manchester School* 22 (2): 139–191.

Marshall, Alfred. 1920. *Principles of Economics: An Introductory Volume*. London: Macmillan and Co.

Mehta, Niti. 2012a. Performance of Crop Sector in Gujarat During High Growth Period: Some Explorations. *Agricultural Economics Research Review* 25 (2): 195–204.

Misra, R.P., ed. 2013. *Urbanisation in South Asia: Focus on Mega Cities*. New Delhi: Cambridge University Press.

Mukhopadhyay, Partha, and A. Maringati. 2014. Articulating Growth in the Urban Spectrum. *Economic and Political Weekly* 49 (22): 44–45.

Mukhopadhyay, Partha, and Kanhu C. Pradhan. 2012. *District-Level Patterns of Urbanisation in India*. New Delhi: Centre for Policy Research Urban Brief.

Nijman, J. 2012. India's Urban Challenge. *Eurasian Geography and Economics* 53 (1): 7–20.

Owusu, George. 2008. The Role of Small Towns in Regional Development and Poverty Reduction in Ghana. *International Journal of Urban and Regional Research* 32: 453–472.

Perroux, François. 1955. Note Sur la Notion de Poles Croissance. *Economic Appliquee*, 1&2: 307–320. Translated by Mette Monsted, 1974.

Planning Commission, Government of India. 2008. *The Eleventh Five Year Plan*. New Delhi.

———. 2011. *Mid Term Appraisal for Eleventh Five Year Plan 2007–2012*. New Delhi: Oxford University Press.

Pradhan, K.C. 2013. Unacknowledged Urbanisation – New Census Towns of India. *Economic and Political Weekly* 48 (36): 43–51.

———. 2017. Unacknowledged Urbanisation: The New Census Towns in India. In *Subaltern Urbanisation in India: An Introduction to the Dynamics of Ordinary Towns Exploring Urban Change in South Asia*, ed. Eric Denis and Marie-Helene Zerah. New Delhi: Springer Nature.

Ramachandran, R. 1989. *Urbanisation and Urban Systems in India*. New Delhi: Oxford University Press.

Raman, B. 2014. Patterns and Practices of Special Transformation in Non-Metros: The Case of Tiruchengode. *Economic and Political Weekly* 49 (22): 46–54.

Rehman, M.R. 2008. Urban Spatial Growth Analysis of Khulna City. www.geospatialworld.net/paper/Application/Articleview.

Rondinelli, D.A. 1983. Towns and Small Cities in Developing Countries. *Geographical Review* 73 (4): 379–395.

Samanta, Gopa. 2014. The Politics of Classification and the Complexity of Governance in Census Towns. *Economic and Political Weekly* 49 (22): 55–62.

Sridhar, K.S. 2010. Determinants of City Growth and Output in India. *Review of Urban and Regional Development Studies* 22 (1): 22–38.

Vaishar, A. 2004. Small Towns: An Important Part of the Moravian Settlement System. In *Cities in Transition*, ed. M. Pak and D. Rebernik, 309–318. Ljubljana: Univerza v Ljubljani.

Verma, L.N. 2006. *Urban Geography*. Jaipur: Rawat Publications.

Wadhwa, Kiran, and S.P. Kashyap. 1985. Inter-Regional Industrialization in India: Role of Urbanisation and Urban Structure. In *Regional Structure of Development and Growth in India*, ed. G.P. Mishra, vol. 1. New Delhi: Ashish Publishing House.

Zhu, Yu. 2000. In Situ Urbanization in Rural China: Case Studies from Fujian Province. *Development and Change* 31 (2): 413–434.

CHAPTER 5

Changing Socio-Economic Profile of Urbanised Villages (Census Towns) in Gujarat

INTRODUCTION

Given the unfolding of transformation processes in Gujarat as embodied in the changing rural economic structure and accelerated urbanization, the specific aim of the present research was to unravel the factors leading to growth of the census towns, these being a major constituent of overall urban growth. In order to satisfy this objective field exploration were conducted for selected census towns, i.e. large villages that have acquired urban characteristics with population expansion and change in the nature of economic activities. The primary research was conducted by following the case study approach. Case study research, allows the exploration and understanding of complex issues. It is increasingly recognized as a tool in many social science studies, and its role in research becomes prominent when issues with regard to education, social and community based problems (Gulsecen and Kubat 2006; Johnson 2006) notably poverty, unemployment, education, impact of government programmes, etc. were raised.

There are limitations of quantitative methods in providing holistic and in-depth explanations of the social and behavioural problems. Case study method enables a researcher to closely examine the data within a specific context. It can be considered a robust research method particularly when a holistic, in-depth investigation is required. Often a case study method selects a small geographical area or limited number of individuals as the

© The Author(s) 2018
N. Mehta, *Rural Transformation in the Post Liberalization Period in Gujarat*, https://doi.org/10.1007/978-981-10-8962-6_5

subjects of study and investigates the contemporary phenomenon through in-depth contextual analysis of events, conditions and their relationships (Zainal 2007). Yin (1984: 23) defines the case study research method "as an empirical inquiry that investigates a contemporary phenomenon within its real-life context; when the boundaries between phenomenon and context are not clearly evident; and in which multiple sources of evidence are used."

Since the case study approach is often criticized in terms of its lack of robustness as a research tool, crafting the design of case studies is of importance. Researchers can adopt either a single-case or multiple-case design depending on the issue in question. According to Yin (1994), generalization of results from case studies, from either single or multiple case approach, stems on theory, rather than behavior of population. By replicating the cases through pattern-matching, a technique linking several pieces of information from the same case to some theoretical proposition, multiple-case design enhances and supports the previous results (Campbell 1975). Case study method, through interviews, journal entries and group discussions thus is a viable method to elicit implicit and explicit data from the subjects; enables systematic recording of a 'chain of evidence'; and lastly can be linked to a theoretical framework (Tellis 1997).

In all fifteen urban centres (as defined by Census) were selected and were the focus of study. The sample primarily included large villages that have transformed as census towns, some of the existing census towns and others that have been designated as statutory towns or have merged with large towns/urban agglomerations. While selecting the urban centres, cognizance was taken of the different agro-climatic regions of the state and towns representing different agro-ecological conditions were taken up for the purpose of the field exploration. At the second level, considerations in selection of towns were: their location near cities or a spatially diffused manner; occurrence along the growth axis/industrial corridor; proximity to transportation route; location in tribal belt or agricultural hinterland. In this manner practically all the facets of development in the state were considered while selecting the case studies. The present chapter gives detailed profile of the selected case studies. Next chapter highlights and identifies underlying growth impulses of the case studies (Fig. 5.1).

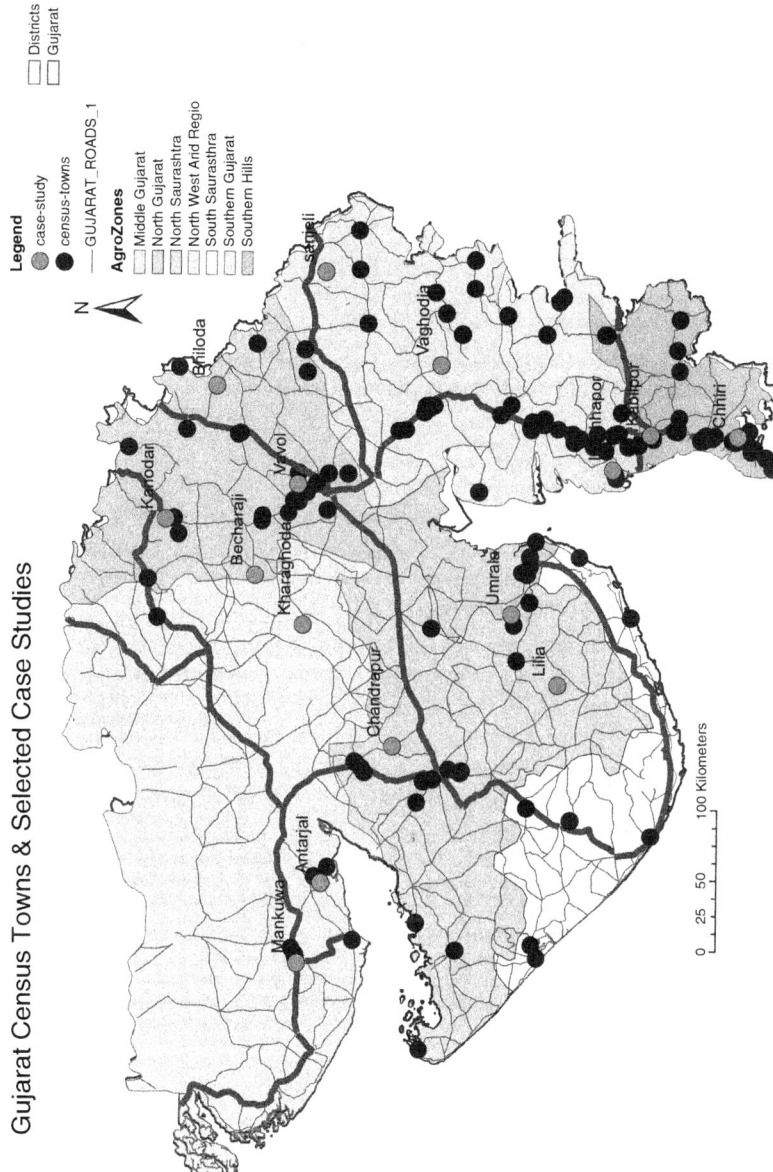

Fig. 5.1 Gujarat census towns and selected case studies. Source: Prepared by author

PROFILE OF CENSUS TOWNS

Tribal Area

Bhiloda, Aravalli District
Bhiloda is a village *panchayat* located in the Aravalli district (earlier part of Sabarkantha district) of Gujarat, and is the *taluka* headquarters. It is situated on the banks of the river Hathmati among the Aravalli hills in the northern Gujarat agro-climatic region. Bhiloda was a part of the Idar state during British rule. After independence in 1947, Idar state was merged with Union of India, and from 1947 to 1956 it was a part of Bombay state in the Idar district. From 1961 to 2013, Bhiloda was a part of Sabarkantha district which was bifurcated and Aravalli district was formed. Bhiloda is identified as a census town, having a population of 16,074 (2011).

Illegal encroachment was the major problem faced by the village panchayat. Several unplanned housing societies and trading establishments were mushrooming in and around Bhiloda. Investment in the real estate sector was being done often by people who were not the actual residents of Bhiloda. Large scale illegal conversion of tribal agricultural land to non-agricultural uses was being reported.

Migration: The main (permanent) migrant communities are Marwaris and Sindhis, and were engaged largely in trading, money lending and real estate sector and were also large landholders. Migrants in large numbers from Rajasthan (Udaipur district), also Uttar Pradesh and Bihar have settled in Bhiloda. A large number of housing societies for such migrants had come up in and around Bhiloda, often on land that was acquired from the tribals. In fact some locals felt that the population in the town could be in excess of that showed by the census. Seasonal migration of tribal labourers from Bhiloda to other parts of Gujarat was a regular feature. Large section of the floating population comprised of daily commuters from surrounding villages. Bhiloda offered employment avenues such as vendors, tailors, and shop owners or as helpers in the retail sector.

Infrastructure: The village had a 40–50 years old cement pipeline for water distribution and under the RURBAN scheme government had approved Rs. 9 crores for the creation of water and sanitation facility, to be implemented with the support of Water & Sanitation Management Organisation (WASMO). This would be implemented for four zones in the town. Currently there were around 3500 tap water (household) connections for purpose of drinking water. In Bhiloda various types of health facilities were available i.e. cottage hospital (20 beds and 2 doctors), private clinics

(2), civil hospital (95 beds), community health centre (1), maternity hospital (6), apart from a panchayat run hospital. Residents reported that the government run health facilities in the village faced shortage of doctors and other staff. In Bhiloda the main arterial, connector and distributor roads were pucca but local roads were semi pucca. PMGSY (Padhan Mantri Gram Sadak Yojana) was operational in the village. There were Panchayat run street lights.

The APMC market in Bhiloda was a well-equipped facility attracting farmers from Himmatnagar, Shamlaji, Bhiloda and other surrounding villages for trading of wheat, cotton and castor. Cotton farmers marketed their produce in Vijapur which had a ginning unit. Wheat procured in Bhiloda was sold in markets in Bombay and Ahmedabad. Cotton seeds were procured by NK Proteins, an oil manufacturing unit located near Shamlaji. The presence of the APMC facilitates dissemination of crop price information periodically that enabled farmers to take timely decisions regarding selling their products in the market. Since prices are declared/supported by the government, local traders in the APMC complained that they could not earn enough profit.

Economic activities: Engagement as agricultural labourers in and around the town was the prime economic activity for a large section of the population. Significant growth in retail trade had occurred in the town, that functioned as a service centre for the rural hinterland. Scheduled tribe (ST) population was largely engaged in tertiary sector activities and was playing an important role in the local economy. A large number of cultivators as well as the service class residents were diversifying into trading activity/shops as Bhiloda is a service cum-market centre for settlements falling within the radius of nearly 10–15 km, including Shamlaji and Ratanpur. A large number of tailoring shops, beauty parlours, mobile repairing and consumer durables shops were existing in Bhiloda. Since nearly all the tribal families had members, quite often multiple members employed in government service or were teachers, the income levels and general living standard of the local inhabitants had noticeably improved, creating a huge demand for goods and services. Assured salaried income had spurred the demand for shops selling consumption goods and tertiary services. This had led to the shift of workers towards retail/repairs and other services besides salaried jobs. By and large the economic betterment of the tribal population (as a result of government jobs) coupled with migration and influx of capital from Rajasthan led the village to grow in size and acquire prosperity.

Various kinds of economic activities were existing i.e. services (mainly tailoring shops, beauticians, laundry services), real estate agents and money lenders, retail trade (there were 7982 shops as of 2012). The existence of Sabar dairy had enabled animal husbandry to emerge as a major household activity. There were no major industries in or around Bhiloda. In fact the town was marked by complete absence of manufacturing or processing activity. There was a GIDC estate in the vicinity but had no functional units.

Agriculture: Agrarian structure shows that 25 per cent of the cultivators were small farmers, 25 per cent marginal, 30 per cent medium farmers, while only 20 per cent were large farmers. There were around 500 landless households. It was reported during group discussion that farmers could tap ground water at a depth of 100 feet around five years ago, but currently farmers were facing acute water related problems and had to go to greater depths for water (up to 150 feet). For irrigation 41 bore wells and dug wells were in existence. Check dams were few; under the IWDP (Integrated watershed Development Programme), two check dams were constructed. No canal or surface irrigation facility was present in the town. Locals felt that the water scenario could change if Bhiloda was supplied water from the Narmada project. Major crops cultivated were cotton, wheat, castor, and vegetables.

Government schemes related to agriculture: AATMA was the main project sponsored by Gujarat Government and Krishi Melas shared information related to land, inputs and agriculture. Green houses had increased in the town in the past few years. Farmers have adopted GM technology and opined that it was effective for crop production. They were aware about Krishi Mohatsav Programme. Farmers also obtained online updates related to agriculture i.e. price information, information on HVY seeds, fertilizers and about agricultural schemes and their benefits e.g. Kisan credit card.

Statutory status: In Bhiloda the impact of urbanization was quite visible, in terms of changes reported in the consumption habits e.g. increased consumption of non-home cooked food, changes in lifestyle, increased emphasis on education, mainly girls' education, as also expenditure on health. Girls, it was reported were increasingly preferring careers in teaching, as also medical education. Awareness levels regarding adoption of new farm technology had enhanced. Nature of housing saw marked change in the recent decades (i.e. preference for tenements/bungalows, row houses, flats) and residents were incurring expenditure on house repairing and modernizing their living environment. Only the poorest sections continued to live in semi pucca houses. The level of physical infrastructure reportedly improved in the recent decades (notably, development of market, banking facilities, etc.).

Due to local political reasons Bhiloda was not declared Nagar palika. Residents felt that local politicians wanted the village to remain a Panchayat as considerable funds were available under the tribal development (TASP) and rural development schemes, which may cease once the village was designated as a statutory town. (Nagar Panchayat status is applicable for towns with population of more than 11,000 but less than 25,000). In the focus group discussions it was felt that the advantages of town status would be:

- More funds for infrastructure could be availed. Problems related to inadequate amenities in the village would be handled with more urban development funds particularly those related to drainage, solid waste management, RCC roads and water supply.
- The health infrastructure could be improved. Currently Bhiloda lacked facilities for critical care and patients travelled to Himmatnagar.
- The village would become an attractive destination for industrial investments (small scale/GIDC), that could go a long way towards employment creation.
- Housing conditions would improve, particularly for the weaker economic sections/slums.

The main disadvantage reported was that taxes would increase. Further, corruption could exacerbate with the presence of a larger number of government employees in the Nagar Palika.

Problems: Observation and discussions revealed that the town suffered from the following problems

- Lack of RCC roads.
- Lack of solid waste management. Bhiloda had no proper management system for solid waste collection. Gram Panchayat provided sweeper and garbage tractor, but they were not sufficient nor worked regularly.
- Lack of drainage facility.
- Slums: In the town most of the people were scheduled tribes but only few were living in slum conditions. Migrants living in slums faced problems related to housing, water, lack of assets and remunerative employment opportunities.

- Lack of the small and large scale industries: It was felt that the government could promote industry in Bhiloda, poverty could be reduced as it was felt that the surrounding areas were dependent on Bhiloda for livelihood opportunities.
- Political issues: In 2001 Bhiloda's population was around 15,000 but it was not declared a census town due to local political concerns.
- It was also opined that the gap between the poor and the rich had widened over the years, mainly due to lack of employment creation and industrial development.

Sanjeli, Dahod District
Sanjeli is located in the eastern tribal belt of Gujarat, belonging to the middle Gujarat agro-ecological region. Sanjeli taluka belongs to the erstwhile principality of Sanjeli, under the administrative control of the Rewa Kantha Agency of Bombay Presidency. Sanjeli is 400 years old and was incorporated as a part of the Baroda Agency, which was a sub division of the Western India States Agency. Its area then was 88 sq. km and it acceded to the Union of India on June 10, 1948. Later the region was merged with the state of Gujarat and is now part of the Dahod district. During the early nineteenth century Sanjeli was appointed as one of the leading princely states of India under the indirect rule of the British administration. Located in the northeastern part of Gujarat, its territory included around 50 villages. The state was bordered by the territory of Sant in the north, by the British territory of Panchmahals in the east, the state of Baria in the south, and by the district of Godhra in the British Panchmahals in the west.

Sanjeli is located 45 km west from district headquarters of Dahod and lies 159 km away from state capital, Gandhinagar. Limkheda is the nearest railway station located at a distance of around 24.7 kms. Sanjeli village progressed after independence under the former Sarpanch Maharaja Rajendra Singh. Before independence his father Maharaja Pusph Singh built a school, water tank, hospital and police station. Earlier Sanjeli was part of a group Gram Panchayat, but now has its own Panchayat, hence it may not be assigned Nagar Panchayat status due to the population criterion. Presently the town shares the Gram Panchayat with Bhuwada village and became the taluka headquarter only a year back. Dominant population comprises of STs, notably Bhils and amongst the settlers are also Dawoodi bohras.

During the 2002 riots in Gujarat a large number of houses, shops etc. were damaged. Post riots, central, state governments and NGOs channelized aid due to which most of the residents have constructed pucca houses. The town also experienced a business/retail boom after 2002, as loans, assistance for the same was easily forthcoming. The town has been on a path of development after the 2002, mainly as a consequence of the attention that was directed in the form of aid for reconstruction/rehabilitation. It was stated that considering the in migrants, total population was as high as 12,000. Amongst the cultivators more than 90 per cent were marginal farmers, 10 per cent medium farmers, having land up to 25 acres. There were no large farmer in the town. Sanjeli is the most developed amongst the surrounding villages and served as a health, education and marketing hub. It attracted labourers from surrounding areas as it offered opportunities for employment.

Infrastructure: In the past decade the village population had seen increase in the level of education, and spending on health care. The town had seven anganwadis, seven primary schools (private and government), two secondary schools, and an ITI. General observation was that the education standard had deteriorated on account of poor quality of teachers, teaching pedagogy and even the quality of students had declined.

There was a PHC and also a CHC with hospital beds that is currently being upgraded. Nearly 15 to 16 private clinics/dispensaries were existing, some with nursing homes too. There is a gynaecology hospital in the town. For secondary/tertiary medical care the villagers had to go to Dahod, Godhra and even to Baroda. There was also a veterinary hospital in the town.

During discussion it was revealed that malnutrition was a major problem amongst women and children, mainly due to iron and B_{12} deficiency. It was mainly ascribed to poverty, poor diet and increased use of junk food. It was opined that the food habits of the adivasis were changing as maize, jaggery etc. were no longer the preferred foods. Excessive use of farm chemicals was also leading to health issues. Sickle cell anaemia was a common ailment in the tribal dominated areas.

There was a water tank in the town used for water chestnut cultivation, and earlier supported fishing activity. Nearly 40 hand pumps and 12 dug wells were used for drinking water purpose. There were also three overhead tanks. It was stated that pipelines were laid from Kadana scheme to provide drinking water, but so far water had not become available. The sump was also constructed at the gram panchayat to collect and redistribute the water.

The different *faliyas*/neighbourhoods in Sanjeli belong to different communities such as *Prajapati, Kalvi, Chali, Thakor, Harijans*. In some of the *falias* tap water connections were installed by WASMO at ten per cent sharing basis. On an average one *faliya* had up to twenty five tap connections. The town had an approach road, but no bus station. It was served largely by private transport (jeeps). Internal roads with street lights exist. Being a princely state, the town had a planned grid pattern of roads. There was a crematorium. However, open drains were visible and the town lacked a sewerage system. Under the RURBAN scheme, sewerage system was proposed by the Gram Sabha.

Land development: There was absence of any real estate agent or contractor/builder in the town. Most of the land dealings were carried out on person to person basis. Since Sanjeli is a taluka centre catering to nearby villages, there was tremendous growth of retail activity. Most of the village main road and market space had been encroached illegally by shops. The village elders felt that such encroachments have led to major problem of traffic and congestion as also cleanliness, especially in the last decade or so. The collector, it was felt could remove such encroachments but political will for such decisions was lacking.

Since the town is now a taluka headquarter, it was felt that all facilities have to be made available, including health, cleanliness etc. Most of the land being held by Adivasis, under section 73AA cannot be sold to non-tribals or converted to non-agricultural uses. Hence tribal population was constrained as they were unable sell the land and engage in non-farm jobs. Since the impact fee for land conversion was very high only the better off farmers undertook land conversion, and not the poor farmers. As of now, not much land conversion or construction activity was visible in the town, unlike in Bhiloda.

Migration: There was large scale migration of labourers from Sanjeli towards north Gujarat, Kutch and Saurashtra. The tribal workers migrated out for eight to nine months and returned to the village during the months of the monsoon. Such migration was carried out by nearly 90 per cent of the adivasi families in Sanjeli. Quite surprisingly there were GSRTC buses that ran directly from Sanjeli to Bhuj and Saurashtra cites, to facilitate the tribal out-migration. Sanjeli also had migrant settlers belonging to *Bohra* community and those from Rajasthan who were primarily engaged in retail and small businesses. In addition workers from surrounding areas came to work in non-farm activities and as agricultural labourers in Sanjeli. However, the ratio of daily commuters from Sanjeli was only around 1 to 2 per cent.

Economic activity: Farming was the main stay of tribal population, also agricultural labour in and around the town. *Panchal* community was engaged in other trades and *Bohras* were carrying out small businesses/ retail trade. Major non-farm trades was observed to be tailoring, laundry, blacksmithy, welding, carpenters, beauty parlours (around 15), and retail sector. There were also shops for provisions, Xerox/mobile repairs, cloth/ garment and scooter showrooms and dealers for agricultural inputs. Of the around 250 shops, nearly 20 to 25 per cent were owned by Rajasthanis. Most of the shops hired local workers and few from surrounding villages. Sanjeli was the main market centre for all types of goods for 52 villages/ hamlets located around it and even as far as Santrampur and Limkheda. Even though Sanjeli functioned as the service/market centre, it was not an attractive destination for jobs for workers from surrounding villages.

Apart from retail trade, engagement in transportation activities, mainly autos, trucks, jeeps and tempos was a major activity, that provided some employment to workers from nearby villages. A few commuting workers were also engaged as carpenters and in sand mining—that is largely an illegal activity. Around five per cent of the households had members engaged in tertiary activities, e.g. as doctors, engineers, lawyers. However, most of these professionals were practicing outside the village. Around ten per cent of the household-heads were teachers (who have been trained outside as there is no college in the town).

There was absence of household based industries in the town. Under the SGSY a few *mandalis* for small savings were formed but these did not undertake economic activity. A starch manufacturing unit existed in the 1960s, that had shut down due to labour problems. Earlier there were also a few rice mills. There were no small or medium scale factories or any GIDC in the vicinity. It was felt that with adequate support from government and training there was potential for small businesses and industries. It was mentioned that few household based industries existed on paper to take the government benefits but were not functioning.

Agriculture and irrigation: Primary crops cultivated were maize, rice, pulses, chickpea and vegetables for own consumption during the kharif season. Agriculture was largely seasonal, as it was rain fed. The main source of irrigation was ground water. Nearly 70 to 80 per cent of the farmers had dug wells that worked with diesel pumps. Water table existed at around 50 feet (300 feet for borewells, depending on the rain in the last season). Farmers were reportedly applying for electricity connections, however due to irregular supply faced difficulties. The electric substation was located nearly 25 km away. In the instance of a fault villagers faced electricity break for 4 to 5 hours at a stretch. The residents opined that since Sanjeli was now taluka centre, it required its own substation.

In 1975 canal lift irrigation was introduced through Chamaria, which led to double cropping. Currently there was no major surface irrigation scheme to serve the region. There was a micro-irrigation scheme called "Kaliyia hill dam" scheme, but lacked water due to drought conditions. It catered to around three villages in the vicinity (Sanjeli, Pratappura, Pisanamuwada, Chamaria). The proposed Bharasimala lift irrigation scheme was not implemented, and there was no water lifting. Agriculture had not seen any major technological innovations, apart from increased use of inputs, mechanization, seeds. There were hardly any sprinkler or drip irrigation systems in the town. Micro irrigation, it was felt was not suitable for rice and maize, but the technology was conducive to cotton, castor and horticultural crops that were not grown in the region. However, due to better extension activity, credit delivery and market/price information was reported. In Sanjeli cultivators are mainly marginal and small farmers with average land holding size of around 0–2 hectare. It was felt during the discussion that farmers preferred non-farm work, as agriculture was under-developed and there were limited irrigation facilities. With irrigation development migrants could be retained.

There was an APMC that catered to the entire taluka. The farmers reported getting good price for their produce here. There were no post-harvest facilities, e.g. storage or processing activities in or around the town. Hardly any impact of rural development schemes was visible in terms of creation of infrastructure in Sanjeli. The total sanitation campaign was not making much dent. Schemes related to drip irrigation, swatchta abhiyan etc. were not implemented due to rampant corruption at lower levels and lack of adequate monitoring. MNREGA was not very popular and hardly any village level infrastructure was created under the scheme. A few instances of pond deepening activity prior to monsoons being undertaken under MNREGA were cited. In Sanjeli MNREGA was viewed largely as riddled with corruption.

Statutory status: The town does not satisfy the population criteria to be designated as a Nagar Panchayat. The major question raised was that till the town expanded in population it could not acquire a statutory status, even though it was felt that the town would definitely be better off if statutory status was given. The potential benefits were cited to be:

- More grants, development funds would help in tiding over the fund related problems for development purposes, particularly for the creation of amenities i.e. education and infrastructure creation (drainage, sewage, cleanliness), solid waste management and water supply. Once Gram Panchayat was converted in Nagar Palika/municipality, it would have a better resource base to engage personnel for conservancy, garbage collection etc.
- Implementation of town development schemes would facilitate planned growth of the town through proper enforcement of building by-laws. Even though the taxes would increase, the people expressed their willingness to pay if development could be stepped up.
- Provision of better health care facilities and also better connectivity would ne enabled. Education facilities would be stepped up as presently there was absence of colleges or training facilities.

Some disadvantages were also cited, mainly that the taxes would increase and addition of new taxes would raise the burden i.e. road and street light tax, increase in property tax. There was apprehension that the corruption level would increase with the number of government employees in the Nagar Palika. It was also felt that criminal activities and related social problems would be exacerbated.

Some household level observations related to enhanced urbanism were, mainly that the people in the town were incurring more expenses on construction of houses, renovation and upgradation. Overall expenditure on consumer durables had increased- an impact of urban influence. Residents also reported increase in conspicuous consumption during marriages, birth and death ceremonies. There were no major changes in social customs as people had to maintain their social stature. Certain communities like Patels were witnessing some changes in lifestyles. Food habits were changing due to changes in the life style over the years. However, there was increase in levels of education and awareness related to rural development schemes and health related problems.

Main Issues

Agriculture was largely seasonal, and ground water was depleting. *Gauchar* land was reportedly totally encroached. A lot of construction activity was being carried out on the *gaucher*, which was a problem for the poor farmers.

Lack of the small and large scale enterprises: There was absence of industries and any employment generating activities, coupled with seasonalilty in agriculture. It was felt that with encouragement from government agencies manufacturing/processing activity could create employment opportunities, thereby reducing poverty.

Gap between the rich and poor had widened: Due to lack of employment opportunities the gap between the rich and poor had increased. Largest section of workers were engaged in farm related work (labour) and earning wages of only about Rs. 150–200/day.

Lack of solid waste management: Lack of proper garbage collection facility and solid waste disposal was reported. In Sanjeli solid waste disposal was a pressing concern as households, commercial establishments and institutions disposed solid waste on streets, in drains, open spaces and nearby water-bodies. This had resulted in dirty streets and clogged drains. Large heaps of garbage all over were glaring vilifying the environment. Further there was overcrowding, noise pollution and encroachment of public spaces by retail activity.

Pollution: Water pollution was a major problem due to open drains and lack of sewerage system. There are only 50–70 households with sewerage connections and the rest had open drainage, exacerbating public health issues. Sanjeli is a market/service center, and the main market area was facing explosive growth and illegal encroachment. Traffic and congestion have increased over the years, causing severe noise pollution.

Corruption was common here, affecting implementation of all rural development schemes, even for taking the benefit of schemes such as IAY etc. It was reported that under MNREGA work initiated, including construction of check dams, farm ponds etc., existed on paper, even though on ground hardly any work was initiated. Completed works were of poor quality. The village had mixed social/economic classes so there was diversity of customs. Social evils such as alcoholism etc. were more prevalent in certain communities.

Location Near Highway/Delhi–Mumbai Industrial Corridor

Kanodar, Banaskantha District
Kanodar census town is located in Banaskantha district in the north Gujarat region. Kanodar has historically been known for handloom production. It is located along the National Highway 8 and it is about 11 km

south from district headquarters of Palanpur, and 116 km from the state capital of Gandhinagar. It is a Muslim dominated village (80%), only 20 per cent of population comprises of Hindus. Maximum population is engaged in non-agricultural activities i.e. services activities (traders, teachers, engineers and doctors) and in repairs (automobile garage, besides manufacturing of auto parts). In this town each house had access to tapped water, and nearly 80 per cent also had drainage facility. Large number of residents had migrated aboard for education and employment. Land rates were high (around 2.5 crore per hectare) due to its location along the national highway. The town is a major hub of automobile repairs (especially Mahindra jeep), body works and manufacture of small auto- ancillary parts.

Migration: In the last decade large number of migrants, around 90–100 families, have come from other states mainly from Uttar Pradesh, Bihar and Rajasthan. Migrant population was working as causal labour/ service in garages. Nearly 200–250 daily commuters from the surrounding villages also worked in the local garages, factories and hotels etc. Migrants were engaged in agriculture as tenants on leased-in land. Nearly 70 to 80 commuters belonging to Kanodar were also working in Palanpur and Chhapi in auto repairs garages/workshops. In addition nearly 150 or more teachers, bank employees, doctors and other professionals commute daily to Palanpur for job/service, besides the students enrolled in the high schools and colleges outside the town.

Infrastructure: Under the MNREGA scheme work for constructing roads, pond deepening and farm bunds was undertaken. MNREGA was not quite successful in this town because the wage rate (Rs. 150/day) is lower as compared to casual labour charges (Rs. 250–300/day) obtained in other non-farm jobs. Labourers were hence not interested to work under MNREGA. Under the RURBAN scheme several village infrastructure development projects were implemented.

The town boasted of thirteen *anganwadis*, four primary schools, one secondary school and an Arts & Commerce College. In Kanodar various types of health facilities exist, notably two government hospitals (30 beds and 2 doctors), a maternity hospital, six private nursing homes and two primary health centres. Diseases related to heart have reportedly increased in the town. Bank branches were present (SBI, Dena Bank, Banaskantha District Cooperative Bank) along with two co-operative societies (a milk co-operative society, and a primary agro-credit cooperative society). The main arterial, collector and distributor roads were pucca even though the local and approach roads were semi pucca.

Economic activities: Two decades ago weaving was the primary source of income, but due to government policies and maintenance expenses of handlooms, the weaving activity has declined considerably (a sharp fall from 500–600 to only 10–12 families operating handlooms in the past two decades or so).
Various tertiary sector activities predominate viz.

- Retail (provision, hardware, consumer durables, garments stores, mobile repairing etc., tailors (25), beautician/saloon (15), laundry (5)).
- Real estate agent/builders (10–12 in number)
- Money Lending
- Doctors (82),engineers (100), lawyers(5), government teachers (250)
- Hotels and Restaurants (6)
- NGOs (4)
- Charted accountants (2–3)

There were more than 200 garages and auto-body part-manufacturing units in Kanodar. Lately a biscuit factory and a chocolate factory catering to markets in Africa have come up though local entrepreneurship. There was a submersible pump-manufacturing unit with its head office in Mumbai.

Decline of weaving: Most of the weaver households were linked to The Gujarat Haathshaal and Hastkala Vikas Nigam Ltd (located on the highway at Palanpur). The Nigam provided raw materials and bought the cloth produced by the weavers. The price of the cloth produced was cited as insufficient by the weavers, as the cost of loom, its maintenance and parts (spindles etc.) was high, and raw material was expensive. The weaving households hired workers, but the labour charges were high (Rs. 100 to 150/day or Rs. 9/meter of material woven) which ate into the profit margin significantly. Although labourers were available locally, the wage rates were quite high.

No major benefits were received by the weavers from the government, except skill development training, and some subsidy for implements; the raw material supplied was inadequate. Weavers complained that mills/factories located in cities were helped by government in terms of marketing support and creation of market linkages, but not so with the home based weavers in Kanodar. The local *bunkars* or weavers were not engaged in any fairs/ melas, handloom expos or other promotional efforts of the government.

The weavers did benefit from product reservation (procurement of *shaal* and towels produced by them by government offices/agencies). Police, government hospitals, offices etc. approached the weavers directly to purchase their products. Weavers were selling their products to private hospitals, and traders in Palanpur too, besides the government requisition. Some also took up orders for traders in Kalupur and Naroda in Ahmedabad.

It was also found that the subsidy for forming cooperatives was not available, despite some efforts by local NGOs. Although 24 hours electricity was available, it did not translate to major economic gains due to other problems besetting the weavers. Furthermore, there was not much product diversification, and there was lack of design inputs and market interface. There was absence of organisation/cooperatives of weavers. No NGO involvement was observed for the revival of the local crafts. Due to these reasons traditional handloom weaving was a dying sector in Kanodar and was being replaced by auto/engineering works.

Agriculture: Most of the farmers were marginal and small, only few farmers had large or medium holdings. In all only five per cent of the population was engaged in farming activity, rest of the workers were engaged in government jobs, secondary sector activities and business activity/retail sector. Earlier farmers obtained groundwater at depths of 200–300 feet but with severe groundwater depletion, water for irrigation even at depths of 600–700 feet was becoming scarce. Due to severe scarcity of water only a miniscule section of the population was engaged in agriculture. Drip irrigation was being adopted. Main crops cultivated were wheat, castor, horticultural crops. Over the years there has been diversification from cereals to vegetables, but there is a near absence of any agro-processing facilities in and around the village. Banas dairy collects the milk from the households.

The conditions for growth of non-farm sector were lack of surface irrigation facilities, increasing depth of groundwater and high cost involved in digging bore wells that had severely impeded any growth in agriculture, and forced people to diversify to non-farm occupations. Farmers also reported inadequate prices received for crops cultivated. In addition Kanodar being a Muslim dominated village, the population possessed considerable traditional skills that fostered growth of repairs and mechanical jobs.

Environment and land: Kanodar was facing falling water table accompanied by increasing salinity of water. Even though the soil is fertile the ground water level is fast receding due to natural reasons. The auto parts industry is not much polluting. All the secondary activities located along the highway were not supplied water by the Panchayat, so face a problem as the small establishments were unable to dig borewells unlike the medium scale factories. However, use of firewood causes air pollution. The town environment was also deteriorating due to inadequate sewerage and absence of waste water collection systems.

There was a construction boom around Kanodar. The most pressing problem was that builders failed to follow the building norms in the new housing societies that were coming up in the vicinity. NA conversions were happening only for residential/retail purposes (nearly 2 to 3 instances were reported each year). The residential societies followed no building norms/bylaws and there was complete absence of land use planning or advance planning for infrastructure facilities. This was considered to be virtually a ticking time bomb, given the scale of real estate development and residential activity around Kanodar.

Statutory status: Residents and *talati* etc. felt that since Kanodar had all the facilities required, there was no need for a statutory town status. In fact the taxation for service delivery may increase and designation as nagar panchayat may lead to increased burden of work and corruption. There could be environmental fallouts too. If the Gram Panchayat was converted into Nagar Palika main disadvantages envisaged were:

- Increase in taxation i.e. road tax, water tax and street light tax, along with rising level of development.
- There could be adverse fallouts at social level, including rise in incidence of robbery and crime.
- Corruption may increase at the local level.
- Lack of transparency.

Problems/issues: Kanodar census town appeared quite clean and most of the amenities were present. Employment creation in secondary and services sectors attracted workers. In this town no major issues were reported.

- There was no significant impact of MNREGA because wages offered were less (around Rs. 120/day), due to which workers preferred other work that fetched higher earnings (Rs. 300–400/day).
- Builders disregarded building byelaws due to absence of regulation; construction limit was up to four floors.
- Health issues: Diabetes and joint related problems were reported due to salinity in underground water.

- Shortage of skilled workers was reported, especially by the engineering units.
- Lack of road facility was also noted by the workshops; the main RCC road was not in a good condition. Moreover the engineering units faced problems related to water and electricity; gram panchayat was paid taxes but services were inadequate. Some of the units reported that infrastructure for piped water was not developed along the highway, where most of the units were located. It was also reported that small industries were getting inadequate support from the government. The taxation policy was complicated for the micro and small scale units and lack of managerial capability was emerging in the expanding repairs/auto parts sector. Migrant workers were preferred in the engineering/repair units as they lacked bargaining capabilities, were needy and hence hard working, unlike the locals.

Chhiri, Valsad District

Chhiri census town belongs to the south Gujarat agro-climatic region. Chhiri is located in Pardi taluka of Valsad district. It lies 32 km south of the district headquarters of Valsad, and three km away from Vapi. Daman and Diu, Amli and Silvassa are the nearby urban centres. Chhiri falls on the border of Valsad district and Diu. Revenue area of the town is 402 hectares, having a population of 18,829 (Census 2011). The town is surrounded by industrial activity and is located along the National Highway 8. Chhiri is a major destination for migrant workers from Bihar, UP, Rajasthan and Maharashtra, coming to work in the industries of south Gujarat. There were around 114 BPL families.

Migration: In-migration to this town was very high, nearly 80 per cent of the residents were migrants, and were engaged in construction activities and as factory workers in units in the GIDC. Labourers working in the surrounding industrial areas (in and around Vapi) also resided in Chhiri due to availability of affordable rental houses and other facilities. It was reported that while the local population was 18,829, nearly 55 to 60,000 residents were migrant industrial/construction workers or pretty traders/businessmen from other states. The village had 18 *falias*/neighbourhoods, of which only seven housed the local population; in the remaining migrant workers resided. About two per cent of the households or members have migrated out (either abroad, or Bombay, Vapi, Valsad, Navsari) for the purpose of education and employment.

Vapi is an industrial hub located close to Chhiri, and offers most of the employment opportunities. Since Chhiri census town is home to largely migrant population, most of the problems regarding service availability/ access to amenities have been created over the years. It was reported that the rural development funds available are insufficient, as funds were allotted on the basis of population while Chhiri abounds with illegal encroachments and settlements of migrant workers who were not counted as the village residents.

Land acquisition: In 1980–1981 agricultural land was acquired by the GIDC from around six villages viz., Karwad, Rata, Kochrwa, Dungara, Chharawada and Chhiri. Land acquired by GIDC rendered many people asset less and without adequate livelihoods. The GIDC acquired agricultural land at the rate of around Rs. 5 to 6 lakhs per acre, at land prices decided as per the government *jantri*. At the time of land acquisition around 97 per cent of the farmers were paid compensation, while the remaining approached the courts as they were not paid adequately for their land. Nearly 80 per cent of the village revenue land was transferred to non-agriculture uses, and was developed for industries.

The current price of the land was around Rs. 15 lakh per acre. When the land was acquired, the District Panchayat approved the NA conversion but water, roads and sanitation facility were not provided. With increased industrial development and creation of employment opportunities, immigrants were attracted on a large scale. Presently there is absence of any land use planning. Since there was no controlling authority, illegal construction activity was happening without the implementation of any building codes and regulation. This caused mismanagement and haphazard development of the town. Chhiri was witnessing considerable residential and retail sector development. Land prices were increasing and locals were getting higher incomes from hiring out the residences. Construction of double storied buildings was allowed.

Slum population: In Chhiri more than 5000 residents (chiefly migrants) dwelled in slum like conditions, in semi-pucca or kutcha habitations that lacked tap water facility, drainage and sewerage connections. No scheme existed for housing for economic weaker sections despite the large presence of industrial workers. Moreover migrants were not entitled to benefits of the government schemes (e.g. for housing etc.) as they did not have permanent residency and held the identification of their place of origin. Overall health condition of the migrant workers was poor as is evident from their life expectancy of around 65–70 years. In addition in the *falias* (mohallas) having migrant workers, many social ills prevailed i.e. crime, robbery, alcoholism.

Infrastructure: Overall there was inadequate infrastructure development, lack of proper drainage facility, existence of open sewerage, even though there is very little open defection. Tap water supply (only 1440 connections) was provided with the help from GIDC. Under the Swajal Dhara Yojana drinking water facility was made available with the beneficiaries contributing ten per cent of the cost. GIDC has also contributed for provision of drinking water facility. Internal paved roads existed. Internal roads also were developed with the residents' contribution. For solid waste collection Gram panchayat had deployed tractors and hired 15–20 sweepers. Bin facility was provided to each house under the Swatch Bharat Mission. The Panchayat had acquired funds for sewerage lines and construction work would be initiated soon, it was reported. Solar street lights were installed by the Panchayat with the help from GIDC. There was lack of bank facilities, as only one bank branch existed. Most of the farmers sold their produce at the APMC located at Vapi.

Although the MNERGA scheme is operational there was not much demand for work under the scheme as industrial wages were nearly Rs. 300 per day, much higher than the MNERGA rate of Rs. 165 per day. No major impact of MNREGA on infrastructure creation was visible.

Economic activity: The main economic activity was work in industries that had led to high income levels. Industries are both large scale (e.g. Micro ink and Bayer industry) and small scale (mainly units of engineering and plastic industry). The "Vapi Industrial Estate" was started by GIDC in 1967, and has spread to 11.4 square kilometres (4.4 sq. mi) having 1400 industrial units, the majority of which are small-scale units. Valsad is an industrial base for chemicals, textiles and paper & paper pulp. Since 1980s textile and chemicals have been the major sectors of investments and employment in the district. The district has also emerged as the horticulture hub of the state. Over 300 medium and large scale units are concentrated in Vapi, that drive the district's economic growth. One of Asia's largest Common Effluent Treatment Plant (CETP) is located at Vapi, owned by the Vapi Waste & Effluent Management Company and promoted by Vapi Industrial Association.

Around 60 per cent of the population of Chhiri worked in the GIDC industrial estate; nearly three-quarters were employed as daily wagers, while only 20 per cent were engaged in regular/salaried jobs. Residents commuted to Vapi, Valsad, Mumbai, Dadra Nagar Haveli, Sari Industrial area for employment. Twenty to twenty five per cent of the residents were also engaged in services, businesses and real estate and construction activity. Service sector workers included workers in salon & parlours (16), street vendors, tailors (30), laundry (10–15), and brokers (15). There was a large presence of retail and small businesses, showrooms etc. that were run by the residents of Chhiri.

Agriculture: In Chhiri more than 90 per cent of the population was engaged in non-farm sector i.e. industry and service sector. Only around 2–3 per cent of the population was engaged in farming related activities. Rice and mango were the major crops cultivated.

Statutory status: The residents indicated their willingness to convert the town into Nagarpalika. They were ready to pay higher taxes for the development of the town and creation of urban facilities. It was opined that service delivery and infrastructure related problems i.e. better road facility, solid waste management system and sewerage connection, could be solved if Chhiri gram panchayat was re-designated as a nagar palika. Presently Chhiri lacked a college; after attaining nagar panchayat status, it was felt that education institutes, health care facilities etc., would be enhanced. For advanced medical care residents travelled to either Vapi or Valsad. With change in status, it was also felt that funds under urban slum rehabilitation and redevelopment schemes could be secured. Disadvantages of change in status cited were increase in level of tax, new taxes, such as for road and street lights, increase in the corruption levels and increase in crime and social evils.

Main Problems

- **Health:** Chhiri residents faced several health issues i.e. malnutrition due to micro-nutrient deficiency, morbidity (tuberculosis, malaria) due to open drainage, unclean and unhygienic living environment.
- **Pollution:** Development of the industrial area has impacted on health, water, and living environment. The unmanaged and scattered growth of industries is causing difficulties in providing necessary infrastructure. After industrialization village environment has changed and various problems have cropped up, such as air and water pollution due to the presence of chemical industries. Rapid

industrialization had led to employment generation, but resulted in unplanned growth of the town and there has been a steady shift in demographic profile of the region. Urbanization with poor infrastructure development has led to most of the environmental issues.

- **Lack of amenities and inadequate housing:** The town dwellers and local authority opined that there were insufficient funds for development due to high rate of in migration and illegal encroachment, leading to problems related to garbage collection, existence of open drains, inadequate and kutcha internal roads that had a detrimental impact on the living environment. There was absence of state transport bus facility and private transportation dominated. Due to high rate of in-migration, some also reported housing scarcity. A large section resides in slum like housing conditions. *Falias* housing the migrant industrial workers stand out in terms of high levels of pollution, lack of basic needs, over-crowded living conditions and high population density.

Industrial District

Vaghodia, Vadodara District

Vaghodia is a census town in the Vaghodia taluka in Vadodara district belonging to the central Gujarat agro-climatic region. It is located 28 km towards the east from district headquarters of Vadodara and 149 km from state capital of Gandhinagar. Vaghodia is the taluka headquarter and is bordered by Dabhoi talukas in the south, Halol taluka towards the north, Sankheda taluka in the east, Vadodara taluka in the west. Vadodara, Padra, Karjan, Rajpipla are the nearby urban centres.

Between the years 1975 to 1980, in the first phase government acquired land from the farmers, at the rate of Rs. 10,000–15,000 per vigha, and in the second phase at Rs. 30,000–35,000 per vigha. About 1100 farmers' land was acquired (a large section reportedly did not receive adequate compensation). The GIDC established its estate in 1985. Vaghodia Industries Association was formed in 1991. Around 393 hectares were declared as Industrial Notified Area under the Government Gazette in 1997 by the state government. The GIDC estate has 3000 plots but houses around 1200 large, medium and small units related mainly to production of rubber, plastics, pharmaceuticals, packaging material, electrical, engineering and agrochemicals goods. The estate employs over 15,000 people, having a turnover of around Rs. 8000 crores, and exports goods worth Rs. 1200 crores. GIDC provides roads, electricity and water facility to the units. The estate is developed with all facilities having road length of nearly 25 kms. It houses leading industries like Apollo tyres, Gujarat cycles, Munjal Auto etc. After Vaghodia GIDC was declared industrial notified area, all the industries started paying taxes to the Vadodara Municipal Corporation, adversely affecting the revenue base of the Vaghodia Panchayat. An R.O Plant is proposed for the Vaghodia taluka in the census town.

Private estates like R R Kabel, Siddhi Infrastructure have also come up in Vaghodia; these are a substantial source of revenue generation for the Gram Panchayat. It was mentioned that overall up to 2000 industrial units were located in and around Vaghodia.

Development Path: Land acquisition → GIDC → Industrial growth/in-migration → Growth in educational institutions → Increase in health services → Growth of census town → Inclusion in Vadodara UA.

The total population of Vaghodia is 17,184 (4200 households, Census 2011). However, the actual population is 35,000–40,000 due to in-migration, largely of population engaged in non-agricultural activities, notably as industrial workers and service sector workers (traders, retailers, vendors, teachers and doctors). It is envisaged that Vaghodia will soon be included in the Vadodara Municipal Corporation.

Migration: Vaghodia is a very attractive destination for migrants due to availability of industrial employment opportunities in the GIDC, presence of educational institutions and health facilities. With the establishment of Vaghodia GIDC and other institutions, migration level in the past decades had increased. Currently there are 20 societies housing migrants mainly from Uttar Pradesh, Rajasthan and Bihar, that contribute to around 60 per cent of the total population. Daily commuters from Vadodara also formed a significant share of the workers in the industries. Only 2–3 per cent residents had migrated out to Vadodara for better education, job opportunities and better life style. Around 45 families had migrated abroad and 665 to other states. Reportedly 163 students had left the town for higher studies.

While GIDC is the prominent source of employment, the town had a large section of workers engaged in service sector activities, viz. lawyers (20), nurses (20), tailors (15), fabricators (03), hair salon/beauty parlours (15), laundry (05), show rooms (03), furniture shops (14), TV etc. repairing shops (12). There were 100 to 110 street vendors who paid Rs. 5 per day to the Panchayat.

Infrastructure: The literacy rate in the town was on an average 70–80 per cent. Recently the town had attracted several institutions of higher education notably, Parul University, Sumandeep Vidyapith and SBKS Medical Institute & Research Centre. There were ten private hospitals, and a PHC. The town had a post office, an APMC and three *wadis*/community centres. Adoption of urban lifestyle was also revealed from the fact that the town had 1708 households having LPG connections.

Revenue collection by the Panchayat was from 70 per cent of the households, and it was stated that 30 per cent of the residents did not pay taxes as they were labourers and poor. The paucity of funds and its administration had adversely affected the service delivery in Vaghodia. The monthly expenditure of the Gram Panchayat was up to Rs. 6.5 lakhs. Annual rural development grants were approx. Rs. 15 lakhs. However, the actual requirement of resources was much higher (officials quoted as Rs. 80 lakhs) due to the pressure of population. After Vaghodia GIDC became a notified area, industries started paying taxes to the Vadodara Municipal Corporation. Officials informed that taxes to Vaghodia gram panchayat had been unpaid since 2008, despite repeated pleas made to the GIDC and taluka officials.

Panchayat officials opined that due to paucity of resources, village development was severely affected and problems of service delivery abounded. Environmental deterioration was glaring as only 400 households had sewerage connections. Only 50 per cent of the drainage facility was completed. Solid waste collection was the other issue as the Panchayat did not have resources to hire sweepers for door to door collection. Though there were two overhead water tanks, one was in a state of disrepair and could not be used. Panchayat had obtained the sanction for one overhead water tank with capacity of 14 lakh litres in the current year. People of Vaghodia welcomed the re-designation of town to a Nagar Palika/municipal status, if that would increase the resource base and enable creation of better amenities and facilities.

Agriculture and irrigation: Only 25 per cent of the households were engaged in farming. Amongst the cultivators, small farmers numbered 144 (1.5 to 2 *vigha*), while 165 and 657 farmers were of medium and large sizes (30 to 40 *vigha*) respectively. The main crops cultivated were rice, wheat, pulses, cotton and vegetables (onion). Canal water through the Dev dam was the main source of irrigation, but was currently dry due to drought conditions. This scheme irrigated around 98 villages. Vaghodia farmers were not receiving water from the Narmada canal despite its proximity to the village (8 kms away). It was learnt that nearly 58 villages could benefit if government provided Narmada canal water.

Chandrapur, Rajkot District
Chandrapur census town is located in the North Saurashtra agro-climatic region of Gujarat, falling in Wankaner taluka in Rajkot district. In the year 2013 Morbi was formed as a separate district. All the census towns falling in Morbi area were merged with MWUDA (Morbi-Wankaner Urban Development Authority). The two cities were proposed to be linked as they have proximate location and possess economic linkages due to the presence of the large ceramic cluster. The census towns that had merged with Morbi Municipal Corporation in 2015 were Saktsanala, Ravapara, Trajpar and Mahendranagar. Chandrapur is located 46 kms north of the district headquarters at Rajkot and 217 km from the state capital Gandhinagar. Distance between Morbi and Chandrapur is 33 kms, while it is only 4 kms away from Wankaner town.

Around 150 acres of land had already been converted to non-agricultural uses, largely for housing and commercial purposes. Chandrapur was proposed to be merged into MUDA (Morbi-Wankaner Urban Development Authority) in 2012, although it was finally merged in 2017. The Gram Panchayat reported total revenue earnings of up to Rs. 8 lakh/annum (mainly through housing tax at Rs. 300–500/year and water tax at Rs. 200/year). Chandrapur was divided in two parts—Chandrapur proper and Bhatia Society.

Migration: Around 10 to 15 per cent of the residents in the town were migrants from Rajasthan, UP, MP, Bihar as well as surrounding areas. This was induced by Chandrapur's proximity to the industrial belt of Morvi-Wankaner and Rajkot. Due to the presence of industries (ceramic, sanitary ware, wall clocks, CFL bulbs etc. in Morbi), job opportunities attracted migrant workers from other parts of Gujarat (largely from the tribal dominated areas). Majority of the clock units in Morbi engaged females from the surrounding villages. Around 20–25 per cent of the families in Chandrapur were commuters to the above locations working in industrial jobs. Around 20 to 25 residents were engaged in teaching and in bank jobs and commuted to Rajkot and Morvi. Also around 30 to 40 families from the town had migrated to Rajkot, Ahmedabad and Surat for better job prospects. Daily commuters travelled from Chandrapur to Toova (Ceramic industry), Amalsar, Talavdi, Kankot, Sindhavadar, Rajkot and Morbi (15–20 kms from Chandrapur).

Under the watershed programme two check dams were constructed in Chandrapur. Under the RURBAN mission, work of sewerage connections was taken up however, only 60 per cent of the households were provided drainage connectivity. Thirty per cent of the population was served by door to door garbage collection service. Due to availability of employment in industries and agriculture, no noticeable impact of MNREGA scheme was reported in terms of both employment generation and creation of assets.

Economic Activities

Industry: Chandarpur had several (around 25) small scale manufacturing units, including ginning mills (15), oil mills (2), looms (8 to 10), and engineering workshops. There were also a few poultry farms. However, in these units most of the labour employed is from out of the town, due to absence of skilled manpower within the town. Around 8–10 families carried out power loom weaving at household level. Samay quartz—a clock unit (located on SH 22) provided employment to women from Chandrapur (the company also provided transportation facility). The agricultural wage rate was Rs. 200/per day, so people preferred to work in industries where the wages were higher (between Rs. 300–400/- per day). Residents also worked in the industrial units located in and around Morbi and Wankaner. Service sector workers were engaged in activities such as, real estate and construction, trading, tailoring, beauty parlours, laundry, teachers, lawyers, doctors, street vendors, provision stores and food outlets.

Agriculture: Agriculture was a dominant activity and the chief crops cultivated were cotton, groundnut, *jowar, bajra*, wheat. In kharif season, 90 per cent of land was devoted to cotton, during rabi 30 to 40 per cent of the land was sown with wheat and *jowar*. Cumin and fodder crops were cultivated during the summer season. Out of 3140 households in the town, 321 families were completely reliant on cultivation related activities. There were 45 large farmers, 200 small farmers, five medium farmers and 100 each of landless farming families and marginal land holders. The town was served by an APMC.

Agricultural production was very low; lack of irrigation availability was cited to be the main constraint. There were two check dams maintained by the villagers, but water was available only for 3 to 4 months. The region is mainly dependent on ground water but the water level was continuously receding. Presently water is available at 300–400 feet and hence expenses incurred in extraction of ground water made farming prohibitive. Farmers also mentioned that only eight hours of electricity supply for irrigation was not sufficient. Moreover, in Chandarpur availability of timely and affordable agricultural labour was also an issue. The bigger farmers hired workers from out of the village for jobs such as cotton picking, as the local labourers were not interested to work in farm related jobs. The farm wages were very low while there were higher paying industrial jobs available easily. Farmers reported increased use of fertilizer and pesticide in the recent years.

Statutory status: Due to proximity to Morbi and Wankaner, the merger of Chandrapur with the Morbi-Wankaner Urban development authority is imminent. In the focus group discussions, the main point raised was that under urban administration, the resource base of the local authority and development grants/funds may increase, aiding the creation of village level amenities and infrastructure and institutions of higher education and health. It was also felt that with urban influence the housing conditions of the residents may improve and other services such as banks, ATM, markets etc. may improve.

It was suggested that along with enhanced development, the taxation base too may increase particularly property tax, road tax, water tax and tax on streetlights etc. Further with urbanism, it was possible that social crimes, robbery and others may get exacerbated. It was feared that with reduced transparency the corruption level in the administrative set up may rise.

At the household level, discussions revealed that in the past decade or so, urban influences had manifested in changes in life style and food habits. Urban culture was being adopted and was reflected in the changing choices of clothing, housing and other consumption habits. There was increased importance of education, especially women's education, although the level of girls education continued to be quite low in certain communities e.g. *Bharwad* and other backward castes.

Within the last couple of years physical infrastructure had improved in the town i.e. banks had set up branches. Reforms in service delivery it was stated, including dedicated electricity supply for 24 hours have been beneficial, giving an impetus to the local non-farm economic activities.

Problems/Issues

Pollution: In Chandarpur within 10–15 years the number of industries had increased leading to increase in the pollution levels. Vehicles have increased contributing to noise and air pollution.

Education: A large segment of children were going to private schools because of better education standards; students going to government schools belonged largely to Muslim community and other backward categories only. Educational facilities needed to be improved, particularly for those who could not afford private schooling and needed to be made more affordable.

Lack of amenities was glaring, particularly RCC roads and sewerage facility. Under the RURBAN project only 25–30 per cent of the households were provided sewerage connections. Around 60–70 per cent of the population had tap water connections, and the rest of the households were dependent on hand pumps and community taps for potable water.

Open defecation: In Chandarpur the incidence of open defecation was high as compared with the other census towns surveyed. Sewerage facility was poorly developed and individual toilet facility was rare, with nearly 30 per cent of the people not having toilet facility at all. There were no community toilets in the town.

Labour: In the local ginning industry, only female workers were interested to work. The male workers lacked interest due to long working hours (10–12 hours), and preferred to work in other industries besides engaging in agriculture related jobs. During cotton harvesting season, farm labour fetched wages as high as Rs. 600–700/day, based of the work quantity and quality. Within Chandarpur, availability of skilled labour was a problem, as reported by the industries. Nearly all the units surveyed reported lack of skilled local labour. People were not interested to work at the current wages and for long hours demanded. Most of the units were running with migrant workers.

Antarjal, Kutch District

Antarjal is a census town in Gandhidham taluka of Kachchh district in Gujarat. It is located 53 kms east of the district headquarters of Bhuj, and 10 kms from Adipur. Adipur was established as a rehabilitation colony for Sindhis after partition and land belonging to Antarjal was also acquired for the purpose. Gandhidham, Bhuj, Jamnagar are the nearby urban centres.

The town had nearly 1000 BPL households. Within five years it is proposed that Antarjal will be merged with the Gandhidham Mahanagar palika (UA). Around five towns will be the part of the proposed Mahanagar Palika i.e. Gandhidham, Adipur, Anterjal, Sinai, Idana, Gadpadar and Mithirohal.

Land

Post-earthquake → Taxbenefits → Industrial growth → Increase in land price →   Land conversion → Construction activity → In-migration.

Post-earthquake incentives for industrial development in Kachchh and emergence of industries in the sorrounding areas were the major contributing factors for the growth of Antarjal. In the post-earthquake rehabilitation phase, land prices increased manifold, industries were set up due to government's policies for industrial development of the district, and this led to increase of (in) migration levels from across the country. The land prices rose from Rs. 1000 to Rs. 1 lakh per acre during this period. A lot of land trading is currently taking place; real estate developers acquire land directly from the farmers for development of housing complexes for workers employed in the industries in the region. Port development had also played a vital role in the development of Antarjal. Most of the land conversion in Antarjal has happened for housing activity/societies. No village revenue land has been converted for industrial uses. Apparently land acquisition problem is not an issue here and most of it is voluntary in nature.

Migration: The town attracted a large number of migrant settlers from Bihar, UP and Rajasthan. Seventy per cent of the residents were migrants employed in the industries in the vicinity. Due to this real estate development was one of the major non-farm economic activities, and had received tremendous fillip during the post-earthquake reconstruction phase. A large number of residential societies were developing or existing within the radius 10 to 12 km. Around 20 per cent of households had members that had out-migrated for employment opportunities to Adipur, Gandhidham, Anjar and Bhuj. Around 500 people were reportedly daily commuters to Adipur for education and occupation.

Antarjal has a government school with a student strength of 600–700, but was up to 8th standard. There was no government high school and students were enrolled in English medium private schools, which abounded in Adipur. While private schooling has increased, girl students from poor families who could not afford to study in private schools dropped out after middle school. Despite presence of private educational facilities in the vicinity, transportation facilities were considered inadequate especially for girls to go to nearby towns to attend high school. The literacy rate had increased over the years and girls' education was also rising despite such problems. However, this is more visible amongst the upscale communities such as *Ahirs*. There were nearly twenty private schools located within the radius of 10 to 12 km of the town, and residents preferred to educate their children in these schools. It was reported that malnourishment was rampant amongst children belonging to the poor sections/labour classes.

Economic Activities

Agriculture: Only dry land agriculture was practised and the ground water level was quite low i.e. around 400–450 feet and for drinking water level is 1000–1200 feet. Monsoon crops, *jowar* (for fodder), and *bajra* were the major crops. Water scarcity prodded the conversion of agricultural land to non-agricultural uses, also spurred by the industrial growth and ports. There have been no major agricultural development initiatives in the recent years. Increasing soil salinity also posed a problem for agriculture.

People preferred to work in non-farm activities and not in agriculture due to scarcity of water and drought situation in the region. This coupled with existence of Kandla port and industrial development offered avenues to engage the residents. A large section of residents were also involved in traditional skills and crafts.

- Nearly 70 per cent of the females were engaged in traditional 'kutchi' handicrafts and weaving activities; and their activity was supported by NGOs and trusts that collected the hand crafted work of the women and marketed it. It was reported that the women earned up to Rs. 25 to 30,000 per month by engaging in this activity. The goods produced were exported to the major cities in Gujarat and outside through various marketing channels.
- Transportation sector (e.g. transport of goods like edible oils to- and fro-Kandla port to storage houses around KPT by trucks) was the other main traditional economic activity in the town due to its proximity to Kandla, Mundra and Tuna ports. While there was little local business/retail activity, local transportation (e.g. owners and drivers of chhakdas, besides truckers) abound. Antarjal was a major transport hub of Gandhidham taluka.
- The Kandla Free Trade Zone existed for the last 20–25 years. A large number of residents from Antarjal were working in 25 to 30 industries in the KFT zone and the ports. Main industries providing employment to the people of Antarjal were Renuka Sugar Pvt. Ltd, SAL steel, Shaifali Rolls (Steel), PSL Pipes, Well spun and IFFCO. A large number of women also worked in the factories in KFTZ. Several migrants working in these industries had also purchased houses/hired houses in and around Antarjal, contributing to the real estate boom.
- Antarjal itself had no factory, godown etc. though considerable residential development was taking place.
- In Antarjal only a few people were engaged in service sector i.e. doctors (2–3), military personnel (40–50), teachers (5), tailors (10–15) and beauty parlour and hair salons (7–8). Few lawyers, and computer related activities also exist. For most of the services, residents were dependent on Adipur.

Statutory status: People's life style had changed over the years, as seen through enhanced expenditure on eating out, clothing, vehicles, consumer durables, conspicuous consumption and aping each other. The expenditure on housing enhanced especially after the earthquake. No major changes in food habits were reported.

- A town planning scheme was reportedly existing, but was not operationalized as was not ratified by the Panchayat. This was because the government proposed to acquire land from the plot holders for roads etc. The scheme was still under implementation.
- Residents wanted the town to become a nagar panchayat as residents aspired to live in an urban area. Services and amenities are envisaged to increase with allocation of greater funds for urban development; it was believed that although tax liability was likely to rise, tax collection would also step up with the town attaining a statutory status.
- It was felt that although taxes would increase with NP status, but there would be assured livelihoods and increased incomes through the creation of more employment avenues.
- The problem of illegal encroachment and lack of building and construction norms would be tackled, and it was recognised as a major problem in the town.
- Land selling and conversion norms would be strengthened. Encroachment of *gaucher* was happening and other village land. It was believed that encroachment would reduce if NP status was attained.
- However, it was felt that with a town status level of corruption would rise. Functionaries will be unknown people and social networks will not function as in a gram panchayat. Moreover voice of poor people will not be heard.

Problems

- Environmental pollution was the main problem cited because of the increase in number of industrial units. However, no major health threat was reported except malnutrition amongst children belonging to poorer sections. It was felt that labour intensive but non-polluting industries should be promoted in the region.
- Alcoholism was prevalent amongst people engaged in the transportation sector. The acquisition of easy money after selling off land and plethora of livelihood opportunities was compounding the problem.

- A proper management system of garbage collection was lacking, even though gram panchayat had provided three wheelers for garbage collection.

Periphery of Urban Agglomeration/City

Mankuwa, Kutch District

Mankuva is a town in the Bhuj taluka of Kachchh district. It is located 14 km west of district headquarters of Bhuj. Bhuj, Mandvi, Adipur, Gandhidham are the nearby cities. Mankuva village is known as an NRI village, falling in the *chauvisi* area of Patels. More than ten per cent of the households (nearly 100) have members who are NRIs. The NRIs leased out their lands for different uses. Mankuva's total population is 11,975; only 711 families fall below the poverty line. Mankuwa Panchayat was awarded "The Gold Medal for the Best Gram Panchayat" in the year 2010–2011. In this town road connectivity was good, and nearly all amenities existed notably, street lights, bus stand and solid waste collection. After the earthquake Navjivan Trust constructed 125 houses for affected residents.

Migration: There was large-scale in-migration of workers to Mankuva (from UP, Bihar and even surrounding places), with the migrants staying in rented houses. There were daily commuters to the town too as it offered jobs in retail trade and other service sector activities. The town was an attractive destination for migrants and commuters. From Mankuva there were very little daily commuters to Bhuj for work; only around 100 persons commuted as construction workers, and in trade related jobs in Bhuj and other nearby villages. Nearly 25 households had members employed in government jobs, and commuted elsewhere for work/job.

Economic Activities

The revenue area was witnessing large scale changes in landuse pattern. Plotting of land for housing purposes was happening. Most of the population was engaged in non-farm activities, such as:

- Retail trade
- Casual labour (Construction and agriculture)
- Auto-rickshaw and other transport related activity
- Small scale service sector activities, such as traders and businessman (8–10), lawyers (3), beauticians (7–8), doctors, teachers (5), tailors (5–10).

- Small scale industry (e.g. engineering/repairs, Gruh Udhyog of pickles, household based food processing) has grown up over the years. Other activities are artisanal based work, carpenters.
- Military personnel

There were no large or medium scale industrial units in or around the town. The non-farm sector had received an impetus owing to the geographic location of Mankuwa. Recurrent droughts (1 in 3 years), water shortage, and unsuitability of land for agriculture made agriculture unviable. For these reasons people moved out of agriculture. The residents stated that livelihood opportunities were sufficient in the town and there was no abject poverty. BPL households had nearly all the facilities and over the years their poverty levels had declined. Nonetheless, it was mentioned that methodology of recognition of BPL households was flawed and required correction.

MGNREGA is not a major scheme in the village, as the wage rates were considerably less, while in other non-farm activities the workers earned higher wages (Rs. 300 or so). No major projects were undertaken under this scheme. *Patels* and *Darbars*, the dominant communities had no interest in working in activities under this scheme.

Agriculture: Around 400–450 households were engaged in cultivation while there were nearly 700 landless agricultural labour households. Fifty per cent of the land belonged to marginal and small land holders and the remaining to medium to large (>14 acres). Agriculture was seasonal, confined to the kharif season and crops cultivated were onion, pulses, groundnut, castor, rapeseed, cotton and horticulture and fodder crops. Agriculture was under developed because of receding ground water table and sandy soil. Water was available at a depth of 500 feet and getting deeper. There were nearly 300 private bore wells for irrigation, that have led to increase in crop output. However, no significant ground water markets existed. Cost of farm labour was also reportedly very high.

Horticultural crops have gained popularity due to profit concerns. The main horticulture crop was pomegranate and around 15–20 farmers were engaged in its cultivation for the last 4 to 5 years, using the subsidy available for drip irrigation. However, drip irrigation posed a problem for saline water. Kesar mango was being adopted in a major way and the output was sold in Bhuj market yard. No major technological changes in the agriculture sector have happened over the years. Farmers were open to adopting genetically modified crops if these enhanced profitability. The last decade witnessed higher use of tractors, farm chemicals and drip irrigation. Credit delivery had improved, better extension and price/market information was reported, mainly on account of newspapers/use of ICT. Post-harvest processing of crops (mainly for pickles, jam etc.) at household level had increased. Private agencies were involved in the storage/warehousing (mainly for onion). So far as irrigation, industrial growth or housing is concerned, no major benefits accruing from rural development schemes were visible.

Land: Land price was reported to be Rs. 5000 to 6000/*vaar* (for housing purpose). The price for exchange of agricultural land was cited to be Rs. 20 lakh/acre. After the earthquake the process of land conversion to non-agricultural uses had increased manifold. There were on an average, five to ten cases of NA conversions reported every year and nearly 5000 to 6000 square meters of land per year was being converted to non-agricultural uses. There was increased fragmentation of land due to demographic pressure. Moreover, haphazard development of housing societies was taking place on converted agricultural land. There was absence of a planning mechanism and inadequate development of roads, facilities, and provision of electricity. Land conversion was particularly common amongst small farmers, mainly of the un-irrigated plots. The farmers either invested in land elsewhere or engaged in some other non-farm activity.

Environment: No major environmental problems were reported. *Gauchar* land was being encroached upon by small farmers, and also by the *maldharis* for livelihood. Depletion of ground water and salinity/alkalinity of the soil was increasing due to natural causes. No adverse health effects/malnutrition was reported. Incidence of diabetes was increasing. Also alcoholism was a major problem (15% of population was affected).

Statutory status: The Panchayat officers and some residents were of the opinion that since all facilities (drinking water, drainage) were already available, with a nagar panchayat status the 14th Finance Commission devolution of funds for urban local bodies will come into practice. This would lead to reduction in grants, particularly for rural development, which will adversely affect the development of the village. Currently tax collection is less compared to the services being offered by the Panchayat however, Panchayat income sources existed (e.g. from petrol pump on Panchayat land). In the last decade or so nearly Rs. 2 crores were made available to the Panchayat as grants for rural development. Once nagar panchayat takes over, personal care/attention would not be given by the officials, welfare of the locals would be compromised and higher degree of corruption will set in. Problems related to management and administration will increase if village acquired a town status. The locals were satisfied with a gram panchayat status and did not desire to be a town. On the contrary, FGD revealed that residents wanted to bifurcate the village Panchayat into two parts on both sides of the highway.

Problems
- No major industry in the village.
- There was no market yard (APMC market) facility in the town and farmers had to transport their produce to Bhuj.
- Door to door waste collection was done only on Saturday and Tuesday, that led to environmental and health problems.
- Ground water level was low, 500 to 700 feet, hampering development of agricultural.
- After earthquake land conversion process had stepped up.
- Alcohol addiction is emerging as a major problem. Diabetes afflicted around 15 per cent of the town population.
- People were not interested in the MNREGA as they get higher wage rates in other labour work (construction), at around Rs. 300/day.
- Encroachment of *gaucher* land was reported to be one of the major problems. Agricultural land was reported to be fertile and suitable for horticulture (Kesar mango) but water availability was a severe constraint. Fodder scarcity was reported that hampered livestock activity.

Vavol, Gandhinagar District
Vavol is a census town of Gandhinagar taluka of Gandhinagar district. It is located four kms towards the west of Gandhinagar. Vavol lies in the proximity to sectors 4, 13, 6, 14 and 12 of Gandhinagar city. Apart from Gandhinagar, Kalol, Ahmedabad, and Dehgam are the nearby cities. This census town is quite large having a population of around 12,628 as per Census 2011 and is part of the Gandhinagar Urban Development Authority (GUDA). Traditionally Vavol was known as the village of *Thakur* community. The literacy rate is quite high at 82 per cent (Census 2011). There are around 65 housing societies of migrant population, who are engaged in industries (GIDC) and service sectors notably, the State Secretariat, also as teachers and doctors. Service activities as well as labour work in industries are the main sources of income. Proximity to Gandhinagar has also spurred the growth and development of Vavol.

Land acquisition: The town falls under the *Patnagar Yojana* (Capital city plan). Under this scheme farmers whose land was acquired for the development of capital city of Gandhinagar were offered either a plot (at concessional rates) or shop in exchange and job for one family member in the state secretariat, suiting the educational qualifications. Plot sizes allotted by the government ranged from 0–80, 80–135 and 250–300 square feet. Further, under the scheme construction up to three stories were permitted. The Government acquired almost all the agricultural land during 1970 (at average rate of Rs. 1600 per *vigha*). The nature of the land holding determined the price fetched, and different rates were given for irrigated and non-irrigated plots.

With a view to undertaking planned growth of the town, a town planning scheme (TPS) was sanctioned in 2006. The TPS area is a part of Vavol village that lies to the west of Gandhinagar Notified Area (GNA). The Kalol-Gandhinagar Highway and the Uvarsad-Kolavada Bypass run through the TPS area. The TPS included the village settlement area of Valol, water bodies and surrounding agricultural lands. It was identified as one of the nucleus villages and is earmarked as residential zone (R7) in the Gandhinagar Development Plan 2011. The total area of the TPS is 175 ha, there are 319 plots and most of the area is vacant. The TPS involved a diverse set of tasks—marking all plots owned by a single owner, planning the road network, delineating plots for public use, delineating final plots, valuing land, designing detailed infrastructure, estimating the costs of development, distributing the costs of development on the owners, calculating betterment charges, modifying the proposals as per suggestions, preparing the documents for publishing the TPS and preparing the final documents for submission to the State Government. Field level observations revealed that in the village large-scale construction activity is going on, possibly due to its proximity to Gandhinagar and Ahmedabad. Several commercial residential societies are being developed under the banner of reputed builders.

Path of development of Vavol:

Post GUDA/post land acquisition act → Increase employment opportunities → Increased migration → Decrease/conversion of agricultural land → Increase in real estate activity → Growth of town.

The life style was quite urbanised, with large number of high rise buildings and existence of housing societies. Vavol has a Gujarati cinema, having a 50–100 seating capacity and is the prime and affordable source of entertainment. Due to the existence of a TP scheme, Vavol has developed akin to Gandhinagar and was an attractive destination for migrants. Most of the houses were pucca, and only 1–2 per cent houses were semi-pucca. Solid waste management was however a pressing problem in Vavol. Gram panchayat engaged sweepers and three tractors are being used for solid waste collection. Also there was open drainage system. Alcoholism was commonly reported amongst the labour classes. Consumption of alcohol was especially high amongst *Thakore* and *Harijan* communities, leading to related diseases.

Migration: In Vavol a large section of the population (around 80 per cent) comprised of migrants. Most of the migrants settled here were from UP, Bihar, Rajasthan as well as from the surrounding rural areas. About five per cent of the original inhabitants had re-settled in Gandhinagar or Ahmedabad. Vavol attracts in-migrants owing to the presence of a GIDC at Gandhinagar that is located close to the town. Other employment opportunities also exist. While the local population was nearly 4000, in-migrants numbered around 8000.

The residents were in favour of conversion to Nagar Palika, if it ensured better amenities, urban facilities and a fast pace of development. Since Vavol was located within GUDA and already had a TP scheme in place it was envisaged that it would soon become part of the Gandhinagar UA.

Economic activities: Large section of the population had jobs in government offices, also in industries in nearby GIDC, Naroda and Kubernagar, and residents commuted to their place of work. There was a GIDC electronics estate at the Vavol-Gandhinagar Highway. Employment in construction activities, retail sector mainly kirana stores and food/tea stalls was also common. Significantly, unemployment problem was quite stark, around 500–700 households have unemployed members, the maximum unemployed belonging to the BPL category. Trade was a vibrant sector in the town which had number of shopping complexes, retail shops, tailors, showrooms, salons and beauty parlours, laundries, medical stores and others. Several tuition classes were also existing in the town. There were around 50 to 60 street vendors.

Agriculture: In this town people were basically engaged in the secondary and service sector activities, and about ten per cent of the land was under cultivation engaging about 5–7 per cent of the residents. Main crops cultivated were *jowar, bajra,* castor, pulses, cotton and vegetables. Unavailability of irrigation was the major constraint in Vavol, the water table was depleting and the depth of groundwater that was 300 feet earlier is now nearly 700 feet. There were six bore wells, mainly privately owned for purpose of irrigation. Farmers in Vavol acquired agro-inputs from Gandhinagar. Gandhinagar was also the chief market for horticultural products, while for the marketing of pulses farmers visit the Kalol and Mansa yards. There was a milk co-operative and an agricultural co-operative society for inputs. Vavol was affected by *neelgai* and farmers had to bear crop losses on this account. Farmers had collectively arranged for a watchman to guard the fields.

There was an irrigation cooperative society called Mahakali Piyat Madali, established in 1997, with a membership of around seventeen cultivators. It was established by the Jal Sampati Nigam of the state government and paid a rent of Rs. 5000/month to the Nigam. The society distributed water to its members at the rate of Rs. 70 per hour. The Madali was not getting regular payment from the farmers, as a result the expenses were borne by the society, leading to problems of administration and maintenance. People in the town were not interested to work under MNREGA scheme because jobs in the industries fetched better wages (wage rate in MNREGA is Rs. 160 to 165 per day).

Kabilpor, Navsari District

Kabilpor is a census town in Navsari District belonging to the South Gujarat agro-climatic region. It is located 2 kms north of Navsari, at a distance of 296 kms from the state capital of Gandhinagar. Navsari, Surat, Valsad, Pardi are the nearby urban centres. Kabilpor is a well-developed town. It is an attractive destination for persons working in Navsari, Surat, Valsad, Vapi and Bombay. The town is well connected with all modes of transportation and has an advantageous location on National Highway No. 8. There is a railway station, as well as an ST bus station.

Kabilpor falls under the Navsari Urban Development Authority (NUDA). Gram Panchayat reportedly earned nearly Rs. 25 lakh as revenue per year and this fund was being utilised for the purpose of infrastructure development. The village lake was a source of revenue generation. The panchayat awarded fishing contracts for the lake to outside parties. Of the revenue generated from the fishing activity, seventy per cent was appropriated by the Kabilpor Panchyat and 30 per cent by Dharagiri Panchyat.

Infrastructure: Kabilpor had a good garbage collection facility. However, garbage disposal was a problem due to unavailability of government land for disposal/fill. This led to haphazard disposal of garbage causing severe health issues. Under the Swatch Bharat Mission a tractor and three workers are provided to the panchayat. The gram panchayat deployed in all five vehicles (tractors, two wheelers) for solid waste collection.

There was a village water committee for solving all water related problems. Internal roads were developed by the panchayat, surfacing (block fitting) was done with the help of people's contribution (10%), and Government grants (90%). Panchayat had a community hall that was available for holding public and private functions. Under the MNREGA scheme toilet construction was undertaken, that also generated some employment. Other than toilets panchayat had not taken up any other work under the MNERGA scheme.

Land acquisition: In 1980, agricultural land in Kabilpor was acquired by the GIDC. With the industrial development in the region large share of agricultural land was converted to non-agricultural uses. This also spurred the demand for land for residential purposes, and many farmers sold off their land to builders for construction of residences. Several large farmers also purchased land in the surrounding villages with the proceeds of their land. Due to the opportunity for land use conversion, the price of land increased to Rs. 1500 to 2000 per sq. feets, resulting into shrinking of agricultural land and decline in cultivation activities. As farmers obtained good price from selling their land to GIDC, residents besides purchasing land in other areas also invested in their housing/upgradation of houses. A significant amount of mango cultivation is happening on the newly acquired land. Despite rapid land conversion for residential purposes, the town lacked a land use plan. In fact, illegal encroachment on government land and even on boundaries of the lake was occurring.

Migration: Development of GIDC led to in-migration. About 60–70 per cent of the residents were migrants from UP, Bihar, M.P, Rajasthan and other states. Only 2–3 per cent of the local population had out migrated—either abroad, to Bombay or Surat. People were settling in Kabilpor due to availability of livelihood opportunities in the industries and several settlers also started their business ventures in Navsari. Private schooling had increased due to increased awareness and importance of education.

Economic activities: Agriculture declined in importance due to land acquisition by GIDC. Major crops cultivated were mango, sugarcane, rice and vegetables during the kharif season. Cost of agricultural labour was prohibitive and timely supply of labour was scarce. Unavailability of labour also adversely affected vegetable cultivation and its production had declined. Mango cultivators largely leased out the orchards directly to traders, who deployed labour and incurred cultivation related costs. Only a few farmers were involved in the cultivation of mangoes and they earned on an average Rs. 3 to 4 lakh annually. Lack of an MSP for mango (unlike rice) was hurting mango cultivation. A *Sahakari Mandali* (cooperative society) existed and was quite active in providing loans and agricultural inputs at reasonable rates to the farmers.

Farming sector in Kabilpor was beset with several problems, notably:

- Farmers reported that supply of single phase electricity for only eight hours was inadequate for irrigation. Besides there were disruptions in the supply. Supply in surrounding areas i.e. Mahua, Gandevi, and other surrounding villages was reported to be better.
- Soil degradation problem was reported, including increased alkalinity.
- Residents reported rampant illegal river-bed sand mining which was causing sea water ingress. Due to this quality of agricultural land was deteriorating.
- Due to reduced supply of agricultural labour farm activities had declined. High labour cost contributed majorly to the high cost of cultivation that was proving to be un-remunerative. Farm wages averaged at Rs. 100 to 150 per day along with lunch and other expenses yet, people were not ready to work in the fields.
- Rice and vegetable were grown only during the rainy season. Major problem reported was theft by the tribals.

Industries: Of the working population in the town, 20–25 per cent were engaged in industries, 25 to 30 per cent had businesses and nearly 55 per cent were engaged as service sector workers. There were around seventy small industries located in the town including food and rice processing units (*Poha*), ceramic, and chemicals. Notable among them were Gufic Pharma (major industry), Padmavati Poha Mill, Ganesh Mill, J.P. Bakery, Prism. Effluent from the units in the GIDC had created unhygienic scenario and people of Kabilpor were becoming victims of mosquito–borne diseases like filariasis. The labourers/workers in industries also suffered from poor health standards and decline in the average life expectancy.

GIDC chemical waste had also resulted in water pollution. Surrounding four villages and Navsari city too was facing health issues due to the discharged effluents and waste generated by the GIDC. While industrial development resulted in employment generation, it had led to increase in health problems, water pollution, and social security problems.

The *Halpathi* community working in chemical industries were facing severe health related problems. Initially the industries provided milk and nutritious food to the workers. Currently mortality amongst workers was reported to be high possibly due to increased exposure to chemicals. In the town, 30 to 40 years aged widows abound whose husbands were working in the chemical units. Due to ill effects on health people were now leaving their jobs in the industries and were getting involved in other labour work. The town suffered from increasing crime rate, often ascribed to poor quality of livelihoods.

Statutory status: Residents were by and large not interested in conversion to Nagarpalika. Panchayat officials and others however felt the need for a statutory status as it would lead to increase in development funds, their power and authority. It was also felt that if Kabilpor merged into the Navsari Municipal Corporation, many of the problems would be tackled effectively such as encroachment, strengthening water, drainage, solid waste disposal and road facilities. It was also reasoned that corruption level in a Nagar Palika would reduce due to greater transparency.

Issues/Problems

- Sewerage problem.
- Effluents from industries have polluted the Poorna River and surrounding villages too were suffering from problem of water pollution.
- Sand mining in the Poorna riverbed was causing sea water ingress during high tides, contributing to soil salinity and land degradation.
- *Halpati* community were traditionally known for labour work, but suffered from alcohol addiction, reduced efficiency due to rise in morbidity and declining life expectancy.
- Living standards of people rose in recent past but quality of life had deteriorated.
- Lack of adequate drainage facility in interiors of Kabilpor.
- Production of horticulture crops had declined due to unavailability of labour and high cultivation costs.

Ichchhapor, Surat District

Ichchhapor town is located at a distance of seven kms from Surat, belonging to the south Gujarat region. It falls under the Surat Urban Development Authority (since 2006). Every urban characteristic is present in the town and it appears to be developed and prosperous (with the presence of gardens, park, community centre). The town was experiencing significant residential development activity, with a sizeable number of residents living in apartments and row houses after shifting out from the Surat city. Basic amenities like garbage collection and sanitation however remain a problem. The *talati* believed that Ichchhapor's merger with Surat Corporation is imminent given its proximity and linkages to the city. Ichchhapor would be affected by the proposed ring road of SUDA. The town was over populated and faced a severe land constraint.

Panchayat's income, mainly grants from corporates (often under CSR) is around Rs. 2 crore per annum, share of government funds is miniscule compared to non-governmental sources. These grants have helped in the construction of roads, piped drinking water, panchayat building and other amenities. The village gained from CSR activities of petroleum complex at Hazira and KRIBHCO. In 2010–2011, Ichchhapor town was bestowed the "Best Gram Panchayat" award in Gujarat.

In Ichchhapor conversion of agricultural land to non-agricultural uses, chiefly for residential purposes was widespread. Land acquisition was the main issue; in 1980 GIDC had purchased agricultural land at the rate of Rs. 65,000/*bigha*. Presently only 50–60 farmers were involved in farming related activities. Nearly the entire workforce was engaged in non-farm activities, such as teachers, businesses, lawyers, tailors, laundry, retail sector and home based workers employed in textile and garments sector, besides employment in the industrial complexes and Surat city.

Migration: A significant population of Ichchhapor comprises of migrant workers from U.P, Bihar, Rajasthan, Tamilnadu and Kerala (reported in-migration is of 6000 persons). Settlers from Surat city have shifted to the town due to increasing residential development. Only 2–3 per cent of residents have migrated from the town (mainly Patel community to Surat and Bombay). A large section of the town's population comprises of daily commuters to Surat, either for work or education.

Economic Activities

- Industrial labour and home based work for textile units.
- Rental housing market
- Service sector activities engaged around 30 per cent of the households.

Ichchhapor-Bhatpore houses GIDC estate (46 ha) on the Hazira road, besides having a Gem and Jewellery park and a Textile Park (64 ha). The first estate houses industries engaged in auto works, transport, fabrication, godowns, engineering, food processing, furniture, plastic and textiles. The second GIDC is an exclusive textile park housing textile and knitted fabric units. In the 1980s nearly 1200 acres of land was acquired by the GIDC in Ichchhapore for industrial development. Farmers were hardly left with any land to cultivate. Around 75 per cent of the people parted with their land willingly, but 25 per cent were not satisfied and had gone to the Court for settlement. It was reported that GIDC made partial payments to the land holders of Ichchhapor. Some reported that till date they had not been paid adequately for their land. The land was acquired at the rate of Rs. 65,000/acre. The big corporations that came up on the land hardly employed the local population. As per *jantri* (2011–2012) rate of land is Rs. 7500 per sq metres and Rs. 8200 per sq mts for commercial purposes.

The presence of GIDC led to land degradation, pollution and worsening of environmental quality. It was reported that this had caused a rise in the incidence of bone and liver related diseases. In group discussions it was conveyed that land acquisition in Ichchhapore and NA conversions had been carried out forcefully. Major industries under the GIDC were Reliance (Hazira), ONGC, KRIBHCO, and the HPCL petro-chemical complex.

In order to provide a flavour of the economic activities in Ichchhapor two cases are profiled in the following paragraphs.

Gujarat Hira Bourse (GHB) has a Gem & Jewellery (GJP) park: GHB unit was registered ten years ago. It has come up with a very ambitious project of developing a world class Gem & Jewellery Park at Ichchhapore. The Project spread across 100 hectares, would house a hi-tech convention centre, trading centre and all relevant infrastructure facilities like roads, electric system, water supply network etc. GHB symbolizes the Gem & Jewellery industry of India with almost all leading entrepreneurs from the industry joining it as members. The managing committee of GHB is determined to provide an international level of infrastructure facilities to the industry and to establish Gujarat/Surat as one of the most favoured destinations in the world.

By 2016 nearly 25 jewellery-manufacturing units started operating from this park. Earlier it was accorded a SEZ status, but was denotified later due to poor response from prospective manufacturers. Land was acquired by the GIDC and given to the GHB for a GJP, after nearly a decade. The park is a boon for diamantaires due to its proximity to the upcoming Surat Diamond Bourse and the DREAM city at Khajod. Many large jewellery manufacturers purchased plots within the park. Once completed the project is expected to house more than 350 gems and jewellery export units.

The park employs around 3500 workers, out of the total only 500 are local workers (from within Ichchhapor) and the rest are daily commuters from Surat, Vapi, Valsad, Navsari and surrounding villages. Basically diamond companies require skilled workers but lack of skilled labour from within Ichchhapor led the units to hire workers from outside. The giant industrial units in Hazira also do not employ the local youth. The GJP is expected to give a major fillip to the cutting/polishing industry through value addition of diamonds into manufactured jewellery, whose proceeds are much higher. Plans are afoot to establish training centres for creating a pool of skilled diamond artisans. It is expected that mining companies/trading centres from across the world would set up their trading offices in Surat, from where manufacturers can source their diamonds.

Initially the Gujarat government granted Special Notified Zone status for trading rough diamonds to the GJP. Nearly 33 per cent of consolidated tax recovered by Notified Area would be given to DRDA for development works in villages whose lands were acquired for the Notified Area. Recently, Gujarat government revised the above policy and constituted a committee under the Chairmanship of District Collector. The development works of the villages whose land has been acquired would be decided and undertaken by this Committee.

RJD Textile Mill: This is the largest textile mill in located within the Ichchhapor textile park, and is basically a manufacturer of "Designer Lehenga and Sari". The textiles unit purchases raw materials from Surat Textiles and sell their finished product to Surat Textiles, as well as sellers in Rajkot, Vadodara and Ahmedabad.

The unit employs around twenty workers including four female workers from Ichchhapor and sixteen male workers from surrounding areas. The unit also employs four designers from Surat. Commuting/migrant workers who are easily available are preferred. Local workers do not prefer to work due to extensive working hours and low wages (around Rs. 300/day). However, female workers have lesser hours of work (9 hours) and enjoy the flexibility to work from home. In Ichchhapor around 15–20 small enterprises (Aashapura handworks, Jagdish handworks) also work

with RJD Textile, and sub-let finishing jobs by employing home based
female workers. The job profile included finishing of saris, hand work,
diamond work, embroidery and stitching work. These women earn higher
wages, between Rs. 1000–1500 per day. The local units delegated work to
the women and collected the finished products.

Dispersed Location

Kharaghoda, Surendranagar District

Kharaghoda town falls in the Patdi taluka of Surendranagar district, located
at a distance of 103 km from Ahmedabad. Kharaghoda is well connected
from Ahmedabad by rail up to Viramgam, and there after by road via
Phulki and Patdi. The town is divided into three parts—Juna gam (Old
Kharaghoda), Nava gam (New Kharaghoda) and Station gam governed by
one panchayat. Kharaghoda had a total population of 11,944 (6343 are
males and 5601 are females). Number of scheduled caste families was 110,
there were 12 scheduled tribe families, and around 1436 OBC families.
There were 322 BPL households (total persons 4153). The literacy rate in
Kharaghoda was 61.1 per cent, lower than the state average of 78 per cent.
Comparatively lower rate of literacy in the town was mainly because a large
section of the population comprised of *Agariya* community or the salt
workers. In Juna village most of the population comprised of Patels,
engaged in farming, also *Thakores, Harijan* and *Rabaris*. In Nava and
Station areas households belonging to *Agariya* (salt workers) and *Thakore*
community were dominant.

   Migration: In Kharaghoda around 200 families have settled from the
surrounding areas and were residing in around four neighbourhoods.
There was seasonal in-migration of people for purpose of employment. In
the last two decades Patel community had migrated to Rajkot, Surat and
Ahmedabad for education and livelihoods. Seasonal migration (of agricultural labour) had stopped/reduced due to mechanization of agricultural
operations. Labour from the town was hardly migrating out or commuting due to the presence of livelihood opportunities in the salt industry.
Currently some 15 to 20 youngsters had reportedly settled in Ahmedabad,
Surat or Rajkot for jobs in the private sector, to work in market yards, and
in the retail sector. A few (10 to 15 individuals) also commuted to Patdi
(taluka headquarter) for work. Upper caste families were migrating to

other places for higher education and in search of better employment opportunities. It was discerned that local politics was interfering in the development of the town and the Panchayat seemed totally ineffective.

Economic Activities

In Kharaghoda large section of workers were engaged in salt related work. There was a large industry, "Hindustan Salt Company". The FGD revealed that there was no stark poverty in the village as labour work was available in the salt industry, even though agriculture was often afflicted with drought-like situation. Since employment opportunities were available in the salt industry, NREGA was not a preferred employment avenue. For nearly all services, purchases, higher education, and marketing of the agricultural produce residents visited either Patdi or Viramgam. There was no major retail activity in Kharaghoda, although a few tertiary and service sector workers (doctors, teachers, lawyers, salon etc.) were present. There was no GIDC or major industry in and around the village, as it is designated as a wild life sanctuary. It was reported that the presence of salty air was not conducive to factories/machinery. Although located close to the Little Rann, it did not have sufficient wind to harness wind energy for generating electricity. It was opined that wind farms were not possible as wind direction was not suitable and there was no height available (the Rann being lower than the sea level).

Salt production: is the major non-agricultural activity, and nearly 70 to 80 per cent of the workers were engaged in salt production. Around 300 families have leased-in land from the government for salt production, although after the entire area was declared as Wild Ass Sanctuary, the traditional leases have been withdrawn. Currently there were co-operative societies (*Rann mandals*) for *agariyas* in which the latter were shareholders. There were in all 70 to 75 such cooperatives with 100 to 150 members in each. The cooperatives leased-in the plots from the government and the members were assigned at least 3 acres of land per household. Every year the leases on the plots were renewed. The members had to pay an amount of Rs. 2500 to the cooperative society after leasing-in the plots in order to avail drinking water, health and other facilities from the society and for the maintenance and salary expenses of the functionaries. Individuals did not possess plots on ownership basis, even though salt making is the traditional work of the salt workers. Level of education had increased in the town over the years, but literacy levels amongst the *agariyas* remained quite low.

The *agariyas* lived in the salt pans for eight months in temporary shelters in abysmal living conditions and returned for four months to the town with the onset of monsoons. In the town too they lived in decrepit houses constructed during the time of British. In the Rann, some NGOs (Gantar, SEWA etc.) provided rudimentary education facilities to children (in bunker schools) and also provided mobile health care. The Panchayat supplied water through tankers to these workers every 15 days. The *agariyas* were tied to traders in Patdi and Ahmedabad (nearly 35 in all). The traders pledged in the beginning of the production season to buy the salt produced by each family. The trader also provided advance payment ranging between Rs. 1 to 1.5 lakhs for a season, (lasting around 8 months), starting from September till May. The price of the salt was decided by the traders. The cost of salt production was borne by each family (including cost of crude oil used to pump out brine from underground to produce salt), tanker cost etc. The salt produced was sold to the traders, and value addition/packaging was done by the traders. Each family annually earned up to Rs. 1 to 1.5 lakh. According to HSL the cost of salt production was not very high, and the price obtained was satisfactory as the *agariyas* had no other livelihood options. However, the government was discouraging salt pan work in the town as the region was declared a sanctuary for endangered species of birds and animals (Wild ass or *Gudkhar*) and the land had an 'option value'.

Hindustan Salt Limited: Hindustan Salts Limited (HSL) was incorporated in the year 1958 as a company fully owned by the Government of India to take over the salt sources at Sambhar, Didwana and Kharaghoda earlier managed by the Salt Department, Government of India. This is the only Central Government public sector undertaking engaged in the manufacture of salt. The company started its business in January 1959. It also involved in salt production from around 23,000 acres of land that it controls around Kharaghoda. It is presently under the department of heavy industries. Hindustan Salt Limited had leased out land under its control to the *agariyas* in the town. The company employed 150 locals (*agariya* families from Kharaghoda), besides a few officers staying in the township of the company. All the workers were third generation salt workers and so were skilled. In the rest of the land (outside company's control), the local *agariyas*, as members of cooperatives produced salt on leased land and sold the output to traders. HSL had developed some infrastructure facilities in the village such as a helipad, sports grounds, an English medium school etc. however, the company had no major stakes in the development activity of the town (except a school). In fact the manager considered the entire settlement as an encroachment on the land controlled by HSL. Most of the buildings, land and infrastructure around Kharaghoda was owned by the company. Since there was a wild life sanctuary no other big industry can be established.

A salt cess was collected (0.5%) from the traders and the cess fund was managed by the Salt Commissioner. This fund was used for the welfare of salt workers. Roads, housing, coolers and ambulance service etc. were operated from this fund. The salt traders were organized (ISMA) and also had stakes in the welfare of workers.

Annual production of salt from the Little Rann is around 20 lakh MT, and the entire output is marketed outside the region. The salt made from brine (inland production) is large consumed in hilly areas (as it slowly absorbs moisture). Out of the total production of 4 lakh tonne by the company, 30,000 MT is by the company itself and the rest is by the *agariyas*. The major cost involved is transportation rather than the salt production. Bromine is a by-product of brine after salt extraction. The brine after salt extraction was acquired by the company and is utilized for pesticide production. Salt production from brine is thus considered an environmentally friendly activity. Bromine is further processed to produce another raw material—magnesium chloride. The bromine plant in Kharaghoda started its operations in 1979 and employs skilled workmen. It was reported that there was potential for a potash plant—that is likely to lead to multiplier effects in terms of job creation, livelihoods, and savings of foreign exchange. The by-product of potash would be low sodium salt. Once this was set up, it may lead to development of the entire region.

Agriculture: Of the total land holdings, large and medium land holders were 50 (15% having >35 *bigha* and 15% had 14 to 35 *bigha*), around 70 small farmers and 46 marginal farmers. Seventy per cent of the small and marginal farmers possessed land less than 14 *bighas*. Farming households (nearly 60 to 70) resided in the Juna gam. In Kharaghoda agriculture was mainly dependent on rainfall, and there was insufficient development of irrigation facilities.

Savada Pond, around 10 to 12 km in diameter, was the main source of irrigation for Kharaghoda; farmers drew water from the pond through underground pipelines for irrigating their fields. When water was available in the pond, it could irrigate around 10,000 acre of land. Of this 1100 acres were irrigated in Patadi village and the rest in other villages like Chikasar, Savada, Khoda and Meetagora. The pond was maintained by

HSL, but its embankment was damaged and was in need of repairs. It was mentioned that despite repeated pleas to the Panchayat, taluka, and district authorities and even HSL, the breech in the embankment had not being repaired and was leading to distress conditions amongst the farmers. The farmers on their own had tried to repair the pond but it remained underutilized (to its full capacity).

Main crops cultivated were caster, cumin, *jowar*, *bajra*, and pulses—mostly rain fed. Crop diversification had happened from cotton to castor. Cotton was threatened by *neelgai* and pigs, forcing the farmers to shift to the cultivation of castor. If there was water in the pond after the monsoons, cumin and fennel were cultivated. Largely *desi* variety of cotton was cultivated and Bt cotton was not common here. APMC facility was available at a distance of 6 km from Patdi. In a good year farmers acquired production of around 25 *mann/bigha*. In a bad year the output was reported to be around 5 to 7 *mann/bigha*. Farmers complained that the cost of cultivation was high and adequate prices for most crops were not forthcoming. Despite 50–60 per cent of the households being engaged in agriculture, severe hardships were faced by the households due to salinity of soil and water, lack of irrigation development, absence of new technology and agriculture development schemes. It was stated that while the soil was fertile and suitable for cropping, dependency on rain hampered agricultural output. Only if sufficient water was available in the Savada pond could the farmers take a second crop, otherwise agriculture remained seasonal.

Price of agricultural land was Rs. 2 lakh to 2.5 lakh/per bigha. No major technological changes were witnessed, except for widespread use of tractors, farm machinery and pumps for lifting water from the tank. Use of fertilisers and chemicals had increased. Water saving devices (drip/sprinklers) were not in vogue. There was poor extension activity as gram sevak was not very active, also there were information asymmetries with regard to market/price information. Local agricultural workers were easily available at Rs. 200 per day and Rs. 100 for half day.

It was stated in the FGD that the Panchayat faced mismanagement of funds leading to inadequate development of amenities. The residents felt that the town was suffering from considerable neglect by government authorities. Despite the presence of a "Kharaghoda" branch canal of Narmada, the town did not receive piped water from Narmada nor was there any sub-minor, even though Patdi obtained water from Narmada. Since the Narmada canal was nearly 10 to 15 kms away the cultivators were unable to lift water from the canal privately. Further the major tank from which water for irrigation was taken was the property of HSL. The tank was filled by monsoon water and currently served five villages all through the summers. If the Savada pond was linked to Narmada canal irrigation capacity could be enhanced and water problem tackled it was reported. However, adequate response to any of these proposals was lacking. No NGOs were active in the region. People wanted to leave agriculture as water availability was a constraint, however if irrigation facilities were created farmers showed willingness to continue farming as land was quite productive. Salt production does not affect agricultural land and was not environment degrading. However salinity ingress in the ground water was a major threat.

Statutory status: No major impact of urbanization or change to urban lifestyles was observed. According to focus group dissension advantages of acquiring an urban status would be better development activity and access to amenities i.e. drainage, solid waste management and water supply. It would lead to the creation of better health infrastructure and connectivity, better education facilities especially colleges, IT institutes, and avenues for vocational training. Development of small scale enterprises and businesses could be encouraged, that would engage the *agariya* households who faced numerous livelihood related issues. As such Kharaghoda was backward with poor development of infrastructure and amenities. The main disadvantages cited were increase in taxation and addition of new taxes/cesses.

The residents were of the opinion that if the panchayat was converted into Nagarpalika it would lead to better employment and business opportunities and more labour intensive work will arise due to the land conversion. If development related work was stepped up, the residents were ready to pay higher taxes. Currently despite availability of funds, there was absence of any planning activity. Interestingly, the major shortcoming cited was that *agariyas* being the dominant community may take over the running/management of the Nagar panchayat and being poorly educated may hamper development prospects. Even though flow of funds may increase, it was feared that problems of mismanagement or corruption may get compounded.

Main Issues

- A solar energy plant was proposed but did not get the approval due to issues at the local level.
- Lack of proper infrastructure facilities i.e. roads, schools (higher secondary school), government hospital, industry. No rural development scheme/programme were implemented adequately due to lacunae at the local level. There was a nearly dysfunctional Panchayat that is affecting maintenance and creation of rural infrastructure (sarpanch was a woman). There was lack of transparency at the Panchayat level.
- Poor condition of salt workers as they lack basic infrastructure, access to amenities and housing facility, besides having inadequate livelihoods. Problem of alcoholism is rampant amongst the *agariyas*.
- Due to the wild life sanctuary farmers faced the nuisance of animals despite fencing. Bajana and Dhrangadhra were the tourist hubs for visitors to the Rann, but Kharaghoda residents did not benefit from the development of tourism in the Little Rann.

Umrala, Bhavnagar District

Umrala belongs to the Saurashtra region. Many of the census towns and large villages in the region have merged with the Bhavnagar Municipal Corporation i.e. Nari, Sidhsar and Malanka. Umrala is a census town and taluka centre in the district of Bhavnagar, Gujarat. It is located at a distance of 33 kms from the district headquarters of Bhavnagar, and 178 km away from Gandhinagar.

Migration: The town does not seem to be an attractive destination for migrant workers. Around 100 households from outside the village, mainly from the Bhal region find employment in agriculture, basically as tenant cultivators on land leased-in from local farmers. These cultivators do share cropping/*bhagya kheti* with the local farmers. From Umrala nearly 160 households have migrated out to work in the Surat diamond industry. Umrala is an attractive destination for teachers and government employees as they come from nearby villages. Due to its proximity to Bhavnagar around 50 to 60 individuals commute daily from the town to Bhavnagar for employment, chiefly in the diamond industry. In addition around 30 teachers commute to other areas. Daily commuters also included around 65 business men/retailers, employees in court, banks, private offices etc. and students who go to Bhavnagar for college education. Around 60 government servants commute to the surrounding villages and Bhavnagar.

Economic Activities

In Umrala there were two ginning mills, which have since closed down. Basically migrants and BPL households were dependent on agricultural activity, as there were no major employment avenues for them. There were several micro enterprises, e.g. diamond polishing, textile weaving, sari and stone work. There was lack of industrial development within and around the town. This coupled with collapse of diamond industry in the region led to increase in the poverty levels over the years. Presently the main economic activities were cultivation, agricultural labour, household based diamond udyog, home based garment related work, services, trade and employment in MNREGA. There was large scale out migration of residents to Surat for jobs in the diamond-processing sector.

Agriculture: Of the 711 land holders, marginal farmers were 237, small 271, medium 145 and 58 were large farmers. There were 862 landless households. Small and marginal farmers dominated the agrarian structure and there was considerable landlessness. Total cattle population was 1485 and animal husbandry was an important supplementary activity.

Good wages persist in agricultural activity i.e. in the cotton-picking season wages were Rs. 600–700/day. Farmers were aware of the new agricultural technology. Irrigation was through canal (155 ha), well/tube wells (20 ha) and area under sprinklers was around 3 ha. For irrigation purpose although there were 415 dug wells but only 40 wells were reported to be functional. Water table was reachable at around 100 feet. The town gets surface irrigation through canal from the Ranghoda Sichai Vibhag. Moreover Kalubhar river had two dams upstream in the Gadhada taluka and water when released irrigates the fields in Umrala. In addition there were three check dams on the Kalubhar river, though water was available from these for only two months after the monsoons. The check dams were dependent on good monsoon rains for filling to capacity. Wells near the river had sweet water. In the past decade only 5–7 per cent of the farmers had adopted drip irrigation.

Main crop during kharif season was cotton (Bt), while the chief rabi crops were cumin, wheat if irrigation water is available, and in summer sesame, *jowar and bajra* was cultivated. A small share of farmers produced cottonseeds for their own consumption and also sold in the surrounding villages. The farmers reported hundred per cent Bt cotton adoption as it gave better output due to less pest attacks. However, cotton farmers were presently reporting more infestation of pink bollworm. The farmers reportedly benefitted from the extension activities under Krishi melas, although there was no agricultural extension officer deputed. An interesting farm innovation was a '*sanedo*', which was a mini tractor (a motorcycle run tractor that could be attached to other farm implements). This was a local innovation and aided tasks in the field (e.g. tilling, weeding, sowing) even where there were close spacing of crops. Moreover, after monsoons the *sanedo* was being used extensively for ploughing instead of use of draught animals. There were a couple of engineering workshops for the service/maintenance of the *sanedo* in the town itself.

Industry: There was no medium or large scale industrial unit but only small/cottage industries. Despite extensive cotton cultivation the town lacked ginning mills or any other agro-processing activity. Cotton was procured by the middlemen who visited the farmers directly. However, there were significant number of small engineering workshops for repairs/service of agricultural implements.

Home based *zari/tikki* work: Women from around 200 households were engaged in handwork on saris, as outsourced and home based piecemeal work. The women earned between Rs. 75 to 100 per day in the off-season, when agriculture related jobs were scarce. There were nearly four such units that engaged women in this activity and were subletting work on behalf of garment units located in Bhavnagar and Surat.

Small scale diamond processing: The proximity to Surat enables easy purchase of raw diamonds and resale of polished products. The diamond polishers/*ghanti* owners procured raw materials and returned the polished products to the middleman known variously as *angadia/dalal/marfatia*. There were around sixty such diamond *ghantis* or micro enterprises engaged in polishing and cutting of diamonds in the town. It took an initial investment of around Rs. 10,000 for setting up a polishing unit. Each unit employed 10–15 workers, and overall 300 or more workers were dependent on this activity. The wages paid to the diamond workers were considered to be quite low. The workers (nearly four per machine) earned up to Rs. 8–10 per diamond and on an average could polish around 20–25 diamonds in a day. Due to low wages in the diamond units, workers felt exploited and wanted to either migrate or divert to agricultural activity. Diamond work was carried out largely in the summer months and was seasonal. In the remaining two seasons, workers preferred agricultural related activity.

Earlier, Bhavnagar had a thriving diamond industry, but lately all the traders/*pedi* had shifted to Surat causing the breakdown of a vibrant regional economic activity. Discussions revealed that income levels had declined as the diamond sector was passing through a bad phase and poverty levels among the workers had increased. There were no other employment diversification avenues in the town. Moreover, there was no initiative taken by traders etc. to set up any manufacturing activity. Umrala being a *taluka* head quarter had spurred service sector activities. There was a market centre that catered to the local customers.

Around 350 families had been working in MNREGA related projects since the last two years. Under MNREGA three check dams have been completed on the Kalubhar river. Canal works were also proposed. The wages received under MNREGA were around Rs. 180/person/day.

Statutory status: Presently, the Panchayat revenue collection is around 60 per cent and does not get sufficient grants for development. If the town was accorded a statutory status, development of amenities could be possible due to increased fund base and tax collection. However, since the population was small in the near future the town cannot be given NP status (eligibility is >11,000 and <25,000 population). By and large the residents were not in favour of urban status and felt that the tax collection base of the panchayat could improve and all development related work carried out from its own resources. It was also felt that corruption levels that were already severe would rise further. Also the funds available for rural development would reduce substantially if urban status was imparted.

Problems/Issues

- Since there were no industries, pollution problem was not there. Soil and land related issues were also absent.
- Around 95 acres of land has been converted into NA for residential purpose. Nearly 35 to 40 plots had been converted to non-agriculture uses, primarily residences (a dalit society). While no other commercial residential society had come up, owners were improving their own land or constructing houses. However, there was absence of any rules for regulating the construction activity. Up to two stories were being built.
- With increasing urbanism, lifestyles had changed, mainly changes in diet. Social customs have seen some changes (purdah, dowry systems had reduced).
- Level of education had improved, in primary segment drop out ratio was zero and most of the children were studying up to tenth standard, even the girls. More and more girls were going for higher education, mainly PTC. The town boasted of a girl enrolled in medical studies besides a boy. Due to greater emphasis on higher education parents were sending their wards out of the town.

Becharaji, Mehsana District

Becharaji is a temple town and *taluka* capital in Mehsana district. It belongs to the agriculturally developed north Gujarat agro-climatic region. The town is associated with Hindu goddess Bahuchara Mata. It is one of the three Shaktipeeths worshipped in Gujarat, the other two being Ambaji and Pavagadh. People bring their children here for the tonsure/*Mundan* ceremony. The sun temple of Modera in the vicinity of Becharaji is a majestic monument and an example of the artistry of Gujarat kings. It was built in AD 1026–27 during the reign of Bhimdev. These two locations attract considerable intra-state tourists.

Becharaji temple was the prime source of the economic activity and resources for the town development. It was a source for employment generation in the village and all development stemmed from the temple and activities that it had spurred so far. Temple trust was also an income source for the village panchayat and the Becharaji Temple Trust aided in crucial panchayat functions (cleanliness etc.), and creation of development infrastructure. Becharaji temple was the focus of the town. Animal husbandry was an important activity in Becharaji. No major industry existed and residents were largely dependent on agriculture and dairying activity for livelihoods, besides a developed retail-trading sector. Becharaji served as a market centre for nearly fifty surrounding villages.

The Panchayat carried out the door to door waste collection by tractor. Under the RURBAN scheme the drainage system had been completed. Temple trust donated Rs. 10 lakh to the panchayat for purchase of tractor, trolley and other equipment required for house to house solid waste collection. The construction of the drainage system had led to considerable improvement in the living environment and health of the residents. Under the RURBAN scheme, Panchayat had also constructed a sump (for collection and distribution of Narmada water) and two overhead tanks from which piped water is proposed to be supplied to all households. Household tap water facility exists. Discussion in FGD indicated that despite being a busy market and temple town, the place did not offer any facilities for leisure/entertainment both for children and adults. Higher education institutions were lacking and posed a major problem for girl students who could not commute to Mehsana for secondary or college education. Mehsana was the major service centre for nearly all requirements.

Land: As residents were not getting much from agricultural land they were converting it into non-agricultural uses (industries, business centers and residential area). For this reason the land prices in the town were very high around Rs. 40 to 50 lakhs per *bigha*, depending on the location. A large number of residential societies were coming up (25 in all existing), on the agricultural land. Nearly 25 more plots were in the pipeline, hence cultivable land was slowly declining. Private builders were active and farmers were voluntarily converting agricultural land to NA due to prevailing prices of agricultural land. Housing activity in Becharaji has received an impetus with the establishment of the Honda plant (20 kms away) and the Maruti plant (4 kms away) in the Mandala–Becharji Special Investment region. In FGD residents opined that the conversion of land to non-agriculture should be stopped, and instead Narmada water for irrigation should be provided at the earliest for the development of remunerative agriculture. However, they also stated that completion of the Maruti plant would enhance employment opportunities for the villagers.

Agriculture: Major crops cultivated in winter were wheat and cotton (*Vagad*, without irrigation), while in kharif season *jowar, bajra,* pulses, castor, cumin and mustard were cultivated. Soil was fertile, and suitable for cash crops. Some farmers were cultivating pomegranate and two were even growing saffron. This was done on an experimental basis on plots of 1.5 *bigha*, instigated by private contacts with farmers of Karampur village located 10 km away and where saffron and pomegranate cultivation is being undertaken. Extension services were poor, and gram sevak was available only for few people. The primary cooperative society had more than 100 members. An APMC was exiting but catered to only cumin, castor and pulses.

In the recent past not much agricultural diversification has happened due to water scarcity. Increase in mechanization (tractors) was reported; availability of farm labour was a serious limitation as manual jobs in construction and retail trade were easily available. Increase in the use of fertilisers, farm chemicals was cited. In the last five years due to water scarcity and irregular rainfall, cumin cultivation had reduced. Drip irrigation was not in use in Becharaji. Farmers were of the opinion that instead of cultivating un-irrigated or *vagad* cotton, they would be willing to adopt Bt cotton if the water situation improved, as it was far more productive. The farmers also showed their willingness to cultivate herbicide tolerant cotton due to the severe shortage of timely farm labour.

Irrigation: There were three bore wells, which were utilized exclusively for irrigation. All were under private ownership and were of 400, 1400 and 600 feet depth. Irrigated land totalled only around 40 to 50 *bighas*. Bore owners sold water to the surrounding fields and charged Rs. 320 per hour of irrigation. However, in a day only 3 to 4 *bigha* of land could be irrigated through this source.

Narmada Canal was situated 25 kms away from Becharaji, and sub minor canal were being constructed. Within a year all minor canals would be completed and the water would be available for irrigation. With sufficient water farmers could diversify to the cultivation of wheat from coarse cereals. Residents complained that piped Narmada water was supplied on a priority basis to the Honda and Maruti plants even though there was a delay in its supply for irrigation. It was revealed that Water Users Associations (*Mandali*) for the sub minor was already in place (in fact the Becharji mandali was one of the oldest), yet no water had been received.

In the FGD residents revealed that with Narmada water for irrigation the agricultural activities in the region can receive a major impetus, and made far more remunerative. The farmers also observed that since it was a water scarce region they should receive priority over industries as far as supply of Narmada water was concerned. It was also stated that allocation of waste lands to industries may increase the employment opportunities in the region.

In Becharaji there was a substantial livestock population (4000 cows and 1000 buffaloes). Becharji had a milk cooperative society linked to the Dudhsagar dairy. It had 150 members and majority belonged to the *Bharwad* community, while the remaining were from Patel and Brahmin communities. Milk was delivered to the society for up to six months in a year. Fodder was easily available during the rainy season and in other seasons dry fodder was purchased. The farmers complained that dry fodder was expensive which resulted in low profit margins from livestock rearing. The village *gaucher* land was encroached for housing/construction activity. *Neelgai* and pigs also posed a major threat to the standing crops. Livestock rearing was increasing as water was available in the village pond, even though not for irrigation purpose.

Non-farm economic activity: In Becharaji a few small scale industrial units related to marble cutting/polishing, wood cutting, automobile parts, ginning and cement works existed engaging around 4–5 labourers each. The largest section of workers were engaged in agriculture and dairying in addition to services. Around 10 to 15 persons were engaged in government service and there were 10 to 12 teachers in government schools. Becharaji being an upper caste dominated village, the residents did not benefit from education/job reservations. Grocery shops, small scale home based businesses (e.g. spice grinding and packaging by women for wholesalers), and masonry work on construction sites were the dominant non-farm activities, in addition to a vibrant retail sector around the temple. Large section of population depended on casual wage work in the temple premises and the small shops around it. Most of the shops catered to the temple devotees and sold products like puja material, grocery, sweetmeat, food stuff and beverages, garments, stationery items or were involved in services such as salons/beauty parlours, xerox and repair shops.

Construction work (as mason) within the town as well as 10 to 15 kms away in nearby villages was a major employment provider. These jobs fetched Rs. 200 to Rs. 250 per day and work was available for 20 days in a month. The town was also an attractive destination for labourers from outside, especially tribals as construction workers (through contractors).

Around 50–100 residents were employed by the Honda Company (18 kms away). More than 300 families have migrated to Becharaji, and were living in the newly constructed housing societies. Inhabitants of these colonies were mostly teachers, traders and people involved in the retail businesses. Around 50 to 60 residents commuted to Mehsana and other nearby places for work. In the last 10 years or so some families have migrated abroad. Nearly 50 to 60 young residents from the village have also migrated to Ahmedabad, Ankaleswar, Baroda for jobs (mainly Patels). Residents stated that absolute poverty had declined with the creation of employment opportunities in and around Becharaji and also in Mehsana.

Statutory status: Residents longed for a statutory town status as it was perceived that it would lead to increase in development funds. They were ready to pay higher taxes in the interest of better facilities and urban amenities. It was believed that a statutory status would ensure planned development of the town instead of the current haphazard growth. Along with increased access to infrastructure/amenities the land prices were likely to escalate with a statutory status. It was felt that rise in the rent of land would increase opportunities, spur competition and improve service delivery and trade. All of this is likely to curb migration. Chief shortcoming cited was that the town may attract more in-migration, increase congestion, pollution etc. Increase in social evils, crime, corruption levels could go up and transparency would be lost, it was feared.

Issues/problems: Increasing urbanism was observed as manifested in the changes in lifestyles, particularly better and improved housing, changes in food habits, and enhanced importance being given to higher education. All vices e.g. alcoholism were on the rise with development. Petty crimes/ thieving etc. though had reduced due to increase in employment opportunities. With industrial growth there was hope for a better future. Tourism had led to changes in eating habits with rising preference for fast food. This had created employment but had led to adverse health outcomes.

A few of the enterprises (marble polishing, trade) interviewed reported that amongst the problems encountered was poor road condition hampering transport of raw materials and finished products to the nearby markets. Lack of basic amenities i.e. water and inadequate electricity hampered smooth running of their operations. Lack of skilled labour was also cited as a major constraint. Despite paying taxes to the gram panchayat water supply was irregular.

Lilia, Amreli District
Recently the government selected Lilia for the smart village scheme. Lilia had won 'The Gold Medal' (Swarnim Puraskar) for the Best Gram Panchayat in the year 2010–2011. The town is located in the Lilia taluka in Amreli district of Saurashtra region. It is the taluka head quarter and located in an agricultural hinterland. Lilia is located 18 km east of the district headquarter at Amreli and 269 km from the state capital Gandhinagar. Lilia taluka is surrounded by Amreli taluka towards west, Lathi taluka in the north, Savarkundla taluka in the south, Gariadhar taluka in the east. Amreli, Savarkundla, Lathi, Palitana are the nearby cities. Lilia has a significant aged population, as younger generation had migrated in large numbers for educational and employment purposes.

Migration: In the absence of opportunities, nearly 30–40 per cent of the residents undertake seasonal migration for employment for eight months and return during the monsoon months. Nearly 2–5 per cent of population have migrated out of the village permanently and a significant share of the working population were daily commuters to the surrounding urban centres.

Lilia Panchayat was resource constrained and not receiving regular grants for their administrative expenses owing to a technical dispute between the panchayat and the Water Supply Board. The panchayat depended on house tax and other sources of revenue however, revenue collection was inadequate and more than half of the households did not pay the requisite taxes. Income earned was sufficient only for conservancy and maintenance of services. There was severe dearth of funds for infrastructure creation and provision of services to all the residents.

The ground water level in Lilia appeared at 50–60 feet but had high fluoride content (up to 11%), and thus was not potable. This was also the cause for widespread occurrence of certain diseases i.e. joint pains and bone related problems. Panchayat has installed three R.O. Plants in the town, which provided up to 60 litres of water per household, at the rate of Rs. 25 per bottle. The Panchayat did not have any concrete plans for improving the supply of adequate potable water.

Economic Activities

Agriculture: Agriculture was the mainstay of the census town. The principal crops cultivated were cotton, groundnut, *jowar, bajra* and onions. Of the total cultivators, there were 440 marginal farmers (up to 3.20 hectare), 510 small farmers (3.2 to 7.2 hectare) and 20 per cent of the population was landless. Overall percentage shares of cultivators indicated that marginal farmers comprised 25 per cent of landholders, 40 per cent were small farmers and the remaining were medium and large farmers. Ground water was the chief source of irrigation, and there were 212 wells and 258 bore wells in the town. Eighty per cent of the farmers had private bore wells. It was difficult to get water for irrigation from the Dhari dam located 60 kms away from Lilia. At Saladi village (6 kms away) there was a big lake which had the potential to irrigate surrounding 8 to 10 villages. However, there was no proposal afoot to develop it.

Agriculture was quite developed and farmers reported using new technology in a big way, mainly drip irrigation (200 farmers), soil testing (605 farmers had soil health cards), adoption of Bt cotton, HYV seeds and increased fertilizer use. While the town had no APMC, the farmers sold their produce in the APMCs located at Babara, Lathi and Savarkundla. The APMCs disseminated information related to agriculture and crop prices. Kisan Sabha and other farmer's awareness programmes were also implemented. The town had 4–5 greenhouses for horticultural crops (tomato and brinjal). Awareness regarding latest agricultural practices was seen to be quite high and farmers had started organic farming for crops such as groundnut, wheat, and horticultural crops.

Diamond cutting: Lilia is a backward *taluka* and there was no significant industrial activity. Gem cutting and diamond polishing is the practice of changing a diamond from a rough stone into a faceted gem. Cutting diamond requires specialized knowledge, tools, equipment, and techniques because of its extreme difficulty. Lilia was a diamond and gem cutting centre in the past having more than 300 diamond polishing units, as of now only 15 to 20 such units exist. In each unit there were around 80–100 diamond cutting machines and on each machine four to five workers were working. Nearly 300–400 persons were currently engaged in such activity in the town. Around 40–50 per cent of the workers were from within Lilia and rest come from the surrounding villages. The working hours were 10–12 hours and wages were decided on the basis of the number of diamonds cut/polished, at the rate of Rs. 6 per unit. Thus there was high degree of worker exploitation coupled with poor work conditions. Overall earnings in this activity ranging between to Rs. 3000 to Rs. 4000 per month were quite low, hence workers preferred alternative livelihoods, including farm labour. Due to this shortage of labour was reported by the units. Erratic supply of electricity was reported as a problem, as diamond work was totally dependent on electricity. It was mentioned that if the state government supported and developed this sector Lilia would benefit given the significant presence of skilled diamond cutters and polishers. Ancillary activities could also be developed generating employment for workers in and around Lilia.

There were four cotton ginning mills. However, the largest segment of workers (75% of the households) were engaged in agriculture and informal service activities, i.e. retailers, barber, vendors, businessman, home based work e.g. sari work, diamond polishing. Two to five per cent of population was engaged in government jobs and other services notably as bankers, teachers, doctors, lawyers and others.

Under MNREGA farm bunds were constructed five-six years ago, since then no major work had been undertaken. There were 500 MNREGA job cards holders, but no work had been carried out in the past few years. There were 53 registered Sakhi Mandals (under "mission mangalam") getting 25 per cent subsidy from government. Members of the sakhi mandals (minimum 11 members in each mandal) contributed Rs. 10 per month that was credited in the bank. Sakhi Mandal members could get loan at a nominal interest for expenditure on health, social functions etc. for a period of 12 months. Members were also imparted occupational training and undertook economic activities such as sari work, agarbatti making, rice crispies and animal husbandry.

Problems/Issues

- Two major problems were reported in Lilia, viz., lack of employment opportunities and irrigation availability, both of which impacted livelihoods. It was mentioned that if government intervened with regard to these two prominent problems the level of outmigration would decline considerably. With government's support harnessing the potential of Saladi lake could benefit not only Lilia but surrounding villages too and the problem of irrigation and employment could be resolved, as water for farming and industry would be available in abundance.
- Inadequate amenities posed a major problem.
- Lack of cleanliness was observed on account of inadequate equipment to perform the work.

- Water scarcity was the main impediment and farmers were totally dependent on rainfall or ground water.
- Labour shortage was reported in Lilia, especially when the crop season started.

Statutory status: If recognised as NP it was opined that the development funds would increase, improving service delivery (including garbage collection, water supply and roads). It would also provide encouragement to set up small and medium industries and training facilities for the youth leading to employment creation, curbing migration and also improve the poverty levels. However, it was felt that the tax liability would increase due to enhancement of services. Corruption would rise, it was felt. Currently the town lacked good institutes of higher education and vocational training and also infrastructural facilities like bank branches. These came in the way of fostering entrepreneurship and availability of credit for self-employment.

CONCLUDING REMARKS

A detailed exposition of the case studies from across the state of Gujarat brings forth some important underlying dimensions associated with the on-going processes of rural transformation and urbanisation. These are summarised briefly in this section as follows:

- It is evident that factors triggering the emergence of census towns in Gujarat are their location and others most notably, proximity to industrial and transportation corridors, nearness to industrial hubs or a GIDC estate, nature of agricultural hinterland and cropping patterns, besides the presence of APMC and retail activity. A large village that functions as the taluka headquarter or its location in proximity to or within an Urban Development Authority also results in a settlement to transform as an urban area. The presence of an APMC or government offices in a taluka headquarter act as a catalyst for the emergence of other agricultural marketing related activity and services (for instance, agricultural inputs, repairs, legal offices, notaries etc.). Eventually such settlements perform the functions of a service centre, often in the absence of a major city in the vicinity.
- Role of large scale industrial enterprises in the economic transition of villages into towns is dominant in Gujarat. Industrial activity predictably leads to the spillover of workers from agriculture sector and also spurs

secondary activities through growth of ancillary units, services etc., besides attracting migrant workers. Growth of non-farm activities is also rooted to the towns' economic base and proximity to hubs of specialization/clusters. Growth of population and changes in worker profile depends on presence of opportunities for self-employment or wage work, for instance availability of opportunities for gems/diamond processing, home based sari/embroidery work, salt manufacturing, ceramic/stone cutting, mechanical repairs, agro-processing, weaving etc. Policy effort to encourage micro enterprises in such towns, including tax benefits is required. This is especially true for the growth and expansion of the traditional non-farm economic activities.

- Also noteworthy is the fact that MNREGA as a scheme has played a limited role in either the creation of productive assets or in generating rural employment—both crucial in reshaping a rural economy. The prevailing wage rates in rural non-farm activities are far more than the wage rates fixed under the scheme in most of the towns surveyed, as a consequence its contribution to poverty alleviation is at best marginal.

- The census towns nearly everywhere are facing haphazard growth and inadequate amenities. The only exceptions, where infrastructure is satisfactory are the towns in the industrial districts of South Gujarat, that are recipients of taxes and income from industries (as CSR funds) or remittances. There is a dire need for formulating village level development plans to minimize the negative externalities and also to use taxes and the funds available under various schemes such as PURA, RURBAN, CSR etc. in a more judicious and coordinated manner.

- The migration patterns are shaped by the nature of the census town. Outmigration from a town is the norm where the economic base does not offer opportunities for income enhancement or for labour absorption or even where avenues for higher education etc. are lacking. Migrants elsewhere form a sizeable proportion, often floating, of the towns' population. Towns in close proximity to industrial estates are recipients of intra- and inter-state migrant workers and offer residential facilities to such workers in addition to services and shops. The industries are a source of water and air pollution and sometimes threaten the wellbeing and health of the residents. The industrial migrant labourers are more than often living in unhygienic and slum like conditions in such towns, threatening the environment. This calls for greater financial devolution to the local bodies for creation of better amenities.

- The other important feature is the attitude towards a town's status. It is quite apparent that while most of the residents in these settlements desire the statutory status, even in the face of higher taxation, there are apprehensions about negative fallouts such as rise in corruption, increasing insensitivity of the municipal machinery to local issues and enhancement of social evils. There were some towns with a substantial revenue base that did not desire a municipal or statutory status for fear of losing out on resources.

- Agriculture and cropping patterns vary but are also sometimes important in diversification of economic activities. One could see that awareness levels about modern techniques and inputs were high amongst the cultivators. Evident also were traces of hi-tech agriculture (mainly, adoption of sprinklers, drip irrigation, innovations in farm machinery, adoption of technology, attitude towards genetically modified cotton, adoption of high value crops etc.). The presence of distress conditions in agriculture, forcing the population to undertake non-farm activities was visible in others. Farmers faced severe constaints, such as lack of adequate irrigation facilities, government support etc. Agriculture overall is a declining activity, even though in some towns that had dispersed or tribal locations it still engaged substantial share of population. Agricultural land is increasingly being diverted to other uses. To that extent, focus of policy has to be directed for the development of the sector per se. A concerted policy effort is also required for skill development of the workers spilling out of agriculture, in addition to providing credit facilities and market linkages for a benign process of structural transformation.

- Nearly everywhere the consumption patterns are changing, especially with increased emphasis on spending on education, health, better lifestyles and diversification of food baskets. While the latter cannot always explain the occurrence of malnutrition and changing morbidity patterns (rising incidence of diabetes, heart related ailments), yet the urban influences are glaring and are here to stay. The emphasis on education and particularly girls' education is a change quite apparent in the countryside. The attraction for technical education, even medical education in some instances is a welcome and desirable trend and could be the fallout of rising employment opportunities for females in the non-agricultural sectors (diamond, apparel, textile, engineering etc.).

Overall, it can be stated that across the agro-climatic regions in Gujarat there is dynamism in the rural society. But for the isolated villages and towns, most of the state is acquiring the potential to assume urban features, without being victims of very high negative externalities. Where industries are located, the environmental factors are becoming important and require stringent enforcement of rules and regulations. Agriculture sector requires policy support to enhance output and labour productivity. Further, the variegated latent factors responsible for the emergence of census towns in Gujarat are not dormant and are increasingly becoming active in explaining the towns' growth and change in character.

REFERENCES

Campbell, D. 1975. Degrees of Freedom and the Case Study. *Comparative Political Studies* 8: 178–185.

Gulsecen, S., and A. Kubat. 2006. Teaching ICT to Teacher Candidates Using PBL: A Qualitative and Quantitative Evaluation. *Educational Technology & Society* 9 (2): 96–106.

Johnson, M.P. 2006. Decision Models for the Location of Community Corrections Centers. *Environment and Planning B-Planning & Design* 33 (3): 393–412.

Tellis, Winston. 1997. Introduction to Case Study. *The Qualitative Report* 3 (2). http://www.nova.edu/ssss/QR/QR3-2/tellis1.html.

Yin, R.K. 1984. *Case Study Research: Design and Methods*. Beverly Hills, CA: Sage Publications.

———. 1994. *Case Study Research: Design and Methods*. 2nd ed. Beverly Hills, CA: Sage Publishing.

Zainal, Zaidah. 2007. Case Study as a Research Method. *Jurnal Kemanusiaan* 9: 1–6.

CHAPTER 6

Census Towns in Gujarat: Economic, Social and Environmental Effects of Rural Transformation

INTRODUCTION

The earlier sections of the book dealt with the discussion on level, growth and casual factors for the emergence of rural non-farm sector at the macro level. The variables associated with the growth of non-farm employment were identified that set the tone for further analysis and explorations. The changes in the non-farm employment structure in rural and urban areas of Gujarat were explored at depth, along with the growing/sunrise sectors that are engaging the non-farm workers in rural areas, and are also fuelling the transformation process. The third chapter examined the tenets of urbanisation in Gujarat, in order to establish the linkages between non-farm employment growth, urban growth and the changing settlement morphology. Factors enabling the growth of census towns were identified. The potential for urban growth and the imminent challenges that require policy focus on account of the on-going transformation of the countryside were explored.

The Census of India presents a rich source of data regarding demography, workforce and amenities for these towns. Apart from using secondary data, a primary survey was conducted (by administering a detailed questionnaire) in randomly selected households to ascertain the social impacts of urbanism and changes in lifestyles and consumption patterns. Recourse was also taken to participatory methods of data gathering (e.g., focus group discussions). The objective was to unravel the nature of changes taking

© The Author(s) 2018   197
N. Mehta, *Rural Transformation in the Post Liberalization Period
in Gujarat*, https://doi.org/10.1007/978-981-10-8962-6_6

place in the rural/urban economic structure, migration/commuting trends social and other impacts of urbanisation. The stress areas in terms of environmental and social impacts, particularly where negative externalities were glaring were sought to be identified through focus group discussion of prominent citizens, chiefly panchayat functionaries and government officers, farmers, farm and non-farm labourers, artisans, teachers, professionals, enterprise owners, and workers belonging to the service sector.

It may be mentioned that the nature of enquiry was primarily limited to fact finding rather than testing of hypothesis. The data gathered through different means was tabulated to draw general inferences and identify peculiarities, if any. It may also be mentioned that although at the outset we had set out to try techniques such as exploratory factor analysis to quantify the economic, social and environmental dimensions of the transformation process, the nature of data gathered was not conducive to carrying out such analysis.

SELECTION OF CASE STUDIES

In the following Table 6.1 some general features and demographic profile of the selected towns are highlighted:

Out of the fifteen case studies, three were recognised as Census Towns (CT) in 2001 itself and remained as such even in 2011, viz., Kanodar, Ichchhapor and Kharaghoda. The remaining were recognised as CTs in 2011. However, five towns viz., Vavol, Chandrapur, Kabilpore, and Chhiri, have been merged with the nearby urban agglomerations as recently as 2015–2016. In the following paragraphs the underlying features of the case studies are highlighted in order to ascertain the enabling conditions for the transformation of large villages into towns.

NATURE OF ECONOMIC ACTIVITIES

Annexure Table 6.8 depicts the locational, demographic and employment aspects of the case studies. The location of the towns has been classified in terms of proximity to highway or location within the DMIC corridor (Kanodar, Chhiri), location within an industrial zone/district (Vaghodia, Antarjal, Chandrapur), tribal dominated region (Bhiloda, Sanjeli), peripheral location (Mankuwa, Kabilpor, Icchhapur, Vavol,) and dispersed location (Becharaji, Kharaghoda, Umrala, Lilia). Urbanization impact, (in terms of living conditions, consumption expenditure, aspects of urbanism) was quite

Table 6.1 Selection of case studies

No.	Census town	District	Population (2011)	Literacy rate (2011)	Sex ratio (2011)	Agro-climatic region	Status (New, existing, merged with city/UA as of 2016)
Tribal area							
1	Bhiloda	Aravalli	16,074	83.5%	936	Northern Gujarat	New
2	Sanjeli	Dahod	7448	83.0%	958	Middle Gujarat	New
Near highway/DMIC							
3	Kanodar[a]	Banaskantha	12,389	89.7%	1020	Northern Gujarat	Existing
4	Chhiri	Valsad	18,829	88.3%	609	Southern Hills	Merged (Vapi)
Industrial district							
5	Vaghodia	Vadodara	16,604	88.1%	909	Middle Gujarat	New
6	Chandrapur	Rajkot	8906	84.4%	929	North Saurashtra	Merged (Wankaner)
7	Antarjal	Kutch	11,256	72.7%	911	North West Arid	New
Periphery of UA/city							
8	Mankuwa	Kutch	11,975	79.7%	999	North West Arid	New
9	Vavol	Gandhinagar	12,628	89.4%	914	Northern Gujarat	New Merged (Gnagar)
10	Kabilpore	Navsari	15,699	90.0%	931	Southern Hills	New Merged (Navsari)
11	Ichchhapor[a]	Surat	12,097	90.0%	851	Southern Gujarat	Merged (Surat)
Dispersed location							
12	Kharagodha[a]	Surendranagar	11,944	61.1%	883	North Saurashtra	Existing
13	Umrala	Bhavnagar	8044	78.8%	931	North Saurashtra	New
14	Becharji	Mehsana	12,574	82.5%	923	Northern Gujarat	New
15	Lilia	Amreli	10,359	80.5%	1020	North Saurashtra	New

Source: Census 2011 and primary survey

[a]Towns that were recognised as census towns in 2001 census

visible in nearly all the towns, with the exception of Umrala, Kharaghoda and Chandarpur. These towns were fairly isolated and dispersed, and fell outside the influence of any major urban centre. Naturally the selected towns may fall in more than a single location typology but for the purpose of classification cognisance is made of the dominant feature of the towns.

Population of the towns varied from 7448 to 18,829 (2011). Examination of the percentage increase in population between 2001 to 2011 reveals that towns located in the proximity to large urban centres, in an industrial district or along the DMIC corridor showed medium to very high increase in population. Towns having a dispersed location or those located in remote regions, even the one along a national highway have shown low population growth between 2001 and 2011.

Predictably rural non-farm sector (RNFS) is the dominant economic activity of all the selected towns, the extent ranging from 63 per cent in Mankuwa to 99 per cent in Chhiri. Table 6.2a shows the relation between locational aspect and nature of RNFS. It can be seen that the dominant non-farm activity appears to be manufacturing or employment in the nearby GIDCs for most of the census towns studied, irrespective of their location category. Towns located in the eastern and northern tribal dominated regions have service activities, particularly retail trade or other tertiary activities as the dominant non-farm activity. Such locations besides having agriculture, also serve as the market/service centres for the surrounding rural settlements. Around a quarter of the workforce in these towns (Bhiloda and

Table 6.2a   Location of towns and dominant RNFS

No.	Nature of rural non-farm sector				
	Location of CT	Service centre/ retail hub	Manufacturing/ GIDC	Farm led growth	None of above
1	Near highway/ DMIC		Kanodar Chhiri		
2	Industrial district		Antarjal Vaghodia Chandrapur		
3	Tribal dominated area	Bhiloda Sanjeli		Bhiloda	
4	Periphery of city/ UA	Mankuwa	Kabilpore Ichchhapor Vavol	Mankuwa	
5	Dispersed location	Lilia	Lilia Kharaghoda		Becharaji Umrala

Source: Annexure Table 6.8

Sanjeli) are still engaged as agricultural workers. It is interesting to note that Sanjeli in Dahod district witnessed a spurt in all round growth (construction, small business, trade) after the riots in 2002, on account of the compensation and subsidies received by the residents as rehabilitation packages. Some of the towns, such as Bhiloda, Lilia and Mankuwa have dominance of more than one economic (non-farm) sector. In Mankuwa (Kutch) located in the proximity of Bhuj, services dominate, in addition to agriculture. Becharaji, Lilia, Kharaghoda and Umrala can be treated as examples of dispersed pattern of urban growth. Becharaji is a temple town, with its activity base geared towards catering to the temple visitors. However, with a special economic zone (Mandal-Becharji SIR as well as Honda company) being developed in the vicinity, manufacturing jobs for the residents are increasing. It is divided into two settlements, with Bechar village largely dominated by agriculturalists. It also serves as the taluka headquarters. Umrala attracts tenant cultivators and workers who commute to other urban areas for employment. Kharaghoda is located in the vicinity of the Little Rann of Kutch, its agriculture is constrained by lack of adequate irrigation facilities. It traditionally is the home of the "*agariyas*" or the salt workers who belong to the town but work in the salt pans for a major part of the year. It also houses the public sector Hindustan Salt Works. Lilia village has transformed into a town led by industrial development in the Liliya GIDC and also serves as a service and market centre for the relatively underdeveloped part of the state, i.e., Amreli. It is also interesting to note that conversion of agricultural to non-agricultural land is not happening in a big way (as observed during field explorations) in Kharaghoda, Umrala and Lilia. Evidently their remoteness and distance from major urban centres precludes major industrial investments or real estate activity.

While secondary sector dominantly engages the workers in Chhiri, Antarjal, Kabilpor and Ichchhapor, these serve more as residential locations for the secondary sector workers engaged in industries and GIDCs in the surrounding Valsad, Vapi, Surat and Hajira belt. These locations have very little manufacturing activity per se, but serve as destinations for industrial workers who are migrants from other states. Some like Kabilpore and Ichchhapor were also emerging as centres for real estate development –an extension or suburb of the nearby UA. After land acquisition by the Gandhinagar Urban Development Agency, Vavol houses a large number of service sector workers (government employees) and industrial workers. Similarly Antarjal has benefitted from the post-earthquake reconstruction activities in Kutch, that led to large scale industrial and port led growth. With the influx of intra-and inter-state migrants, the town has emerged as a major site for real estate and residential activity. It also houses the workers employed in Gandhidham, Adipur, and Kandla areas. Kanodar is a manufacturing hub of auto parts and automobile repairs—an activity that has benefited by virtue of its location along the Ahmedabad-Delhi highway.

In order to get a deeper insight into the changes in economic activities, the towns were cross tabulated in terms of location and percentage change in category of "other workers" (Table 6.2b) Census workforce data suffers from certain inadequacies, notably, non-farm workers are classified as those engaged in "household industries" and the remaining are clubbed as "other workers". Workers engaged in the former category form a minuscule share of the workforce, ranging from 0.3 per cent (Kharaghoda) to 10.4 per cent in Umrala. However, other workers is the most dominant industrial category in all the towns surveyed, engaging workers ranging from 57.1 per cent in Sanjeli to 96 per cent in Kharaghoda. It may be mentioned that this category is inclusive of allied activities, non-household manufacturing and all the tertiary sector activities. Change in this category of workers is the driver for non-farm sector growth and subsequently a village being recognised as a town, in addition to density and population criteria.

The largest increase in share of other workers was observed in the towns located either in an industrial region (Chandrapur, Vaghodia), near transport corridors (Kanodar) or those growing independently and away from the influence of large urban bodies (Becharaji, Unrala, Kharaghoda, Lilia). This is possibly the underlying reason for conversion of villages to towns. With the exception of Vavol, the remaining towns showed either a low or negative change in this category of workers, thereby indicating that popu-

Table 6.2b Location of town and change in "other workers"

No.	Location of CT	Per cent point change in other workers (2001–2011)			
		High > 10	Moderate 5–10	Low < 5	Negative
1	Near highway/ DMIC		Kanodar		Chhiri
2	Industrial district	Chandrapur	Vaghodia	Antarjal	
3	Tribal dominated area			Bhiloda, Sanjeli	
4	Periphery of city/ UA	Vavol		Kabilpore	Mankuwa, Ichchhapor
5	Dispersed location	Becharji, Umrala	Kharaghoda, Lilia		

Source: Based on Census 2001 and 2011 data

lation expansion and density played a more important role in these towns being recognised as urban settlements. As will be seen in the subsequent sections, migrant workers and settlers have played a major role in bringing about changes in the economic profile of these towns.

Annexure Table 6.9 provides a profile of the micro, small and medium enterprises in the selected towns, based on the data from the MSME Census. It can be noted from the data that manufacturing, processing, assembling and job work was the dominant activity within the MSMEs, followed by repairs and services. Also, all the units have developed independently, and are not part of any industrial cluster. Annexure Table 6.10 depicts the details of the agriculture sector in the towns surveyed. As was observed in the earlier paragraphs, agriculture is an activity that is losing its importance in these towns. We look at the effect of location on share in agricultural employment in Table 6.3, based on Table 6.10. During 2011, agriculture employed workers ranging from 1 per cent (Chhiri) to 40 per cent (Lilia). Engagement in agriculture is the largest i.e., more than 20 per cent of the workforce in towns located in tribal hinterland and those having a dispersed location, due to inadequacy of avenues for employment diversification. Becharaji also belongs to this location category, but has around 11 per cent of its workforce engaged in primary activities. Mankuwa located at the periphery of Bhuj (Kutch) also has dominance of agriculture, due to absence of secondary sector job opportunities.

Agriculture is a shrinking activity can be observed from the decline in the magnitude of workforce engaged in agriculture sector during 2001 to 2011 in nearly all the towns. The decline in share of agricultural workforce ranged from −1.7 percentage points (Chhiri) to −13.3 percentage points (Vavol) during 2001 to 2011. The decline was also quite noticeable in case of Chandarpur (−12.5% points), followed by Kharaghoda (−7.5% points)

Table 6.3   Location and agricultural employment (2011)

Location of CT	Share of agricultural workers		
	<10%	*10 to 20%*	*>20%*
1 Near highway/DMIC	Kanodar, Chhiri		
2 Industrial district	Antarjal	Vaghodia, Chandrapur	
3 Tribal dominated area			Bhiloda, Sanjeli
4 Periphery of city/UA	Kabilpore	Vavol, Ichchhapor	Mankuwa
5 Dispersed location	Kharaghoda	Becharji	Umrala, Lilia

Source: Based on Census 2001 and 2011 data

and Becharaji (−6.4% points). Apart from Sanjeli, Ichchhapur (Surat) was the other case that depicted gains in the share of agricultural workforce (by around 3.8 per cent points). These are the two towns with predominance of cash crops, namely, wheat, rice, horticulture and sugarcane and also have irrigation available through surface water sources (dams and canals). Thus availability of irrigation from surface sources is essential for agriculture to remain a sustainable activity. Dependence on ground water in rain fed regions was often the primary reason for employment diversification. Ground water was the predominant mode of irrigation across all the towns, except Middle and Southern Gujarat towns.

The changes in area devoted to agriculture would have been a far more critical variable in this respect. As per the recent revenue records available from the Gram Panchayats, it is evident that the extent of cultivated area was the highest in Umrala, Lilia (83%), Becharji (78%), Mankuwa (71%) and Vavol (69%). It was the least in Chhiri, Ichchhapur (less than 25%) and Kharaghoda (39%). However, inadequate temporal data for all the case studies does not allow detailed investigation into the land use changes over time. Nonetheless, on comparing information available for cultivated area from Census 2001 with the recent revenue records, it can be seen that cultivated area declined from 69 to 20 per cent in Bhiloda, from 98 to 56.4 per cent in Sanjeli, from 68 to 55 per cent in Vaghodia and from 96 to 17 per cent in Chhiri. Not much change was visible in Mankuva, Vavol, Chandrapur, and Lilia. In the remaining, i.e., Becharaji and Umrala there was some increase in cultivated area. It is also noteworthy that except Vaghodia, in all the towns landholding pattern was dominated by small and marginal cultivators, that may have spurred increased engagement in non-farm jobs for income enhancement. Presence of APMC markets in the agriculturally developed cases (Bhiloda, Sanjeli, Umrala, Lilia) add to their role as service centres for the surrounding villages. This is also true for Becharaji and Vaghodia (Table 6.10).

MIGRATION AND COMMUTING PATTERNS

During the course of the field study we tried to ascertain whether the increase in the population across the settlements was on account of migration and whether the town was an attractive destination for migrants and commuters. The nature of activities that attracted migrants to the town were investigated. The extent and purpose of out-migration from the town was also explored. The information from the primary survey, focus group discussions and interviews of prominent citizens is summarised in Table 6.4.

Table 6.4 Details of migration/commuting patterns

No.	District	Census town	Is CT attractive destination for immigrants/commuters	Activities migrants are engaged in the CT	Activities commuters are engaged in CT	Is the CT having outmigration	Purpose of migration/commuting
1	Aravalli	Bhiloda	Yes	From surroundings as owners of real estate, retail trade (Sindhis & Rajasthanis), construction labour, govt. service	Services such as tailors, retail trade, casual labour in agriculture	Yes	Education, employment to cities, govt service, teachers
2	Dahod	Sanjeli	Yes		Agricultural labour, retail trade, services (e.g., tailors, artisanal activity), teachers, professionals and govt services	Yes	Agricultural labour to all parts of Gujarat, urban employment, higher education
3	Banaskantha	Kanodar	Yes	Owners of industry, engg workshops and services (teachers), real estate dev for housing purpose	Workers in SSI (Auto, repairs, food processing, engineering, Agricultural labourers)	Yes	Abroad, education, regular employment in Gujarat cities, jobs in Palanpur, Siddhpur
4	Valsad	Chhiri	Yes	Workers in GIDC/industries from other states residing in CT	GIDC and industries in Vapi, Valsad	Yes	Employment in Valsad, Vapi, Navsari, Surat, Mumbai etc
5	Vadodara	Vaghodia	Yes	Intra- and inter-state migrants residing and working in GIDC, industries, educational institutes	Industry owners commuting from Vadodara, workers in GIDC	Yes	Daily commuters to Vadodara, (govt service, teachers, service sector), GIDC, higher education

(continued)

Table 6.4 (continued)

No.	District	Census town	Is CT attractive destination for immigrants/ commuters	Activities migrants are engaged in the CT	Activities commuters are engaged in CT	Is the CT having outmigration	Purpose of migration/ commuting
6	Rajkot	Chandrapur	Yes	Workers residing in CT, working in agriculture and Wankaner GIDC	Education, employment	Yes	For employment to Rajkot, Morbi, Wankaner
7	Kutch	Antarjal	Yes	Port/SEZ/FTZ workers from within state/outside Gujarat residing in CT, employed in services, teachers, transport workers	Govt employees, service activities and teachers etc.	Yes	Women workers employed in garment etc. units in FTZ, workers in ports, transport sector, urban employment, higher education
8	Kutch	Mankuwa	No		Workers in trading, construction, Kutir Udhyog, from Bhuj, agricultural workers	Yes	Abroad (Patels), higher education, employment
9	Gandhinagar	Vavol	Yes	Housing purpose	Industrial and service sector workers	Yes	Govt job and jobs in GIDC (Gandhinagar)
10	Navsari	Kabilpor	Yes	Workers in GIDC from other states, Navsari residing in CT	GIDC, govt service	Yes	For employment in other Gujarat cities, abroad
11	Surat	Ichchhapor	Yes	Workers in GIDC (Diamond/textile units) from other states residing in CT, real estate development	GIDC, govt service	Yes	For better jobs in big cities (Surat, Mumbai)

12	Mehsana	Becharji	Yes	Not known	Jobs in cement/marble industry, retail trade & temple services, repairing enterprises, teachers, govt service, agricultural labour	Yes	Higher education, urban employment in Mehsana etc.
13	Surendranagar	Kharagodha	Yes	Govt. sector, services (tailor, lawyers, priest, teachers)	Salt works, govt. sector	Yes	Agariyas working in Rann for up to nine months, higher education, jobs in Patdi, Surendranagar and other cities
14	Bhavnagar	Umrala	Yes	Agricultural labour, tenant cultivators, workers in diamond units, GIDC	Retail trade, casual labour in industries and agriculture	Yes	Some diamond unit owners shifted to Surat/Bhavnagar, higher education, employment in cities
15	Amreli	Lilia	Yes	Workers from other states residing & working in diamond units, textile units, NGOs, Liliya GIDC	From Amreli/sorrounding areas to work in SSIs like diamond, agarbatti etc., retail trade, services	Yes	To Amreli & other cities in govt service, higher education and employment

Source: Primary survey and focus group discussions

From the table above it can be discerned that these towns have been recipients of migrant population (from within and outside the state) that has contributed to the increase in their population size. The migrants were largely residing in these towns and working elsewhere. This has led to considerable real estate development in most of the towns located in peripheral locations or within industrial zones. The absence of building regulations is fostering unprecedented growth in construction activity, mainly for residential purposes in and around the towns surveyed. Proximity to large urban centres (Vavol, Ichchhapor, Kablipor), and availability of employment opportunities in the vicinity (Vaghodia, Kanodar) is also spurring the growth of housing societies in these towns. Even in Bhiloda, tribal land is being converted for residential purposes by settlers, often by unfair means. Sanjeli has seen a spurt in renovation and construction of new houses after the riots. Thus construction activity, often boosted by influx of migrant workers is an important driver for the transformation of these towns.

ACCESS TO PHYSICAL AND SOCIAL INFRASTRUCTURE

Annexure Tables 6.11 and 6.12 depict the physical and social amenities data for the selected towns, as derived from Census 2011 and the primary survey.

The picture across the towns appears to be dismal with respect to the physical amenities. It can be observed from the data that most of the towns located at the periphery of UAs or and along the industrial corridors are densely populated. Household electricity connections were found to be rather low in Sanjeli, Ichchhapor and Chandrapur. Majority of the towns housing industrial workers were lacking in tap water facility from treated sources. Most of the towns, with the exception of Kanodar, Ichchhapur Becharji and Bhiloda also suffered from either inadequate drainage and toilet facilities or solid waste disposal facilities.

Predictably the towns having peripheral location or near major transportation arteries were better off in terms of road connectivity and quality. Surprisingly, tribal towns had the highest per capita ratio of pucca road length. Industrial towns and ones having dispersed location were worse off in this respect. Public facilities such as street lights, fire fighting services and bus routes were severely lacking in all the towns surveyed. Availability of fire fighting services is of considerable importance as most of the towns studied were marked by congested nature of habitation. Further the expansion of built up area, often without regard for basic tenets of town planning and building regulations increases the vulnerability of the populations residing in these towns. However, as the detailed narrative of each town separately had revealed the towns, especially the taluka headquarters were benefitting from the RURBAN scheme of the government that aimed at creation/upgradation of village level infrastructure facilities.

Health and educational infrastructure are depicted in Annexure Table 6.12. Census of India and Panchayat sources were the main sources of information. However, census information pertains to 2011 and since then considerable developments have occurred, especially in the towns at the periphery of UAs. Chhiri, Chandrapur, Antarjal, Kabilpor, Kharaghoda have inadequate health and education facilities, while Kanodar, Lilia, Umrala, Sanjeli had relatively more developed health facilities. For referral and tertiary care, none of the towns surveyed had multi-speciality hospitals or diagnostic services and the residents had to travel to the nearest urban centre. While anganwadis and primary schools are present in all the towns, most of the towns lacked institutions for higher education. It was ascertained during field investigations that for college education, the students were largely commuting to the nearby large city. Becharaji, Vaghodia and Lilia had arts and commerce colleges. Notably, science and technical education facilities were nearly absent in all the towns surveyed, that does not bode well for the future employment prospects of the younger generation. Banking infrastructure is pivotal for financial inclusion, and it can be observed that Chhiri, Kanodar, Antarjal and the peripheral towns had a lower density of bank branches. Overall, it is observed that the tribal locations were better served with social infrastructure. However, community halls, auditoriums and reading facilities were quite sparse. It was a common refrain amongst the respondents that facilities for extra- and co-curricular activities, entertainment and leisure were lacking in the towns and with changing aspirations and urban influences such facilities were being increasingly desired.

IMPACT OF URBANISATION

Lifestyles and Consumption Habits

In order to assess the changes in lifestyle, consumption habits and to ascertain social impacts of rural transformation, a primary survey of 154 households was conducted in the selected case studies with the help of a structured questionnaire. The samples were selected randomly, by adopting a snowball technique of sample identification. Care was taken to cover different strata of residents from each census town. Table 6.5 provides an overview of the sample households by pooling data gathered from all the selected towns. Nearly two-thirds (61%) of the households belonged to the general category, and average size of the household was 5.3. Nearly half of the household heads reportedly had completed school education, 12 per cent possessed a graduate degree/diploma and 8 per cent had professional qualifications. Almost 60 per cent of the households were non-

Table 6.5 Profile of respondents of primary survey

Total respondents	154
Males (%)	93.5
Females (%)	6.5
Average age of household head (years)	46
Social group (%)	
General	61.2
OBC	20.4
SC	4.8
ST	13.6
Average size of household (No.)	5.3
Education level of HH head (%)	
Illiterate	17.5
Primary	18.8
Middle	5.8
Secondary & HS	48.9
Diploma/Graduate	12.3
PG & Professional	7.8
BPL card holders (%)	14
MNREGA card holders (%)	1
Household type (%)	
Self-employed in Agriculture	37.7
Self-employed in Non Agri.	35.6
Agricultural Labour	2.1
Casual Labour	14.4
Others	10.3
Principal industry of household head (%)	
Primary sector	36.6
Manufacturing/Construction	18.3
Trade/Repairs/Hotels	15.0
Transport/Communication	3.3
Services	26.8

Source: Primary survey

cultivating households, (36% self-employed in non-agriculture and 14% casual labour and 10% others). With regards to principal industry of head of the household, agriculture and allied activity engaged only 37 per cent of the respondents, while 18 per cent had secondary sector jobs. Nearly a third of the respondents had non-traditional service activity as their principal occupation.

The influence of urbanisation was quite visible in the living standards of the respondents. Table 6.6 shows some features of the living standard of the households surveyed. It may be noted that 85 per cent of the respondents lived in *pucca* dwellings, and 94 per cent of the respondents owned their houses. A miniscule share lived in rented premises. The quality of life is reflected by the fact that 72 per cent of the respondents possessed a two-wheeler and three per cent had an automobile. In fact a quarter of the respondents possessed both two-wheelers as well as a four wheeler. Except for four per cent, all other households had bank or post office accounts. Only 21 per cent of the respondents reported hiring domestic servants, and such a trend was not yet common in the towns surveyed.

Observations during the field survey revealed that most of the households surveyed possessed amenities that were ubiquitous in middle class

Table 6.6   Lifestyle characteristics of respondents

Type of dwelling unit (%)	
Pucca	82.4
Semi pucca	12.4
Kuccha	5.2
Ownership of house (%)	
Own	94.0
Hired	6.0
Ownership of vehicle (%)	
Two wheeler	72.1
Four wheeler	2.9
Both	25.0
Bank/post office account holder (%)	96.1
Hiring HH servant (%)	20.5
Primary source of HH energy (%)	
LPG	81.3 (56.0)
Fire wood	14.7 (36.0)
Kerosene	4.0 (8.0)

Source: Primary survey

Note: Figures in brackets show the situation in this respect 10 years ago

urban households, viz. television, radio, computer, air-conditioner/air coolers, refrigerator, furniture and house furnishings, consumer durables and kitchen utilities etc., with the exception of BPL households. Enquiry into the energy use pattern revealed that presently nearly 81 per cent of the households were using LPG, while only 19 per cent were using other sources, mainly firewood. However, some changes were observed in the past decade. The respondents were asked to recall the fuel used by the household 10 years ago. It was reported that only 56 per cent of the households were using LPG a decade ago, and nearly 36 per cent were using firewood. Thus there has been a positive change with nearly 25 per cent of the households having shifted to the use of LPG in place of firewood or stove.

The food and non-food consumption patterns and changes therein due to urban influence can be viewed from the information summarised in Table 6.7a.

The data collected does not permit us from having a temporal view of the consumption habits of the residents in the census towns. Nonetheless the pattern of expenditure on food items reported is quite revealing. Nearly 54 per cent of the food expenditure is on milk and dairy products, fruits, vegetables and dry fruits etc., while only 29 per cent is on purchase of food grains (cereals and pulses and product thereof). The remaining share is for expenditure on spices, sugar, intoxicants, beverages etc. Thus the weightage of the expenditure on expensive and diversified food items is starkly more. This indicates that households residing in these towns have been witnessing diversification of diets. Furthermore, the share of expenditure on food items per capita was (for average household size of 5.3) 38 per cent of the total expenditure, quite close to that estimated for urban areas in Gujarat using NSS data (2010–2011) at 42 per cent (Mehta 2012b).

Overall share of expenditure on non-food items was 62 per cent, again indicating aspects of urbanism. Within the average non-food expenditure, it was heartening to note that the largest share was devoted towards education (47%), followed by health (11%). However, this also shows that considerable private expenditure is being incurred on such services even in the semi-urban areas, thereby indicating the inadequacy of government action on these fronts. In fact the respondents expressed their distress and concern about a sharp rise in expenses on private school and college education. Rent and taxes also reportedly formed around 16 per cent of the yearly expenditure. Expenditure on entertainment and leisure, household consumer goods and transport shared around 7 to 8 per cent of total non-food expenditure. Albeit miniscule, expenditure on consumer services

Table 6.7a Effect of urbanisation on consumption patterns

Average expenditure on non-food consumption (Rs/year/HH)		
Entertainment	10,500	(7.0)
Furniture/consumer durables	12,215	(8.1)
Consumer services	5918	(3.9)
Education	70,726	(47.1)
Medical	16,010	(10.7)
Transportation	11,331	(7.6)
Rent/taxes	23,355	(15.6)
Average expenditure on food consumption (Rs/month/HH)		
Cereals & products	1272	(16.6)
Pulses & products	968	(12.6)
Milk & products	2304	(30.0)
Vegetables, fruits, dryfruits	1852	(24.1)
Sugar, spices, beverages	893	(11.6)
Pan, tobacco	394	(5.1)
Ratio of food to total expenditure/capita	38%	
Change in food consumption habits in 10 years (% reporting)		
Yes	52.7	
No change	47.3	
For HHs reporting yes, increase up to 25%	33.8	
Increase bet 25–50%	9.1	
Cannot say	57.1	
Changes in non-food consumption in 10 years (% reporting)		
Yes	65.5	
No change	34.5	
For HHs reporting yes, increase up to 25%	42.9	
increase bet 25–50%	9.1	
Cannot say	48.1	

Source: Primary survey

Note: Figures in brackets are percentage to total

(tailors, beauticians, laundry etc.) also accounted for 4 per cent of non-food expenditure.

The respondents were posed queries regarding any changes observed in household consumption expenditure and increased importance to certain items of expenditure in the last decade or so. Nearly all the respondents indicated considerable shifts in the expenditure patterns and lifestyles, as indicated in Table 6.7a. About 53 per cent reported changes in food consumed over the period of time, including enhanced consumption of fruits, vegetables, processed foods, dairy products and outside food. Amongst those who reported a change, nearly a third reported increase of up to 25 per cent and nine per cent also reported increase up to 50 per cent. A larger share of respondents—66 per cent conceded to change in non-food consumption expenditure—i.e., better clothing/footwear, furniture, quality of house, consumer durables, entertainment, education, health and social expenditure etc. Forty three per cent amongst these households indicated increase of such expenses by nearly 25 per cent, while nine per cent mentioned increase of up to 50 per cent. A large share of the respondents was reticent about indicating changes in their household expenditure patterns, for fear of attracting unnecessary attention and official scrutiny. However, with the limited information it can be easily deduced that residents of the census towns were undergoing several changes in their consumption habits that were in tune with the urban way of life.

Social and Environmental Impacts

From Table 6.7b, it can be observed that urbanisation and transformation of the villages in to census towns led to certain social impacts. More than three-quarters of the respondents observed that urbanisation was accompanied by greater emphasis on higher education. This observation came from all strata of respondents and was also emphasised in the focus group

Table 6.7b   Social impacts of urbanisation (% reporting)

Impact on higher education	
Increase	77.9
No change	22.1
Impact on girls' education	
Increase	67.5
No change	32.5
Impact of media on lifestyles	
Yes	66.2
No change	18.8
Cannot say	14.9
Marriage expenditures have increased	93.5
Social reform[a]	49.6
Adverse health impact (Malnutrition, cancer, diabetes, heart problem, joint pain and others)	75.8

Source: Primary survey

[a]Social customs indicate relaxation in death customs, superstitions, and reduction in social expenditures

discussions. As agriculture was losing its importance and with the urban areas/cities holding greater opportunities for employment, it was widely felt that higher education and professional degrees was the key towards a better life and economic progress. For that most of the respondents were willing to spend more. Besides reflecting a desire for a stable economic life, the cross-cutting spending on education also points to the perceived fragility and dissatisfaction with the current occupation in the local non-farm economy, which to many is simply a survival strategy. Across social categories, respondents recognised and acknowledged the value of education, which alone can enable their children to find regular salaried jobs and pull them out of agriculture. However, they also realised that the currently available education in local schools is unlikely to be of help. In the town and outward fringes of the towns, a variety of private education providers had emerged. The presence of tuition and coaching centres, private English-medium schools, reveals a demand for education, distant from urban centres of education, to be able to procure and provide educational services for their children.

More than two-thirds of the respondents also indicated that in the present context girls' higher education (up to higher secondary or even college) was important for their economic and social advancement. Girls were also being given greater opportunity to enrol for technical education. The most common avenue for girls were reported to be teaching, nursing, vocational training and engineering. Given this, there appears to be presence of a serious gap in the aspirations of people and the facilities available on ground.

Questions were also posed before the respondents pertaining to awareness generation due to spread of print and digital media. A very high share—66 per cent of the respondents conceded that exposure to information through varied avenues was having its impact on living standards, general village development, enrolment in education institution, social events and expenditure etc. Only 19 per cent said that such impacts were not affecting their life styles, while 15 per cent declined any social impact of urbanisation and awareness generation.

Nearly half of the respondents agreed that urbanisation and spread of education had impacted positively in bringing in social reforms in the traditional village society. This was most visible in the relaxation of death/birth related and other social expenditures, as also superstitious beliefs. However, around 94 per cent conceded that with the opening up of communication channels and urban influences, demonstration effect in consumption related expenditure had gone up; this was especially visible in marriage related expenses. Discussion also revealed that the negative side of changing food habits, particularly junk food and eating out was being manifested in malnutrition and adverse health outcomes and morbidity (blood pressure, diabetes, cancer etc. and other lifestyle related diseases). Nearly 76 per cent of the respondents indicated this.

During the field explorations and discussion with residents, the negative externalities of the urbanisation and rural transformation process on environment were ascertained (Table 6.7c). These can be broadly categorised into two viz., (a) relating to land and (b) living environment. A widely reported externality of urban growth and industrialisation was pollution (89%). In some towns in the vicinity of industries mention also was made of declining fertility of land due to water, air pollution and degradation, leading to declining output levels.

It was most commonly mentioned that population expansion was taking a toll on the water levels and was reflected in water scarcity conditions. The towns were marked by inadequate storage capacities and proper management of water resources. Most of the towns had open drains, absence of potable water, apart from *kuccha* roads and inadequate sewage facilities. In the towns where agriculture was still a dominant activity the farmers complained of inadequate irrigation development leading to over drawal of ground water and reported its negative impact on overall farm profitability. This was inevitably forcing the people to shift to non-farm sector as agriculture was failing due to declining output levels and water scarcity. Under such conditions, non-farm sector growth can be viewed as arising from 'push' factors.

Village *gaucher* lands were being encroached upon by the poor and this was causing considerable hardship to sections of marginal farmers. Conversion of agricultural to non-agricultural land was seen as a major negative fallout of the urbanisation process by 67 per cent of the respon-

Table 6.7c Environmental impacts of industrial growth and urbanization (% reporting)

Decline in soil fertility due to high use of fertilizer/pesticide	8.5
Decline in average rainfall and climate change	50.9
Environment pollution i.e., air, water and noise pollution	88.8
Depletion of water (high demand of water, poor storage system, over exploitation of water, lack of management)	93.5
Gaucher encroachment	5.2
Agricultural land converted in non—agricultural uses (due to lack of water, electricity, lack of labour, fragmentation of land holdings, land acquisition) (except Umrala, Lilia)	66.6

Source: Primary survey

dents. The reasons for this were diverse, i.e., land acquisition, lack of irrigation, supply bottlenecks of labour, uneconomic holdings due to land fragmentation etc. While it resulted in escalation of the land value and monetary benefits, a sharp feeling of dispossession prevailed. It also led to enhanced unemployment, particularly for those sections that had given up agriculture and were bound to do non-remunerative non-farm activity. Despite the stringent controls on conversion of tribal land, this process was commonly observed in the two case studies and had increased with the influx of migrants. Land scarcity due to commercial exploitation also cropped up in a number of FGDs as a negative fallout of urbanisation.

There was absence of any village/town level development plan in the census towns other than those falling in TP Scheme areas, and it was observed that landuse changes were happening in the towns indiscriminately. Towns in Southern Gujarat housing the industrial workers had slum like conditions. That the urban amenities were inadequate across the case studies has been mentioned earlier. Most of the census towns visually displayed congested living environment with under developed infrastructure. Even though land conversion was happening in a big way, the new colonies and real estate development was happening in a haphazard manner without adequate planned facilities and services. While the builders were acquiring land and constructing residential colonies, these did not provide for water availability, roads, or sewage systems. FSI norms were often being disregarded and building bye-laws were being flouted. Encroachment on roads and an explosion of retail activity had led to problems of traffic and congestion in some of the towns surveyed. In the long run deterioration of the living environment could prove to be hazardous and detrimental to the growth of these settlements.

CONCLUDING REMARKS

The focus of this section was to unravel the underlying changes taking place in the rural economic structure, migration/commuting trends, as well as impacts of urbanisation process on consumption patterns and societal norms. The stress areas particularly where negative externalities are emerging were sought to be identified. The findings can be summarised as follows:

- Existence of a relation between locational aspect and nature of RNFS cannot be denied. Towns located in the tribal dominated regions have service activities, particularly retail trade or other tertiary activities as the dominant non-farm activity. Such locations serve as the market/service centres for the surrounding rural settlements. Presence of APMC markets in the agriculturally developed cases add to their role as service centres. Evidently their remoteness and distance from urban areas precludes major industrial investments or real estate activity. Towns in the midst of industrial districts even though housing little manufacturing activity per se, serve as destinations for industrial workers who are migrants from other states.

- Change in 'other workers'" category is the driver for non-farm sector growth and subsequently a village being recognised as a town. The largest increase in the share of other workers was observed in towns either located in an industrial region, near transport corridors also in those growing independently and away from the influence of large urban bodies. Agriculture is an activity that is losing its importance in the census towns. Engagement in agriculture is the largest in towns located in tribal hinterland and those having a dispersed location.
- Migrant workers and settlers have played a major role in bringing about changes in the economic profile of the towns. Some towns have been recipients of migrant population (from within and outside the state) that has contributed to the increase in the size of population. This has led to considerable real estate development in most of the towns located in peripheral locations or within industrial zones. The absence of building regulations is fostering unprecedented growth in construction activity, often boosted by influx of migrant workers and has been an important driver for the transformation of these towns.
- The picture across the towns appears to be dismal with respect to the physical amenities. Predictably the towns having peripheral location or near major transportation arteries were better off in terms of road connectivity and quality. Public facilities such as street lights, fire fighting services and bus routes were severely lacking in all the towns surveyed. The RURBAN scheme of the government is helping to ease some of the infrastructure bottlenecks and creation of village level facilities.
- The towns are lacking in specialised health care, or diagnostic services. Most of the towns also lack institutions for higher education forcing commuting, sometimes for long distances. Moreover, facilities for extra-and co-curricular activities, entertainment and leisure were lacking but strongly desired with the changing aspirations and urban influences.
- There was considerable improvement in the lifestyle of the residents surveyed. Households residing in these towns have been witnessing

diversification of diet and changes in consumption in tune with urban way of life. The share of expenditure on food items per capita was 38 per cent of the total expenditure, quite close to that estimated for urban areas in Gujarat. Within the average non-food expenditure, the largest share was devoted towards education followed by health indicating considerable private expenditure on such services, and points towards the inadequacy of government action on these fronts.

• Traditional societal norms were weakening; urbanisation and spread of awareness through media channels (print, TV, internet) had impacted positively in bringing about reforms in the traditional village society. However, the negative feature of changing food habits was being manifested in malnutrition and adverse health outcomes. Urban influences were manifested in importance being accorded to private schooling and to higher education and its percieved role in attaining better livelihoods. Facilities though rarely matched with the people's aspirations.

• Environmental impacts related to land and the living environment. Apart from air, water and land pollution due to industrial activity, population expansion was cited to cause water scarcity conditions. Also, inadequate irrigation development was reported to have negative impact on overall farm profitability. This was inevitably forcing the people to shift to the non-farm sector. Moreover, land conversion to non-agricultural uses while valorising land and providing monetary benefits, often resulted in dispossession of productive assets and has exacerbated unemployment.

• The absence of a village/town level development plan and planning mechanism contributed to indiscriminate landuse changes and haphazard growth of the towns. Added to that, the encroachment of commons and explosion of retail activity was causing problems of traffic and congestion in some of the towns surveyed, akin to that experienced in bigger cities. In the long run deterioration of the living environment could prove to be hazardous and detrimental to the growth of these settlements.

From the discussion it emerges that policy focus is desired on all of these fronts for a smooth process of rural economic transformation. This is also imperative in the interest of emergence of a sustainable and functional settlement hierarchy that in future eases the constraints being faced by the explosive metropolitan expansion.

ANNEXURE

Table 6.8   Demographic & general details of selected census towns

No.	Census town	Nearest city & distance in km	Population 2011	% change (2001 to 11)	Urbanization impact	Location of CT[a]	Nature of CT[b]	Main worker
1	Bhiloda	Shamlaji 17	16,074	13.6	Y	3	3.1	77.6%
2	Sanjeli	Dohad 59	7448	22.2	Y	3	1	64.1%
3	Kanodar	Palanpur 13	12,389	11.3	Y	1	2	94.9%
4	Becharji	Mehsana 35	12,574	17.8	Y	5	0	95.4%
5	Vavol	Gandhinagar 5	12,628	79.5	Y	4	1.2	84.5%
6	Vaghodia	Vadodara 22	16,604	23.2	Y	2	2	77.3%
7	Kharagodha	Surendranagar 65	11,944	9.3	N	5	2	89.2%
8	Umrala	Bhavnagar 38	8044	−0.01	N	5	0	88.5%
9	Chandrapur	Morvi 32	8906	47.5	N	2	2	87.4%
10	Lilia	Rajkot 120	10,359	4.6	Y	5	1.2	81.9%
11	Mankuwa	Bhuj 12	11,975	20.9	Y	4	1.3	86.9%
12	Antarjal	Gandhigham 2	11,256	86.5	Y	2.4	2	94.9%
13	Kabilpor	Navsari 2	15,699	34.3	Y	4	2	92.2%
14	Chhiri	Vapi 2	18,829	79.5	Y	1	2	96.0%
15	Ichchhapor	Surat 14	12,097	45.9	Y	4	2	93.5%

Source: Census 2001, 2011 and primary survey

[a]Location of CT:
  1. Near Highway or DMIC corridor
  2. Industrial district
  3. Tribal area
  4. Periphery of city/UA
  5. Dispersed location

[b]Nature of CT:
  1. RNFS led by Services/Retail
  2. RNFS led by Manufacturing/GIDC
  3. RNFS led by Agricultural Growth
  0. None of Above

Marginal worker	Agricultural workers	HH industry	Other workers	% point change in other workers (01–11)	% point change in agri Worker (2001–2011)	Whether land conversion taking place	If yes, to what uses	Proximity to GIDC
22.4%	26.9%	2.8%	70.4%	4.8%	−4.9	Y	Housing	N
35.9%	33.6%	9.3%	57.1%	0.0%	3.8	Y	Housing Retail	N
5.1%	5.4%	1.3%	94.3%	6.3%	−2.0	Y	Industry, Housing, Retail	Palanpur, Siddhpur
4.6%	10.7%	1.5%	87.9%	11.5%	−6.4	N		N
15.5%	12.8%	2.0%	85.3%	15.1%	−13.3	Y	Industry Housing	Electronic Park, Bhat
22.7%	17.1%	1.2%	81.7%	5.0%	−2.7	Y	Industry	Vaghodia
10.8%	3.7%	0.3%	96.0%	8.2%	−7.3	N		N
11.5%	29.4%	10.4%	60.2%	28.6%	−1.1	N		Bhavnagar
12.6%	20.1%	2.7%	77.2%	14.9%	−12.5	Y	Housing	Wankaner
18.1%	40.2%	0.7%	59.1%	6.5%	−3.4	N		Liliya
13.1%	37.0%	2.6%	60.4%	−1.7%	3.4	Y	Housing Retail Industry	Mankuwa, Bhuj
5.2%	2.9%	1.1%	96.1%	1.7%	−1.9	Y	Housing Education	Anjar, Gandhidham
7.9%	3.8%	1.4%	94.8%	1.5%	0.06	Y	Industry Housing	Kabilpore, Bilimora
4.0%	0.9%	3.6%	95.5%	−1.4%	−1.7	Y	Industry Housing	Vapi
6.5%	10.0%	0.7%	89.3%	−3.9%	3.9	Y	Industry Housing	Ichchhapore-Bhatpore, Sachin

Table 6.9 Details of registered MSME units

No.	Census town	Major manufactured commodities	No. of registered MSMEs	Nature of activity (% units)			Part of cluster	Source of power	Total employees
				Manufacturing, processing, assembling, job work	Repair/ maintenance	Services			
1	Bhiloda	Cotton	67	60	28	12	No	16% no power 84% electricity	242
2	Sanjeli		54	33	6	61	No	100% electricity	160
3	Kanodar	Handloom cloth, mechanical tools, spare parts	94	36	29	35	No	2% no power 98% electricity	288
4	Becharji	Cotton	13	38	46	16	No	100% electricity	26
5	Vavol		17	35	12	53	No	100% electricity	46
6	Vaghodia	Cotton	3	100	0	0	No	100% electricity	71
7	Kharagodha	Magnesium chloride, salt, cotton	35	89	9	2	No	6% oil 3% no power 91% electricity	255
8	Umrala	Cotton	110	87	5	8	No	4% no power 96% electricity	319
9	Chandrapur	Cotton	50	88	6	6	No	100% electricity	203
10	Lilia	Cotton	35	69	14	17	No	100% electricity	92
11	Mankuwa	Cotton	13	85	15	0	No	100% electricity	36
12	Antarjal		5	20	40	40	No	100% electricity	12

Source: MSME Census, 2007

Table 6.10 Nature of agriculture

No.	Name	Geog Area (ha)	Cultivated (ha)	Irrigated (ha)	Source of irrigation	Main crops	APMC	Cultivators (%)	Agricultural labourers (%)	Marginal farmers (%)	Small farmers (%)	Medium farmers (%)	Large farmers (%)	Awareness & adoption of new technologies
1	Bhiloda	974	197 (20.2%) [69.5%]	150 (76%)	Tube well	Cotton, wheat, castor	Yes	16.8	10	38.0	32.5	28.9	0.0	Yes
2	Sanjeli	303	171 (56.4%) [98.9%]	171 (100%)	Kaliya Hill Dam, tubewell	Rice, maize, pulses, wheat and horticulture	Yes	10.8	22.8	30.4	24.5	43.7	1.4	Yes
3	Kanodar	788	NA	NA	Wells, drip irrigation	Wheat, castor, horticulture	No	1.5	2.9					Yes
4	Becharji	877	681 (77.7%) [68.1%]		Wells and tubewell	Jowar, bajra, cotton, pulses	Yes	2.3	8.4					Yes
5	Vavol	761	524 (68.9%) [70.6%]	175	Tubewell	Jawar, bajra, castor and cotton	No	2.7	10.1	23.9	39.3	36.8	0.0	Yes

(continued)

Table 6.10 (continued)

No.	Name	Geog Area (ha)	Cultivated (ha)	Irrigated (ha)	Source of irrigation	Main crops	APMC	Cultivators (%)	Agricultural labourers (%)	Marginal farmers (%)	Small farmers (%)	Medium farmers (%)	Large farmers (%)	Awareness & adoption of new technologies
6	Vaghodia	1502	828 (55.1%) [68.0%]	NA	Canal	Rice, jowar, cotton, wheat and horticulture	Yes	5.9	11.1	0.0	14.9	17.0	68.1	Yes
7	Kharagodha	1157	447 (38.6%)	178 (40%)	Wells, tank	Caster, cumin, jowar, bajra, pulses	No	1.2	2.4	40.0	60.0	0.0	0.0	Yes
8	Umrala	1452	1213 (83.5%) [77.0%]	155 (12.8%)	Drip irrigation, canal & tube well	BT cotton, wheat, cumin, fodder	Yes	11.2	18.2	36.5	47.0	16.5	0.2	Yes
9	Chandrapur	2785	1470 (52.8%) [58.6%]	NA	Borewell	Cotton, fodder, wheat	No	11.4	8.7	22.2	10.0	46.0	0.0	Yes
10	Lilia	1815	1521 (83.8%) [84.7%]	NA	Borewell (285), drip irrigation	Cotton, fodder, wheat	Yes	12.4	27.9	21.2	37.0	41.1	1.0	Yes
11	Mankuva	1958	1390 (71.0%) [72.5%]	232 (16.7%)	Tubewell (drip irrigation)	Ground nut, castor, horticulture	No	14	23	15.0	27.0	53.4	4.6	Yes

No.	Village				Source of irrigation	Main crops							
12	Antarjal	964	NA		Rainfall	Bajra and fodder	No	0.7	2.2				Yes
13	Kabilpor	253	NA			Mango, sugar cane & rice	No	1.7	2.1				Yes
14	Chhiri	402	70 (17.4%) [96.0%]	25	Canal, tube well	Rice, mango	No	0.3	0.6	26.0	28.0	46.0 0.0	Yes
15	Ichchhapor	912	205 (22.5%)	190	Canal	Sugarcane	No	3.3	6.7				Yes

Source: Primary survey & Census 2001, 2011

Note: Figures in square brackets in col. 4 are % in 2001

Table 6.11   Village level amenities

Census town	Location	No. of HHs	Density of pop (persons/ sq.km)	Electricity-domestic connection (Nos)ᵃ	Electricity-industrial connection (Nos)	Electricity-commercial connection (Nos)	Tap water from treated source
Bhiloda	Tribal area	3464	1167	3610 (100.0)	10	70	Yes
Sanjeli	Tribal area	1381	2458	916 (66.3)	32	221	Yes
Kanodar	Nr Highway/ DMIC	2625	1572	2404 (91.6)	6	65	Yes
Chhiri	Nr Highway/ DMIC	4757	9096	4310 (90.6)	310	260	Yes
Vaghodia	Industrial district	3604	1394	3374 (93.6)	NA	2634	No
Chandrapur	Industrial district	1860	790	1500 (80.7)	45	200	No
Antarjal	Industrial district	2426	1168	2100 (86.6)	0	60	No
Kabilpor	Peripheral	3486	6205	3103 (89.0)	NA	120	Yes
Vavol	Peripheral	2807	1659	2900 (100.0)	6	236	Yes
Mankuwa	Peripheral	2476	612	2210 (89.3)	12	275	Yes
Ichchhapor	Peripheral	2870	3816	2100 (73.2)	140	200	No
Kharagodha	Dispersed	2308	1032	2300 (99.7)	45	75	Yes
Umrala	Dispersed	1608	518	1400 (87.1)	120	26	Yes
Becharji	Dispersed	2709	1434	2377 (87.7)	6	807	No
Lilia	Dispersed	1970	571	1871 (95.0)	82	472	Yes

Source: Primary survey and Census 2011

ᵃFigures in brackets are share of households

ᵇPucca road density km/sq. km in brackets

ᶜRoad light connections per 100 population in brackets

Drainage system (open-1/ closed-2/ both-3/)	Latrines- Flush/Pour flush (Nos)[a]	Solid waste facility	Pucca road length (kms.)[b]	Kutcha road length (kms.)	RCC roads	Bus route road distance (in kms.)	Road lighting connection (No)[c]	Fire fighting service
2	3389 (97.8)	Yes	30 (2.18)	0.0	No	0	930 (5.8)	Yes
3	1296 (93.8)	Yes	9 (2.97)	2.0	Yes	26	7 (0.1)	No
2	2304 (87.8)	Yes	6 (0.76)	1.0	Yes	0	300 (2.4)	No
3	4475 (94.1)	Yes	6 (2.9)	2.0	Yes	0	40 (0.2)	No
2	2621 (72.7)	Yes	3 (0.25)	2.5	Yes	0	78 (0.5)	Yes
2	1010 (54.3)	Yes	2 (0.18)	6.0	No	4	251 (2.8)	No
3	1411 (58.2)	Yes	10 (1.04)	2.0	Yes	2	35 (0.3)	No
3	2965 (85.1)	Yes	10 (4.0)	2.0	Yes	0	325 (2.1)	No
2	2022 (72.0)	Yes	5 (0.66)	0.0	Yes	0	250 (2.0)	No
1	2308 (93.2)	Yes	12 (0.61)	5.0	Yes	0	345 (2.9)	No
2	2763 (96.3)	Yes	3 (0.95)	2.0	Yes	0	260 (2.2)	No
3	2142 (92.8)	No	8 (0.69)	3.0	No	0	350 (2.9)	No
1	1100 (68.4)	Yes	3 (0.19)	2.0	Yes	0	1 (0.01)	No
2	2502 (92.4)	Yes	4 (0.46)	2.0	No	0	2100 (16.7)	No
1	1503 (76.3)	Yes	6 (0.33)	6.0	Yes	0	280 (2.7)	No

Table 6.12   Social infrastructure

S. no.	Census town	Location	Hospital/ CHC/PHC/ TB centre/ nursing home/ maternity home (No.)	Health facility/1000 pop	Non-government medicine shop (No.)	Veterinary hospital (No.)	Educational institutions (No.)
1	Bhiloda	Tribal area	4	0.2	8	1	37
2	Sanjeli	Tribal area	4	0.5	3	1	16
3	Kanodar	Nr Highway/ DMIC	6	0.5	4	0	21
14	Chhiri	Nr Highway/ DMIC	1	0.1	0	0	14
6	Vaghodia	Industrial district	5	0.3	3	1	15
9	Chandrapur	Industrial district	1	0.1	1	0	7
12	Antarjal	Industrial district	1	0.1	0	0	9
11	Mankuwa	Peripheral	2	0.2	3	0	22
5	Vavol	Peripheral	3	0.2	1	1	8
13	Kabilpor	Peripheral	1	0.1	1	0	20
15	Ichchhapor	Peripheral	2	0.2	5	0	17
7	Kharagodha	Dispersed	2	0.2	0	0	17
8	Umrala	Dispersed	5	0.6	2	1	13
4	Becharji	Dispersed	3	0.2	0	1	11
10	Lilia	Dispersed	5	0.5	3	1	24

Source: Census 2011, primary survey

Edu insttns/1000 pop	Aangawadi	Primary school	Sec. & HS school	Institute/ college & ITI centre	Auditorium/ community hall (No.)	Public library/ reading room (No.)	Bank branches/1000 pop
2.3	17	11	8	1	1	2	0.31
2.1	7	3	6	1	1	0	0.67
1.7	13	5	3	(Palanpur)	1	1	0.16
0.7	11	3	0	Vapi	1	0	0.05
0.9	7	6	2	3	0	2	0.36
0.8	5	2	0	Wankaner	1	0	0.22
0.8	7	2	0	Aadipur	0	0	0.00
1.8	13	7	2	Bhuj	6	0	0.33
0.6	4	2	2	Gandhinagar	1	2	0.08
1.3	8	7	5	Navsari	0	0	0.13
1.4	6	5	6	Surat	0	0	0.17
1.4	13	3	1	Patdi	0	3	0.84
1.6	7	3	3		0	2	0.25
0.9	11			2	4	7	0.48
2.3	11	8	5	2	2	1	0.39

CHAPTER 7

Conclusion and Policy Suggestions

The rural transformation process in Gujarat, as in India, has several under-lying dimensions. Analysis and discussion in preceding chapters reiterates that emergence of the rural non-farm sector (RNFS) today is not so much a result of prevailing conditions in the agriculture sector but is an indepen-dent phenomena, possibly also an outcome of trickling down of urban influences. A country as vast as India is marked by existence of a dual econ-omy i.e. rural/subsistence sector coexisting with urban/capitalist sector. Growth led RNFS expansion accompanies urbanization, literacy and irriga-tion led agricultural development. Impact of urbanization on the growth of rural non-farm employment can be seen from the lens of increase in the net additions of town in Census 2011, that have not received statutory status. Given the population pressure and shrinking of livelihood opportunities in rural areas and to earn the higher incomes the pathways have been to shift to non-farm employment opportunities, often engagement in multiple jobs and finally out-migration. Out migration from rural areas could be the result of a combination of push and pull factors. Moreover, the influence of urbanism and emerging rural-urban networks impact on the socio-eco-nomic and political landscape of rural areas and also change the inter-caste relationships. The changes happening in the countryside as well as in the rural economy require focus of policy and appropriate interventions for a smooth and sustainable transition. In this chapter we highlight some of the major findings from the study undertaken.

© The Author(s) 2018
N. Mehta, *Rural Transformation in the Post Liberalization Period in Gujarat*, https://doi.org/10.1007/978-981-10-8962-6_7

EMPLOYMENT PATTERN AND SECTORAL GROWTH

The rural non-farm sector after decades of stagnancy emerged in 2004–2005. In the period following 2004–2005, RNFS is demonstrating accelerated employment generation. Labour absorption in the farm sector continues to show negative growth (1% per annum). The heartening development is that for workers dependent on agriculture and allied activities, labour productivity shows a high growth (4.6% per annum). There is also evidence of accelerated urban growth having a trickledown effect on the rural economy. Unlike the experience of the last decade, the rapid developments in the urban sector are deepening the rural-urban linkages and the rural areas are no more isolated or bounded spaces. The pace of rural poverty decline has accelerated in all the major states.

There seem to be overcrowding in construction activities as can be visualized from the declining per worker productivity in this sector. All the other non-farm sectors i.e. manufacturing, utilities, trade, transportation and services are absorbing workers at rising productivity levels. The RNFS sector has grown in all the states reflecting the reversal of earlier prevalent dualism and existence of a rural and urban divide. Together with rising farm productivity levels, the rural areas are showing indications of greater integration with the rest of the economy. The increase in non-farm employment opportunities has meant that the labour market is no longer dependent overwhelmingly on agriculture. Mechanization and technical change are leading to a relative decline in labour demand in agriculture. The agrarian economy is moving towards a market-based system, with enhanced rural to urban migration and tightening of labour markets. Such trends, no doubt, indicate the need to step up the creation of social and economic infrastructure in villages.

In rural Gujarat up to 1999–2000 the relative importance of the primary sector increased. Between 1999–2000 and 2011–2012, the share of primary sector in the workforce declined, though it continued to engage three-fourths of the workforce. Industries sector witnessed a reduction by nearly 2.5 percentage points, even though tertiary activities, mainly trade, transport, storage etc. recorded enhanced share of workers. Rural occupational diversification, at least at the aggregate level gained vigour. Non-primary sectors that gained in terms of share of workers in the 2000s decade were largely construction, trade and hotels. Manufacturing and other services depicted weak gains. Transport and communication sector at the aggregate level remained unchanged. Employment in construction activities in urban areas is dominant over rural areas (60%). Employment in enterprises belonging to wholesale and retail trade, communications and hospitality sectors is predominantly urban based and continued to record an increasing share here. Service sector employment seen in isolation though dominantly urban, was shifting to rural areas by 2012 as compared to 1998. Shift towards rural areas was steeper for community, personal and other services than financial and business services

The process of rural industrialisation needs an impetus. It is imperative that the manufacturing sector witnesses technological up-gradation to increase productivity levels. Household based industry and traditional sectors in addition also require support in the nature of easy access to raw materials, credit, technology, marketing and product support etc to emerge as viable employment generators and providers of sustainable livelihoods.

The per capita income from construction sector turned negative between 2005 to 2012, possibly due to overcrowding in this sector. Per capita income growth accelerated in trade and restaurants sector, financial and business services as well as transport and communication sector. Overcrowding of workers in the manufacturing sector does not bode well as seen from the declining productivity levels. Trade (retail and wholesale) seemed to be the last resort for the workers spilling out from the primary activities earlier but lately the acceleration in per capita productivity levels (by more than 10% annual increase) indicate that employment increase in trade and hospitality sectors has stalled. The communications revolution is causing the growth in transportation sector- both formal and informal, engaging workers at increasing productivity levels. These are the activities that are operating as depositories of surplus labour and where the surplus rural labour is finding a space. It remains for the state to create an environment where these activities become productive and viable and get integrated with the mainstream economic sectors, in addition to promoting investments in rural-based manufacturing activities.

STRUCTURAL TRANSFORMATION AND URBAN GROWTH

Rural employment structure is changing with the growth in the non-agricultural workforce. Population expansion in large villages is due to in-situ growth and migration. Urbanisation in the state is led by smaller towns; smaller towns are growing faster than larger towns and the activity base of smaller towns is also undergoing rapid change, that often functions as pull forces for rural migrants.

Recognition of statutory status of a CT or urban village involves complex decisions at the village level. The mapping of the development schemes of the government over urban/rural areas is a crucial factor in the reluctance of villages to acquire urban status, besides the laxity in crucial regulations. Increase in the number of census towns indicates underestimation of the number of urban areas and rural administered urban areas. It is a reflection of the state policy and reluctance to give a statutory status to the CTs. Results of the regression analysis indicate that emergence of census towns is related to base urbanization level and the growth rate of urban population, besides the non-agricultural male workforce. Growth of towns and transformation of rural areas is occurring both in the proximity of large urban centres in developed districts, along industrial and urban corridors, and also in a dispersed fashion in remote and less developed pockets. In less developed districts too large villages are emerging as service/retail centres, irrespective of industrial growth.

With relaxation of census urban definition, urbanisation levels in Gujarat, as in the country could be much higher. Nearly a third of the rural population is on the threshold of acquiring urban nature. This has a bearing on the provision of equal standards of public goods and services to all settlements. However, due to lack of recognition as a statutory town/urban area growth of large villages leads to settlements suffering from gross neglect of basic amenities available for healthy, productive and sustainable urban living. Lag in the development process and distribution of gains needs to be viewed with caution, as it may have adverse human development and social outcomes. The smaller settlements or larger villages are providing avenues for economic advancement and non-farm jobs even though these may not be recognized as towns. These are also bearers of social emancipation and fulfil functions of cities. The Government needs to focus on investment to provide adequate urban (economic and social) infrastructure in smaller urban areas, census towns and large villages. There is a need for reforming institutions and governance and building capacity of local government bodies to analyse, assess and implement urban interventions. Area based schematic mapping should be rethought.

IMPACTS OF RURAL TRANSFORMATION

The case studies of selected census towns representing varied development scenarios in Gujarat unravelled the tangible and intangible changes taking place in the rural economic structure, migration/commuting trends, as well as impacts of the urbanisation process on changes in consumption patterns, lifestyles and societal norms. That there is existence of a relation between the locational aspect and nature of RNFS has been underscored by the field analysis. Towns located in the tribal dominated regions have service activities, particularly retail trade or other tertiary activities as the dominant non-farm activity. Such locations serve as the market/service centres for the surrounding rural settlements. Presence of APMC markets in the agriculturally developed cases supplement their role as service centres. Evidently their remoteness and distance from urban areas precludes major industrial investments or real estate activity. Towns in the midst of industrial districts even though housing little manufacturing activity per se, serve as destinations for industrial workers who are migrants from other states. The largest increase in the share of 'other workers' was observed in towns either located in an industrial region, near transport corridors and also in those growing independently and away from the influence of large urban bodies. Agriculture is an activity that is losing its importance in the census towns. Engagement in agriculture is the highest in towns located in tribal hinterland and those having a dispersed location. However, amelioration of distress conditions in agriculture in such areas requires immediate focus of policy and the creation of supporting infrastructure.

Migrant workers play a major role in bringing about changes in the economic profile of the towns. Considerable land conversion and real estate development in most of the towns located in peripheral locations or within industrial zones is a consequence of migrant workers populating certain categories of settlements. The absence of building regulations and land use planning is fostering unprecedented growth in construction activity, although this has been an important driver for the transformation of these towns.

Nearly all the census towns suffer from shortcomings with respect to the physical amenities. Predictably the towns having peripheral location or near major transportation arteries were better off in terms of road connectivity and quality. Public facilities such as street lights, fire- fighting services and bus routes were severely lacking in all the towns surveyed. The RURBAN scheme of the government is helping to ease some of the infrastructure bottlenecks and creation of village level facilities. The towns are lacking in specialised health care or diagnostic services. Most of the towns also lack institutions for higher education forcing commuting, sometimes for long distances. Moreover, facilities for extra-and co-curricular activities, entertainment and leisure were lacking but strongly desired with the changing aspirations and urban influences. The rural transformation process is manifested in the considerable upscaling of the lifestyle of the residents surveyed. Households are witnessing diversification of diets and changes in non-food consumption patterns in tune with the urban way of life. The share of expenditure on food items per capita was estimated to be quite close to that ascertained for urban areas in Gujarat. However, in these towns substantial proportion of household expenditure is being earmarked for attainment of education and health services, indicating the inadequacy of government action on these fronts.

Traditional societal norms were weakening; urbanisation and spread of awareness was having positive impact in bringing about reforms in the traditional village society. However, the negative feature of changing food habits was being manifested in malnutrition and adverse health outcomes. Urban influences had increased awareness regarding the importance of higher education for attaining better livelihood opportunities and its role in reducing dependence on agriculture as the primary source of earnings.

There were considerable negative externalities associated with urban growth, notably, impacts related to land and the living environment. Apart from air, water and land pollution due to industrial activity, population expansion was cited to cause water scarcity conditions. Moreover, land conversion to non-agricultural uses while providing monetary benefits, often resulted in dispossession of productive assets and even exacerbated unemployment levels.

In the absence of planned development at low levels of settlement hierarchy and indiscriminate land use changes, the towns were facing haphazard pattern of growth. Added to that, the encroachment of commons, and explosion of retail activity was causing problems of traffic and congestion in some of the towns surveyed. In the long run deterioration of the living environment could prove to be hazardous and detrimental to the growth of these settlements.

De-peasantisation or the movement of workers out of agriculture into non-farm sectors is a fall out of the declining labour use is agriculture, due to rising capital intensity as well as non-viability of agriculture among small and marginal farmers. Nonetheless policy interventions for infrastructure creation and technology are imperative to make agriculture a more profitable venture for the communities dependent on the sector. Subsequent policy actions therefore require sensibility and should be driven by in-depth research that targets the core of the issues. While the policies such as creation of smart cities are useful, these will make development more top-heavy. It is imperative for the urban policymakers to develop and implement plans that lead to a more balanced and inclusive form of development. Adoption of a 'regional' approach is the need of the day that is increasingly getting dissipated.

The policy priorities should include investing more in agricultural technology and rural infrastructure, eliminating market distortions on agricultural and rural growth and fostering a better business environment to promote private sector investment. Strengthening institutional reforms for rural land and finance would enable the poor to access agricultural land and credit. There is also a need to decentralize fiscal responsibilities and funding so that lower-level authorities can allocate resources according to the local needs. A major area of action is to prioritize job creation in the rural non-farm economy, and in services and industries in urban and semi-urban settlements. Rural transformation is a complex and on-going process and its effects extend beyond the transformation of the agricultural sector and the economic transformation and are accompanied with some negative effects in the developing countries. However, its direction and effects can be shaped and steered to mitigate the negative impacts and produce outcomes that are beneficial for rural populations. A policy agenda is thus required that addresses rural transformation process by making it more ecologically sustainable and socially as well as economically inclusive.

REFERENCES

Alagh, Yoginder K. 2012. *Rural-Urban Continuum*. Inaugural Address at ITDC-TTI Workshop on Rural-Urban Linkage, at Institute of Rural Management, Anand, 21 August, Mimeo.

Alam, Ashfaque, and Binayak Choudhury. 2016. Spatio-Functional Determinants of Small Towns: A Case Study of Selected Indian Small Towns. *Review of Urban and Regional Development Studies* 28 (2): 75–88.

Ali, Md. Julfikar, and Deepika Varshney. 2013. Spatial Modelling of Urban Growth and Urban Influence. *Environment and Urbanization ASIA* 3 (2): 255–275.

Arya, Anita, and Niti Mehta. 2011. *Performance of Gujarat Economy: An Analysis of the Instability Aspect*. SPIESR Working Paper No 7, November.

Bagchi, Amiya Kumar, Panchanan Das, and Sadhan Chattopadhyay. 2005. Growth and Structural Change in the Economy of Gujarat, 1970–2000. *Economic and Political Weekly* 40 (28): 3039–3047.

Basant, Rakesh, and B.L. Kumar. 1989. *Rural Non-Agricultural Activities in India: A Review of Available Evidence*. Working Paper No 20. Ahmedabad: Gujarat Institute of Area Planning.

———. 1990. *Non-Agricultural Employment in Rural Gujarat—A Review of Evidence*. Working Paper No 28. Ahmedabad: Gujarat Institute of Area Planning.

Basant, R., and R. Parathasarathy. 1991. *Inter-Regional Variations in Rural Non-Agricultural Employment in Gujarat, 1961–81*. Working Paper No 36. Ahmedabad: The Gujarat Institute of Area Planning.

Basant, R., B.L. Kumar, and R. Parthasarathy, eds. 1998. *Non-Agricultural Employment in Rural India: The Case of Gujarat*. Jaipur: Rawat Publications.

© The Author(s) 2018
N. Mehta, *Rural Transformation in the Post Liberalization Period in Gujarat*, https://doi.org/10.1007/978-981-10-8962-6

Basole, Amit. 2017. What Does the Rural Economy Need. *Economic and Political Weekly* 52 (9).

Basu, D.N., and S.P. Kashyap. 1992. Rural Non-Agricultural Employment in India: Role of Development Process and Rural-Urban Employment Linkages. *Economic and Political Weekly* 27 (51/52): A178–A189.

Bathla, Seema, Thorat Sukhadeo, P.K. Joshi, and Bingxin Yu. 2017. Where to Invest to Accelerate Agricultural Growth and Poverty Reduction. *Economic and Political Weekly* 52 (39): 10.

Berdegué, Julio A., Tomás Rosada, and Anthony J. Bebbington. 2014. The Rural Transformation. In *International Development: Ideas, Experience, and Prospects*, ed. Bruce Currie-Alder, Ravi Kanbur, David M. Malone, and Rohinton Medhora. Oxford Scholarship Online.

Berry, B.J.L. 1961. City Size Distributions and Economic Development. *Economic Development and Cultural Change* 9 (4): 573–588.

Bhagat, R.B. 2011. Emerging Pattern of Urbanization in India. *Economic and Political Weekly* 46 (34): 10–12.

Bhalla, Sheila. 1993a. Tests of Some Prepositions About the Dynamics of Change in the Rural Workforce Structure. *The Indian Journal of Labour Economics* 36 (3): 428–439.

———. 1993b. Patterns of Employment Generation in India. *The Indian Journal of Labour of Economics* 36 (4).

———. 2000. *Behind Poverty: The Qualitative Deterioration of Employment Prospects for Rural Indians*. IHD Working Paper Series 7. New Delhi: Institute of Human Development.

———. 2005a. *India's Rural Economy: Issues and Evidence*. Working Paper Series No 25. New Delhi: Institute of Human Development.

———. 2005b. Rural Workforce Diversification and Performance of Unorganized Sector Enterprises. In *Rural Transformation in India: The Role of Non-Farm Sector*, ed. Rohini Nayyar and Alakh N. Sharma. New Delhi: Institute for Human Development.

———. 2005c. Rural Workforce Diversification and Performance of Unorganized Sector Enterprises. In *Rural Transformation in India: The Role of Non-Farm Sector*, ed. R. Nayyar and A.N. Sharma, 75–104. New Delhi: Institute for Human Development.

———. 2005d. *India's Rural Economy: Issues and Evidence*. Working Paper Series No 25. New Delhi: Institute for Human Development.

Bhowmick, S.K., Shubhashis Gangopadhyay, and Shagun Krishnan. 2009. Reforms and Entry: Some Evidence from the Indian Manufacturing Sector. *Review of Development Economics* 13 (4): 658–672.

Binswanger-Mkhize, Hans P. 2012. India 1960–2010: Structural Change, the Rural Non-Farm Sector, and the Prospects for Agriculture. In *Stanford Symposium Series on Global Food Policy and Food Security in the 21st Century*. Stanford: Center for Food Security and the Environment, Stanford University.

———. 2013. The Stunted Structural Transformation of the Indian Economy Agriculture, Manufacturing and the Rural Non-Farm Sector. *Economic and Political Weekly* 47 (26&27): 5–13.

Cadène, Philippe, and Mark Holmström, eds. 1998. *Decentralized Production in India: Industrial Districts, Flexible Specialization and Employment*. New Delhi and London: Sage.

Campbell, D. 1975. Degrees of Freedom and the Case Study. *Comparative Political Studies* 8: 178–185.

Chakraborty, Saurav, Subhanil Chowdhury, Utpal Roy, and Kakoli Das. 2017. Declassification of Census Towns in West Bengal Empirical Evidences from Patuli, Bardhaman. *Economic and Political Weekly* 52 (25&26): 25–31.

Chand, Ramesh, and S.K. Srivastava. 2014. Changes in the Rural Labour Market and Their Implications for Agriculture. *Economic and Political Weekly* 49 (10): 47–54.

Chand, Ramesh, R. Saxena, and S. Rana. 2015. Estimates and Analysis of Farm Income in India, 1983–84 to 2011–12. *Economic and Political Weekly* 50 (2): 139–145.

Chandrasekhar, S. 2011. Workers Commuting Between the Rural and Urban: Estimates from NSSO Data. *Economic and Political Weekly* 46 (46): 22–25.

Chandrasekhar, S., and Ajay Sharma. 2014. *Urbanization and Spatial Patterns of Internal Migration in India*. Mumbai: Indira Gandhi Institute of Development Research.

Christaller, Walter. 1966. *Central Places in Southern Germany*. Englewood Cliffs, NJ: Prentice-Hall.

Clark, Colin. 1940. *The Conditions of Economic Progress*. Macmillan and Co. Ltd.

Coelho, K., and M. Vijayabaskar. 2014. On the Charts, Off the Tracks. *Economic and Political Weekly* 49: 49–79.

Currie-Alder, Bruce, Ravi Kanbur, David M. Malone, and Rohinton Medhora. 2014. *International Development: Ideas, Experience, and Prospects*. Oxford Scholarship Online.

Dandekar, Ajay, and Sreedeep Bhattacharya. 2017. Lives in Debt: Narratives of Agrarian Distress and Farmer Suicides. *Economic and Political Weekly* 52 (21): 77–84.

Datta, Amrita. 2016. Migration, Remittances and Changing Sources of Income in Rural Bihar (1999–2011): Some Findings from a Longitudinal Study. *Economic and Political Weekly* 51 (31).

Datta, Amrita, Gerry Rodgers, Janine Rodgers, and B.K.N. Singh. 2014. Contrasts in Development in Bihar: A Tale of Two Villages. *Journal of Development Studies* 50 (9).

de Janvry, Alain, and Elisabeth Sadoulet. 2010. Agricultural Growth and Poverty Reduction: Additional Evidence. *World Bank Research Observer* 25: 1–20.

Denis, E., and K. Marius-Gnanou. 2011. Toward a Better Appraisal of Urbanisation in India. *Cybergeo: European Journal of Geography* 569.

Denis, Eric, P. Mukhopadhyay, and Marie-Helene Zerah. 2012. Subaltern Urbanization in India. *Economic and Political Weekly* 47 (30): 52–62.

Dholakia, R.H. 2000. Liberalisation in Gujarat—Review of Recent Experience. *Economic and Political Weekly* 35 (35–36): 3121–3124.

———. 2007. Sources of Economic Growth and Acceleration in Gujarat. *Economic and Political Weekly* 42: 770–778.

Dholakia, Ravindra H., Manish B. Pandya, and Payal M. Pateriya. 2014. *Urban-Rural Income Differential in Major States: Contribution of Structural Factors.* Ahmedabad: Indian Institute of Management.

Directorate of Census Operations. 2011. *Primary Census Abstracts, Census – 2001 and 2011,* Gujarat State, Series-25. Gandhinagar.

Directorate of Economics and Statistics. 2000. *Report on Fourth Economic Census, 1998, Gujarat.* Gandhinagar: Government of Gujarat.

———. 2006. *Report on Fifth Economic Census, 2005, Gujarat.* Gandhinagar: Government of Gujarat.

———. 2015. *Socio-Economic Review of Gujarat State, 2013–14.* Gandhinagar: Government of Gujarat.

———. 2017. *Report on Sixth Economic Census, 2012, Gujarat.* Gandhinagar: Government of Gujarat.

Dixit, A. 2009. Growth and Non-Farm Employment: The Case of Gujarat. *The Indian Journal of Labour Economics* 52 (3).

DNA (Daily News & Analysis) (2011). Urbanisation Has Touched Even Tribal Areas in Gujarat, October 17 Issue.

Dutta, Puja, Rinku Murgai, Martin Ravallion, and Dominique van de Walle. 2014. *Right to Work? Assessing India's Employment Guarantee Scheme in Bihar. Equity and Development.* Washington, DC: World Bank.

Ellis, Frank, Milton Kutengule, and Alfred Nyasulu. 2003. Livelihoods and Rural Poverty Reduction in Malawi. *World Development* 31 (9): 1495–1510.

Freidmann, John. 1961. Cities in Social Transformation. *Comparative Studies in Society and History* 4 (1): 86–103.

Gaiha, Raghav. 2016. The Overrated Urban Spinoff. *The Indian Express,* November 2.

Gandhi, V.P., and N.V. Namboodiri. 2010. The Economics and Contribution of Cotton Biotechnology in the Agricultural Growth of Gujarat. In *High Growth Trajectory and Structural Changes in Gujarat Agriculture,* ed. R.H. Dholakia and S.K. Datta. Macmillan Publishers India Ltd.

Gandhi, Sahil, and Abhay Pethe. 2017. Emerging Challenges of Metropolitan Governance in India. *Economic and Political Weekly* 52 (27): 55.

Garcia-López, Miquel-Àngel, Camille Hémet, and Elisabet Viladecans-Marsal. 2016. *Next Train to the Polycentric City: The Effect of Railroads on Subcenter Formation.* Working Paper 2016/14, Institut d'Economia de Barcelona.

Gelman, Andrew, and Jennifer Hill. 2007. *Data Analysis Using Regression and Multilevel/Hierarchical Models.* Cambridge: Cambridge University Press.

Gelman, A., J.B. Carlin, H.S. Stern, and D.B. Rubin. 1995. *Bayesian Data Analysis*. Chapman and Hall.

Glaeser, E.L. 2011. The Challenge of Urban Policy. *Journal of Political Analysis and Management* 31: 111–122.

Government of India, Labour Bureau. 2016. *Report on Fifth Annual Employment – Unemployment Survey (2015–16)*, Volume 1. Chandigarh.

Guin, Debarshi, and D.N. Das. 2015. New Census Towns in West Bengal – 'Census Activism' or Sectoral Diversification. *Economic and Political Weekly* 50 (14): 68–72.

Gujarati, D.N. 1995. *Basic Econometrics*. 3rd ed. New York: McGraw-Hill, Inc.

Gulsecen, S., and A. Kubat. 2006. Teaching ICT to Teacher Candidates Using PBL: A Qualitative and Quantitative Evaluation. *Educational Technology & Society* 9 (2): 96–106.

Haggblade, Steven, Peter B.R. Hazell, and Thomas Reardon. 2007. *Transforming the Rural Nonfarm Economy Opportunities and Threats in the Developing World*. Baltimore, MD: International Food Policy Research Institute, The Johns Hopkins University Press.

Hayami, Y., and V.W. Ruttan. 1971. *Agricultural Development: An International Perspective*. Baltimore, MD: Johns Hopkins Press.

Himanshu. 2007. Recent Trends in Poverty and Inequality: Some Preliminary Results. *Economic and Political Weekly* 42 (6).

———. 2011. Employment Trends in India: A Re-Examination. *Economic and Political Weekly* 46 (37): 3729–3748.

Himanshu, Bhavna Joshi, and Peter Lanjouw. 2016. Non-Farm Diversification, Inequality and Mobility in Palanpur. *Economic & Political Weekly* 51 (26 & 27): 43–51.

Himanshu, Peter Lanjouw, Rinku Murgai, and Nicholas Stern. 2013. Non-Farm Diversification, Poverty, Economic Mobility and Income Inequality: A Case Study in Village India. *Agricultural Economics* 44: 461–473.

Hirway, Indira. 1995. Selective Development and Widening Disparities in Gujarat. *Economic and Political Weekly* 30 (41–42): 2603–2618.

———. 2000. Dynamics of Development in Gujarat: Some Issues. *Economic and Political Weekly* 35 (35).

———. 2003. Identification of BPL Households for Poverty Alleviation Programmes. *Economic and Political Weekly* 38: 4803–4808.

Hirway, Indira, S.P. Kashyap, and Amita Shah, eds. 2002. *Dynamics of Development in Gujarat*. New Delhi: Concept Publishing Co.

Hirway, Indira, Amita Shah, and Ghanshyam Shah, eds. 2014. *Growth or Development – Which Way Is Gujarat Going?* Oxford University Press.

IIPA. 2010. *A Study of Bihari Migrant Labourers: Incidence, Causes and Remedies*. Indian Institute of Public Administration. Sponsored by Department of Labour Resources, Govt of Bihar.

International Fund for Agricultural Development. 2016. *Rural Development Report 2016: Fostering Inclusive Rural Transformation*. Rome: Quintily, September.

Jatav, Manoj. 2010. Casualisation of Workforce in Rural Non-Farm Sector of India: A Regional Level Analysis Across Industries. *The Indian Journal of Labour Economics* 53 (3): 501–516.

Jatav, Manoj, and S. Sen. 2013. Drivers of Non-Farm Employment in Rural India. *Economic and Political Weekly* 48: 26–27.

Jayaraman, Raji, and Peter Lanjouw. 1998. *The Evolution of Poverty and Inequality in Indian Villages*. Policy Research Working Paper, 1870, The World Bank.

Jodhka, Surinder. 2006. Caste and Democracy: Assertion and Identity Among the Dalit of Rural Punjab. *Sociological Bulletin* 55 (1): 4–23.

———. 2014. Emergent Ruralities: Revisiting Village Life and Agrarian Change in Haryana. *Economic & Political Weekly* 49 (26&27): 5–17.

Jodhka, Surinder, and Adarsh Kumar. 2017. Non-Farm Economy in Madhubani, Bihar: Social Dynamics and Exclusionary Rural Transformations. *Economic and Political Weekly* 52 (25&26).

Johnson, M.P. 2006. Decision Models for the Location of Community Corrections Centers. *Environment and Planning B-Planning & Design* 33 (3): 393–412.

Johnston, B.F., and J.W. Mellor. 1961. The Role of Agriculture in Economic Development. *American Economic Review* 51 (4): 566–593.

Jurnal, Kemanusiaan. 2007. *Case Study as a Research Method*. Malaysia: Universiti Teknologi, Faculty of Management and Human Resource Development.

Kashyap, S.P. 1995. Irrigation Induced Agricultural Growth, Occupational Diversification and Poverty Alleviation: Experience of a Prosperous District in Gujarat. In *Growth, Employment and Poverty: Change and Continuity in Rural India*, ed. G.K. Chaddha and Alakh N. Sharma. New Delhi: Indian Society of Labour Economics, Vikas Publishing House Pvt Ltd.

———. 2011. Emerging Tendencies in Rural Non-Farm Enterprise Sector: Role of Policy. *Sampada* 67 (9).

Kashyap, S.P., and Niti Mehta. 2005. Rural Non-Farm Sector in Gujarat: Growth and Emerging Nature. In *Rural Transformation in India: The Role of Non-Farm Sector*, ed. Rohini Nayyar and Alakh N. Sharma. New Delhi: Institute for Human development.

———. 2007. Non-Farm Sector in India: Temporal & Spatial Aspects. *Indian Journal of Labour Economics* 50 (4): 611–632.

Kasturi, Kannan. 2015. Comparing Census and NSS Data on Employment and Unemployment. *Economic and Political Weekly* 50 (22): 16–19.

Khasnabis, Ratan. 2008. The Economy of West Bengal. *Economic and Political Weekly* 43 (52): 103–115.

Krishna, Anirudh, and Devendra Bajpai. 2011. Lineal Spread and Radial Dissipation: Experiencing Growth in Rural India, 1993–2005. *Economic and Political Weekly* 46 (38): 44–51.

Krugman, Paul. 1991. Increasing Returns and Economic Geography. *The Journal of Political Economy* 99 (3): 483–499.

Kumar, Satendra. 2016. Agrarian Transformation and the New Rurality in Western Uttar Pradesh. *Economic & Political Weekly* 51 (26&27): 61–71.

Kumar, Dinesh M., A. Narayanamoorthy, O. Singh, M.V.K. Sivamohar, Manoj Sharma, and Nitin Bossi. 2010. *Gujarat's Agricultural Growth Story: Exploding Some Myths*. Occasional Paper No.2-0410, Hyderabad: Institute of Resource Analysis & Policy.

Kundu, Amitabh. 1983. Theories of City Size Distribution and Indian Urban Structure – A Reappraisal. *Economic and Political Weekly* 18 (31): 1361–1368.

———. 2011a. Politics and Economics of Urban Growth. *Economic and Political Weekly* 46 (20).

———. 2011b. Method in Madness: Urban Data from 2011 Census. *Economic and Political Weekly* 46 (40): 13–16.

Kundu, Amitabh, and Shalini Gupta. 1996. Migration, Urbanisation and Regional Inequality. *Economic and Political Weekly* 31 (52): 3391–3398.

Kundu, Debolina, and D. Samanta. 2011. Redefining the Inclusive Urban Agenda in India. *Economic and Political Weekly* 46 (5): 55–63.

Kuznets, S. 1966. *Modern Economic Growth: Rate, Structure and Spread*. New Haven: Yale University Press.

Lanjouw, Jean, and Peter Lanjouw. 2001. The Rural Non-Farm Sector: Issues and Evidence from Developing Countries. *Agricultural Economics* 26: 1–23.

Lanjouw, P., and R. Murgai. 2009. *Poverty Decline, Agricultural Wages, and Non-Farm Employment in India: 1983–2004*. Policy Research Working Paper No 4858. Washington, DC: World Bank.

Lanjouw, Peter, and Abusaleh Shariff. 2004. Rural Non-Farm Employment in India: Access, Incomes and Poverty Impact. *Economic and Political Weekly* 39 (40).

Lewis, W.A. 1954. Economic Development with Unlimited Supplies of Labour. *The Manchester School* 22 (2): 139–191.

———. 1956. *Theory of Economic Growth*. Great Britain: George Allen & Unwin Ltd.

Lipton, M. 1968. Strategy for Agriculture: Urban Bias and Rural Planning. In *The Crisis of Indian Planning*, ed. P. Streeten and M. Lipton. London: Oxford University Press.

Lobo, Lancy, and Jayesh Shah, eds. 2012. *Globalization, Growth and Employment: Challenges and Opportunities*. New Delhi: Rawat Publications.

Mahadevia, Darshini. 2014. Dynamics of Urbanization in Gujarat. In *Growth or Development: Which Way Is Gujarat Going?* ed. I. Hirway, A. Shah, and G. Shah. New Delhi: Oxford University Press.

Majumdar, Surajit. 2012. *Agriculture-Industry Dynamics and Rural Transformation in India*. Presented at ITDC-TTI Workshop on Rural-Urban Linkage, at Institute of Rural Management, Anand, 21 August.

Marshall, Alfred. 1920. *Principles of Economics: An Introductory Volume*. London: Macmillan and Co.

Mehta, Niti. 2001. *Development Process and Occupational Diversification: A Case of Kheda*, Ph.D. Thesis. Ahmedabad: Gujarat University.

———. 2006. Imbalances in Development Between Regions and Social Groups: Evidences from Gujarat. *Anvesak* 36 (1): 1–12.

———. 2012a. Performance of Crop Sector in Gujarat During High Growth Period: Some Explorations. *Agricultural Economics Research Review* 25 (2): 195–204.

———. 2012b. Food Security Aspects and Diversification of Demand in the Context of Gujarat. *Anvesak* 42 (1&2).

———. 2013. Employability of Rural Labour in the Neo-Liberal Era: A Study of Gujarat. *Indian Journal of Labour Economics* 56 (2): 243–267.

———. 2014. *Gujarat Over Time: Progress Towards Growth, Development and Inclusiveness*. Paper Presented at the Seminar on "Status of Social Science Research in Western India: Critical Engagement and Future Direction", November 14–16, 2014, ICSSR Western Regional Centre, Vidyanagari, SantaCruz (E), Mumbai.

Mehta, Niti, and S.P. Kashyap. 2002. An Approach Towards Identifying Sunrise Industries: A Regional Perspective. *Manpower Journal* 38 (2&3).

Mellor, J.W. 1966. *The Economics of Agricultural Development*. Cornell University Press.

———. 1986. *Agriculture on the Road to Industrialisation*. Washington, DC: IFPRI.

Misra, R.P., ed. 2013. *Urbanisation in South Asia: Focus on Mega Cities*. New Delhi: Cambridge University Press.

Misra, Sangita, and Anoop K. Suresh. 2014. *Estimating Employment Elasticity of Growth for the Indian Economy*. RBI WPS (DEPR): 06/2014. Mumbai: Reserve Bank of India.

Morris, Sebastian. 2014. A Comparative Analysis of Gujarat's Economic Growth. In *Growth or Development: Which Way Is Gujarat Going?* ed. I. Hirway, A. Shah, and G. Shah. New Delhi: Oxford University Press.

Mukhopadhyay, Partha, and A. Maringati. 2014. Articulating Growth in the Urban Spectrum. *Economic and Political Weekly* 49 (22): 44–45.

Mukhopadhyay, Partha, and Kanhu C. Pradhan. 2012. *District-Level Patterns of Urbanisation in India*. New Delhi: Centre for Policy Research Urban Brief.

Nadhanael, G.V. 2012. Recent Trends in Rural Wages: An Analysis of Inflationary Implications. *Reserve Bank of India Occasional Papers* 33 (1&2).

National Sample Survey Office, Government of India. 1997. *Employment and Unemployment in India, 1993–94*. Report No. 409, NSS Fiftieth Round (July 1993–June 1994). New Delhi: MOSPI.

———. 2001. *Employment and Unemployment Situation in India, 1999–2000*. Report No. 458(55/10/2), NSS 55th Round (July 1999–June 2000). New Delhi: MOSPI.

————. 2006. *Employment and Unemployment Situation in India, 2004–05.* Report No. 515(61/10/1), NSS 61st Round (July 2004–June 2005). New Delhi: MOSPI.

————. 2014. *Employment and Unemployment Situation in India, 2011–12.* Report No. 554(68/10/1), NSS 68th Round (July 2011–June 2012). New Delhi: MOSPI.

Nayyar, Rohini, and Alakh N. Sharma, eds. 2005. *Rural Transformation in India – The Role of Non-Farm Sector, Institute of Human Development.* New Delhi: Manohar Publishers & Distributors.

Nijman, J. 2012. India's Urban Challenge. *Eurasian Geography and Economics* 53 (1): 7–20.

Owusu, George. 2008. The Role of Small Towns in Regional Development and Poverty Reduction in Ghana. *International Journal of Urban and Regional Research* 32: 453–472.

Pant, Chandrashekhar, and Rakesh Mohan. 1982. Morphology of Urbanisation in India – Some Results from 1981 Census. *Economic and Political Weekly* 17 (39).

Papola, T.S., and P.P. Sahu. 2012. *Employment Growth and Structure: Policies, Performance and Prospects.* (Mimeo). New Delhi: Institute for Studies in Industrial Development.

Patel, Surendra. 1991. Growing Regional Inequalities in Gujarat. *Economic and Political Weekly* 26 (26): 1618–1623.

Perroux, François. 1955. Note Sur la Notion de Poles Croissance. *Economic Appliquee,* 1&2: 307–320. Translated by Mette Monsted, 1974.

Planning Commission, Government of India. 2008. *The Eleventh Five Year Plan.* New Delhi.

————. 2011. *Mid Term Appraisal for Eleventh Five Year Plan 2007–2012.* New Delhi: Oxford University Press.

————. 2013. *The Twelth Five Year Plan.* New Delhi.

Pradhan, K.C. 2013. Unacknowledged Urbanisation – New Census Towns of India. *Economic and Political Weekly* 48 (36): 43–51.

————. 2017. Unacknowledged Urbanisation: The New Census Towns in India. In *Subaltern Urbanisation in India: An Introduction to the Dynamics of Ordinary Towns Exploring Urban Change in South Asia,* ed. Eric Denis and Marie-Helene Zerah. New Delhi: Springer Nature.

Ramachandran, R. 1989. *Urbanisation and Urban Systems in India.* New Delhi: Oxford University Press.

Raman, B. 2014. Patterns and Practices of Special Transformation in Non-Metros: The Case of Tiruchengode. *Economic and Political Weekly* 49 (22): 46–54.

Ranis, Gustav, and Frances Stewart. 1999. V-Goods and the Role of the Urban Informal Sector in Development. *Economic Development and Cultural Change* 47 (2): 259–288.

Reddy, D.N., Amarender A. Reddy, N. Nagaraj, and C. Bantilan. 2014. *Rural Non-Farm Employment and Rural Transformation in India*. Working Paper Series No 57. Patancheru: International Crops Research Institute for the Semi-Arid Tropics.

Rehman, M.R. 2008. Urban Spatial Growth Analysis of Khulna City. www.geospatialworld.net/paper/Application/Articleview.

Reserve Bank of India. 2012. *RBI Releases Time Series Data on Average Daily Wage Rates in Rural India for Men*. Press Release-2012-2013/465, September 18.

Rodgers, Gerry, and Janine Rodgers. 2011. Inclusive Development? Migration, Governence and Social Change in Rural Bihar. *Economic & Political Weekly* 46 (23): 43–50.

Rondinelli, D.A. 1983. Towns and Small Cities in Developing Countries. *Geographical Review* 73 (4): 379–395.

Ruttan, Mario. 1995. *Farms and Factories: Social Profile of Large Farmers & Rural Industrialists in West India*. Delhi: Oxford University Press.

Saha, Partha, and Sher Verick. 2016. *State of Rural Labour Markets in India*. ILO Asia-Pacific Working Paper Series, May.

Saleth, Maria R. 1997. Occupational Diversification Among Rural Groups: A Case Study of Rural Transformation in Tamil Nadu. *Economic and Political Weekly* 26: 1908–1916.

Samanta, Gopa. 2014. The Politics of Classification and the Complexity of Governance in Census Towns. *Economic and Political Weekly* 49 (22): 55–62.

Sarkar, Abhirup. 2006. Political Economy of West Bengal. *Economic and Political Weekly* 41 (4).

Schultz, T.W. 1968. Institutions and the Rising Economic Value of Man. *American Journal of Agricultural Economics* 50 (5): 1113–1122.

Seidman, David. 1976. On Choosing Between Linear and Log-Linear Models. *Journal of Politics* 38: 461–466.

Sen, Abhijit, and Himanshu. 2004. Poverty and Inequality in India, Parts I and II. *Economic and Political Weekly* 39 (38): 4247–4263.

Shah, A.M. 2002. *Exploring India's Rural Past: A Gujarat Village in the Early Nineteenth Century*. Delhi: Oxford University Press.

———. 2012. The Village in the City, the City in the Village. *Economic and Political Weekly* 47 (52): 17–19.

Shah, Rajiv. 2013. *Rural Proletarianization: Census 2011 Data Suggest Sharper Rise in Agricultural Workforce in Gujarat than Most of India, May 2*. Counterview.org.

———. 2017. *"Model" Gujarat Agricultural Wages One of the Lowest in India, Gender Gap Is Market Driven: Union Ministry Report, October 17*, Counterview.net.

Shah, Amita, and Biplab Dhak. 2014. Labour Migration and Welfare in Gujarat: Recent Evidence and Issues. In *Growth or Development: Which Way Is Gujarat*

Going? ed. I. Hirway, A. Shah, and G. Shah. New Delhi: Oxford University Press.

Shah, Amita, and Jharna Pathak, eds. 2014. *Tribal Development in Western India*, 344. New Delhi: Routledge.

Shah, Tushaar, Ashok Gulati, P. Hemant, Ganga Shreedhar, and R.C. Jain. 2009. Secret of Gujarat's Agrarian Miracle After 2000. *Economic and Political Weekly* 44 (52): 45–55.

Shaw, Annapurna, ed. 2005. *Indian Cities in Transition*. Hyderabad: Orient Longman.

Singh, Sukhpal, and Shruti Bhogal. 2014. Depeasantization in Punjab: Status of Farmers Who Left Farming. *Current Science* 106 (10): 1364–1368.

Singh, N.K., and Nicholas Stern. 2013. *The New Bihar, Rekindling Governance and Development*. New Delhi: HarperCollins.

Sita, K., and R.B. Bhagat. 2005. Population Change and Economic Restructuring in Indian Metropolitan Cities: A Study of Mumbai. In *Indian Cities in Transition*, ed. Annapurna Shaw. Hyderabad: Orient Longman.

Sivaramakrishnan, K.C., Amitabh Kundu, and B.N. Singh. 2005. *Handbook of Urbanisation in India*. Delhi: Oxford University Press.

Solarin, Sakiru Adebola, and Yuen Yee Yen. 2016. A Global Analysis of the Impact of Research Output on Economic Growth. *Scientometrics* 108 (2): 855–874.

Sridhar, K.S. 2010. Determinants of City Growth and Output in India. *Review of Urban and Regional Development Studies* 22 (1): 22–38.

Srivastava, Ravi. 1998. Migration and the Labour Market in India. *Indian Journal of Labour Economics* 41 (4): 583–616.

Sundaram, K. 2007. Employment and Poverty in India, 2000–2005. *Economic and Political Weekly* 42 (30): 3121–3131.

Tacoli, C., ed. 2006. *The Earthscan Reader in Rural–Urban Linkages*. London & Sterling, VA: Earthscan.

Tellis, Winston. 1997. Introduction to Case Study. *The Qualitative Report* 3 (2). http://www.nova.edu/ssss/QR/QR3-2/tellis1.html.

Timmer, C. Peter, and Selvin Akkus. 2008. *The Structural Transformation as a Pathway out of Poverty: Analytics, Empirics and Politics*. Working Paper Number No 150, July. Washington, DC: Centre for Global Development.

Unni, Jeemol. 1998. Non-Agricultural Employment and Poverty in India: A Review of Evidence. *Economic and Political Weekly* 33: 36–44.

Unni, Jeemol, and G. Raveendran. 2007. Growth of Employment (1993–94 to 2004–05): Illusion of Inclusiveness? *Economic and Political Weekly* 42: 196–199.

Vaidyanathan, A. 1986. Labour Use in Rural India – A Study of Spatial and Temporal Variations. *Economic and Political Weekly* 21 (52): 130–146.

Vaishar, A. 2004. Small Towns: An Important Part of the Moravian Settlement System. In *Cities in Transition*, ed. M. Pak and D. Rebernik, 309–318. Ljubljana: Univerza v Ljubljani.

van Duijne, Robbin. 2017. What Is India's Urbanisation Riddle? *Economic and Political Weekly* 52 (28): 76–77.

Verma, L.N. 2006. *Urban Geography*. Jaipur: Rawat Publications.

von Thünen, J.H. 1826. *The Isolated State*. English Translation by C.M. Wartenberg (1966). Oxford: Pergammon Press.

Wadhwa, Kiran, and S.P. Kashyap. 1985. Inter-Regional Industrialization in India: Role of Urbanisation and Urban Structure. In *Regional Structure of Development and Growth in India*, ed. G.P. Mishra, vol. 1. New Delhi: Ashish Publishing House.

Wang, Gabe T., and Xiaobo Hu. 2007. Small Town Development and Rural Urbanization in China. *Journal of Contemporary Asia* 29 (1): 76–94.

World Bank. 2007. *World Development Report 2008: Agriculture for Development*. Washington, DC: The World Bank.

World Bank and the International Monetary Fund. 2013. *Global Monitoring Report 2013: Rural-Urban Dynamics and the Millennium Development Goals*. Washington, DC: The World Bank.

World Bank Group. 2006. *World Development Report 2007: Development and the Next Generation*. Washington, DC: The World Bank.

Yin, R.K. 1984. *Case Study Research: Design and Methods*. Beverly Hills, CA: Sage Publications.

———. 1994. *Case Study Research: Design and Methods*. 2nd ed. Beverly Hills, CA: Sage Publishing.

Zainal, Zaidah. 2007. Case Study as a Research Method. *Jurnal Kemanusiaan* 9: 1–6.

Zhu, Yu. 2000. In Situ Urbanization in Rural China: Case Studies from Fujian Province. *Development and Change* 31 (2): 413–434.

Zhu, J. 2002. Urban Development Under Ambiguous Property Rights: A Case of China's Transition Economy. *International Journal of Urban and Regional Research* 26 (1): 41–57.

Zhu, Yu. 2014. *In-Situ Urbanisation in China: Processes, Contributing Factors and Policy Implications*. World Migration Report 2015. www.iom.int/sites/default/fi les/our_work/ICP/MPR/WMR-2015.

Zhu, Yu, X. Qi, H. Shao, and K. He. 2009. *The Evolution of China's In Situ Urbanization and Its Planning and Environmental Implications: Case Studies from Quanzhou Municipality*. www.ciesin.columbia.edu/repository/pern/papers/urban_pde_zhu_etal.

Zimmerman, Frederick J., and Michael Carter. 2003. Asset Smoothing, Consumption Smoothing and the Reproduction of Inequality Under Risk and Subsistence Constraints. *Journal of Development Economics* 71 (2): 233–260.

INDEX

© The Author(s) 2018   251
N. Mehta, *Rural Transformation in the Post Liberalization Period*
in Gujarat, https://doi.org/10.1007/978-981-10-8962-6